As we celebrate Scottsdale Bible Church's 50th anniversary, we are devoting the entire year to remembering all the ways God has glorified Himself through our church, rejoicing over all the blessings God has lavished upon us, and renewing our commitment to be people of unwavering faith who choose to trust the Lord every day.

This precious book is a Spirit-fueled resource to help you remember, rejoice, and renew your faith in 2012. While working in our bookstore, God gave Susan Phipps the vision to collect devotionals from our own pastors, elders, staff, teachers and missionaries. This book is the compilation of insights and reflections from many of our gifted leaders and teachers, designed to help you draw near to the Lord every day.

I am so grateful that this book is one way we chose to commemorate our anniversary celebration. Our goal is to have this be a yearlong prayer of thanksgiving to God for all He has done for us. Therefore, a devotional makes sense. Each author prayed and asked God for a verse for their entries. There are repeated Scriptures, but unique messages stemming from their walk with God designed to encourage you in your walk with God.

Enjoy. Consider. Pray. Obey. Glorify God.

Your pastor and friend,

Jamie Rasmussen

Acknowledgements

Some of the entries were adapted or excerpted from other work:

Darryl DelHousaye's work adapted from: Today for Eternity, *(J. Christopher 1997)*

Holly DelHousaye's work adapted from: *www.SoulWork.org,* "I've Been Thinking..."

Don Farr's work adapted from: Becoming a Whole-Life Follower of Jesus and Living Life With the End in View, *(publication pending)*

Wayne Grudem's work adapted from: Christian Beliefs, *(Zondervan 2005)* and Business For the Glory of God *(Crossway 2003)* "Biblical Ethics, An Overview", ESV Study Bible *(Crossway 2008)*

Tim Kimmel's March 20 work excerpted from: *Extreme Grandparenting: the Ride of Your Life (Tyndale House 2007)*

Quoted works:

Mere Christianity, *(New York, Macmillan 1960)*

Muller as quoted by A.T. Pierson in George Muller of Bristol p. 216

Our Daily Bread, *(April 21, 1997)*

Sources:

Scripture quotations taken from The Holy Bible English Standard Version (ESV), Copyright 2001 by Crossway, a publishing ministry of Good News Publishers. Used by permission. All rights reserved.

Scripture quotations taken from the New American Standard Bible, Copyright 1960, 1962, 1963, 1968, 1971, 1972, 1973, 1975, 1977, 1995 by The Lockman Foundation. Used by permission.

Scripture quotations taken from the Amplified Bible, Copyright 1954, 1958, 1962, 1064, 1965, 1987 by The Lockman Foundation. Used by permission.

Scripture taken from the New King James Version, Copyright 1982 by Thomas Nelson, Inc. Used by permission. All rights reserved.

Scripture quotations taken from the Holy Bible New International Version. NIV. Copyright 1973, 1978, 1984 by Biblica, Inc. Used by permission of Zondervan. All rights reserved.

Scripture quotations taken from the Holy Bible New Living Translation, Copyright 1996, 2004. Used by permission of Tyndale House Publishers, Inc. Wheaton, Illinois 60189. All rights reserved.

Scripture quotations taken from The Holy Bible New Century Version. Copyright 1987, 1988, 1991 by Word Publishing, Dallas, Texas 75234. Used by permission.

Scripture taken from The Message (MSG) Copyright 1993. Used by permission of NavPress Publishing Group.

Great thanks to

There are so many people to acknowledge that made this devotional possible. First, Susan Phipps had the vision to bring together the leaders of our church to write this devotional. She worked tirelessly to round up pastors, elders, teachers, leaders and missionaries to submit their lessons of faith to make this work complete.

Thanks goes to the following authors for contributing:

Larry Anderson
Bill Anthony
Barry Asmus
Adrian, Sandra &
Augustina Azzati
Sherrill Babb
Don Baltzer
Fred Beasley
Kristin Beasley
Jackie Benedict
Darien Bennett
Jim Borror
Joe Bubar
Bob Cain
Lucas Cooper
David Cottrell
Darryl DelHousaye
Holly DelHousaye
Walt Edman
Scott Edwards
Steve Eriksson
Don Farr
Roy Fritz
Margi Galloway
Dale Galloway
Jeff Goble
Ron Goble

Tracy Goble
Joe Gordon
Wayne Grudem
Brooke Hellestrae
Nate Hughes
Bill Keyes
Tim Kimmel
Esther Kriskova
Wayne Lehsten
Lauren Locker
Nonie Maupin
Bryan McAnally
Steve & Jean McLurg
Susan Miller
John Milligan
Ronald Moe
Bob Moffitt
MaryAnn Morton
Cathy Myers
Jessica Neill
Tom & Deborah Nite
Stan & Barbara Orth
Christy Osborn
David & Donna Otto
Troy Peterson
Gary Phipps
Susan Phipps

Fanny Pineda
Deb Pirtle
John Politan
Jamie Rasmussen
Larry Roberts
Lyndall Rothery
David Scholl
Kory Schuknecht
Dan Scruggs
Tom Sharda
Gary & Char Shingledecker
Patrick Sullivan
Don Sunukjian
John & Cindy Trent
Mark Upton
Marilina Vega
Ota Vozeh
David Walther
Paul Wegner
J & S W.
Ed Willmington
Cathy Wilson
Archie Wright
Isaias Colop-Xec
Jim York
Dave Zehring.

As a note, each devotional is the personal property of each author.

Also, hundreds of hours went into editing and formatting this book for publication. Without these behind the scenes people, this book would never have gotten into your hands!

Thanks to Susan Phipps , Patti Scott-Sellers, Ginger Aretakis, Lucas Cooper, Tracy Goble, Michael Ludwig, Nicholas Palomo, Michael Oliveros, Amy Farrugia, Jim York, Kelli McAnally, Don Baltzer and Bryan McAnally .

Most importantly, all thanks goes to Jesus Christ, Who has authored and perfected our faith. *What a joy to serve the God of the Universe Who cares about us personally!*

Table of Contents

remember
rejoice
renew

Daily **Devotionals** for

our **5**0th year

TRUTH

My sheep hear My voice…and they follow Me. (John 10:27)

God's very words of Scripture are more than simply true; they are truth itself (John 17:17). All the words in the Bible are God's words. Therefore to disbelieve or disobey them is to disbelieve or disobey God Himself. Since the Old and New Testament writings are both considered Scripture, it is right to say they are both, in the words of 2 Timothy 3:16, "Breathed out by God." This makes sense when we consider Jesus' promise that the Holy Spirit would "bring to" the disciple's "remembrance" all that Jesus said to them (John 14:26).

But the claims of Scripture only become our personal convictions through the work of the Holy Spirit in an individual's heart. The Holy Spirit makes readers realize the Bible is unlike any book they have ever read. Just as our physical lives are maintained by daily nourishment with physical food, so our spiritual lives are maintained by daily nourishment with the Word of God.

—Wayne Grudem

Prayer Starter: *Lord, help me to prayerfully read Your word so that Your truth will be revealed to me.*

LISTENING WELL

Each one of you should be quick to listen... (James 1:19)

Oftentimes the value of a particular Biblical principle becomes painfully clear to me when I behave otherwise. Have you ever felt that way? For example, I had a conversation recently in which I was "quick to speak." I was too busy defending my viewpoint to understand the hurt that the other person was experiencing. I was trying so hard to be "right" (and convince the other person, too!) that I failed to listen well. You can probably guess how that conversation turned out for me.

What I love about this verse in James is that it's active, not passive. "Be an active listener!" it says, not just "hear." When I listen well, I should share in a person's joy or in their hurt, not just be able to repeat what they have said.

As you think about your responsibilities over the next few days—family, school, work, friendships—where is God calling you to "get active" about listening? Where might He want you to look past the circumstances and really listen to a hurting heart?

—Lucas Cooper

Prayer Starter: *Father, teach me to be an active listener.*

COUNT IT ALL JOY

Consider it all joy, my brethren, when you encounter various trials, knowing that the testing of your faith produces endurance, And let endurance have its perfect result, so that you may be perfect and complete, lacking in nothing. (James 1:2–4)

Perhaps in the midst of a difficult event (a job loss, a broken relationship, or prolonged illness), a well-meaning friend has told you to "count it all as joy…"

As you were sinking low, unable to think or feel beyond your immediate circumstances and feeling crushed, pressed in on all sides, the words sounded like, at best, an ethereal platitude – words intended to comfort your uncomfortable friend rather than you. James, however, has nothing trite in mind when he exhorts the twelve Tribes. James offers a perspective that thrusts us out of the earthly, temporal realm and circumstances, into our reason for being - to glorify God and enjoy Him forever. One way we glorify God, or enhance His appearance, is by becoming more like Him, reflecting Him in the image of Him according to which we are created. According to James, difficult events, diverse trials, tests, and temptations help us do that. They work for our benefit! Given an ongoing, deep trusting in Christ, when tests come, patience and endurance will be tempered and strengthened to a greater degree. This endurance or fortitude has its "perfect work:" righteousness, Christlikeness. As we endure in faith in Christ, we will "…be perfect and complete, lacking in nothing." Can you imagine a more significant, fulfilling end? What joy!

—David Walther

Prayer Starter: *Lord, in the midst of our difficulties, please remind us of our ultimate end in You. Lord, be our comfort and help us to endure well, knowing as we trust in You that You will bring about Your perfect work.*

GREAT IS THE LORD

Yours, O Lord, is the greatness and the power and the glory and the victory and the majesty, for all that is in the Heavens and the earth is Yours.
(1 Chronicles 29:11)

A.W. Tozer once said, "There is scarcely an error in doctrine or a failure in applying Christian ethics that cannot be traced finally to imperfect and ignoble thoughts about God."

How big is your God? Tim Keller helps us answer this question in his book, <u>The Reason for God,</u> writing: "For organic life to exist, the fundamental regulations and constants of physics—the speed of light, the gravitational constant, the strength of the weak and strong nuclear forces—must all have values that together fall into an extremely narrow range. The probability of this perfect calibration happening by chance is so tiny as to be statistically negligible." Believing that the world "just happened" would be the same as believing a tornado blowing through a junkyard created a Boeing 747 airplane. Even the atheist Stephen Hawkins concludes, "It would be very difficult to explain why the universe had begun in just this way, except as the act of a God who intended to create beings like us."

—Barry Asmus

Prayer Starter: *Dear Lord, as we consider all the world's Thy hands have made, we stand in awe of the truly indescribable.*

THE TURNSTILE

The gate is small and the way is narrow that leads to life, and few are those who find it. (Matthew 7:13–14)

Here is piercing truth: there are not hundreds of options. There are only two. Two gates. Two ways. Two destinies. One gate is wide, and "many"- most go through it. The other is narrow, and few will find it. We all reach a crossroads, and must choose which of the gates we will enter.

All religions of this world are "in order to" faiths–individuals gaining enough merit "in order to" go to some Heavenly experience. For these faiths, one word describes their essence: *Do!*

But the Christian faith is a therefore faith. Jesus has already finished the work of providing a way to God by paying the debt for our sin on that cross … therefore we are accepted by and in Jesus. The word is not Do, but Done! That's what makes the way narrow, the gate small. The gate is like a turnstile - only one at a time, responding in personal faith. This is no groupie deal. And no baggage is allowed. The wide gate lets you bring all the baggage you want: selfishness, self-indulgence, and self-righteousness. There is no self-denial. That's why so many will always go after the self-made religions.

Are you still stuck in the turnstile? Or do you know you have committed your life to following Christ? Did you hear the Gospel – that Jesus paid the debt for your sin? Did you enter the narrow gate, leaving all baggage behind, trusting only what He did for you on that cross?

—Darryl DelHousaye

Prayer Starter: *Lord, help me put all my trust in You.*

A NEW SONG

He put a new song in my mouth, a song of praise to our God; Many will see and fear and will trust in the Lord. (Psalm 40:3)

Have you ever wondered what song the birds are singing so early in the morning? Perhaps it is "I Exalt Thee", or "Great is Thy Faithfulness" or maybe "How Great Thou Art." I believe it is new every morning, knowing that "every day with Jesus is sweeter than the day before."

Their focus is so pure, so simple, so balanced. They have full days with tasks to complete, nests to build and reinforce, young to tend, and yet their song continues throughout the day. They don't need smart phones, they don't have five-year plans, and they don't have endless to-do lists. Birds sing because they have a song.

"Every day with Jesus"—What if we woke up singing praises to our King with a new song everyday? What if our focus was to trust instead of fear? What if we took time not only to fly but to soar like the eagles? What if we viewed our world from above?

God's view is from above, He holds the five-year plan. He knows what to put on the pages of our calendars and He knows how to balance it all. Together let's trust God to show us how to make this day "sweeter than the day before."

—Jessica Neill

Prayer Starter: *Lord, please put a new song in my heart so I can sing praises to You through-out the day with my trust securely in You.*

REJOICE IN TOIL

I perceived that there is nothing better for them than to be joyful and to do good as long as they live; also that everyone should eat and drink and take pleasure in all his toil – this is God's gift to man. (Ecclesiastes 3:12-13)

Recently I finished studying Ecclesiastes, and at such a perfectly appointed time in my life, as the Lord is always so faithful to arrange. Without completely disclosing my age, I will share the fullness I am blessed to be experiencing all at once as I consider the toil described in the verse noted. I am raising two incredible teenage daughters who keep me running. I have an amazing husband who after 23 full years is still my heart. I also delight in a brand new nephew, deeply love and cherish my aging parents, and thrill at my 95 year-old grandmother who can run circles around all of us!

The busy-ness of full lives from 1 month to 95 years is not a burdensome toil; it is an honor to see all the God-ordaining that I can sometimes see as distractions to my calculated course. As verses 19 and 20 of chapter 3 continues: "Everyone also to whom God has given wealth and possessions and the power to enjoy them, and to accept his lot and rejoice in his toil—this is the gift of God. For we will not much remember the days of our lives because God keeps us occupied with joy in our heart." That's it! God gives us all ages and stages for the purpose of His joy in our heart.

—Brooke Hellestrae

Prayer Starter: *Heavenly Father, thank You for blessing me with the earthly toil of living for You*
—I joyfully honor You. Thank You for this gift!

RELATIONSHIP WITH JESUS

He is the image of the invisible God, the firstborn of all creation. For by Him all things were created, in Heaven and on earth, visible and invisible, whether thrones or dominions or rulers or authorities—all things were created through Him and for Him. (Colossians 1:15–16)

When the Scriptures say that we were created through Christ and for Christ, that doesn't mean that Christ needs us to serve Him (Mark 10:45). It means that our ultimate purpose is to be in a relationship with Him.

If someone loses a key to their house, they would call a locksmith to inject a mold through the lock in order to make a duplicate that would operate that lock. Since the duplicate key was literally created through the lock, it would only fit that one lock. Its very purpose was limited to that very lock it was created through.

In the same way our purpose in life is to be in a relationship with Jesus! It's only through Jesus where we will find purpose and true pleasure.

—Joe Gordon

Prayer Starter: *Lord, help me live a life that finds its fulfillment in Christ rather than in the things of this world.*

IN THE ARMS OF THE LORD

*Deep calls to deep at the sound of Your waterfalls; All Your breakers and
Your waves have rolled over me. (Psalm 42:7)*

I was visiting my daughter in California and drove along the Oceanside Highway near
Cyprus Point. I watched as the waves roared and crashed against the rocks. Great gusts of
mist rose high into the wind breaking up after assaulting the rocks. I got quite a visual of
this Psalm unfolding in front of me. David is in great distress. His enemies are after him and
they are unrelenting in their pursuit. When he feels like he may have a breath coming, he is
hit with another problem—more trouble—more stress. "Breakers and waves" come crashing
down upon him (just as in our lives) while yet another wave builds in the distance.

The Hebrew word here for "deep" is *tehom* and it refers to a primeval abyss, or a depth of
chaos. This word describes the chaos that existed from which the earth was formed during
the creation verses in Genesis 1:2. What a graphic. Forced by the chaos of trouble from
without, the distress I feel within increases and I cry out to the Lord right now in my life,
just as David did. The problems of life in a fallen world beat us up and shape us violently at
times. The problems run "deep" within me.

I look closer at this psalm and I find that it is a *mastic*...which means it is a teaching
Psalm. "Now, what can I learn from my distress?" I ask myself.

The very next verse says it all: "The Lord will command His lovingkindness in the
daytime, And His song will be with me in the night." The forces of chaos can never overwhelm me when I am in the arms of the Lord. I am only an earshot away from hearing
His voice humming a song of safety and security to calm my fears and ease my distress.

—Dan Scruggs

Prayer Starter: *Help me to listen quietly, wait patiently and be still during the
chaos that is breaking around me.*

FROM BONDAGE TO FREEDOM

Now the Lord is the Spirit; and where the Spirit of the Lord is, there is liberty. (2 Corinthians 3:17)

I am often asked, "What does freedom in Christ mean?" It's easy for me to share my joy about the freedom that comes with knowing and living Jesus Christ!

The more you become like Jesus, the more He releases your God-given potential and you experience a freedom that can only be found in Him. Jesus moves us from a state of bondage to a state of freedom. He moves us from a state of sorrow to a state of joy. Jesus makes you free, so trust Him and follow Him. His truth makes you free, so study His Word, believe it and obey it. Following Him leads you out of darkness and takes you from despair to hope.

Oswald Chambers says it best: "Freedom is life controlled by God's truth and motivated by His love. Bondage is life controlled by lies we believe and motivated by our selfishness. Freedom is the result of a loving relationship with Jesus Christ – walking with Him, talking with Him and learning from Him."

Let the freedom of Christ ring with every beat of your heart!

—Susan Miller

Prayer Starter: *Lord, change my heart today. Release me from bondage that I might clearly see and understand the freedom of Your truth and love.*

LISTENING TO GOD

My people did not listen to My voice; and did not obey Me, so I gave them over to the stubbornness of their heart, to walk in their own devices.
(Psalm 81:11-12)

Listening takes work. I find it difficult to sit in quiet reflection and think about what God is saying to me when I read the Bible. Can you relate? This year I am trying to read through the Bible. In the busyness of life, my natural tendency is to read the passage assigned for the day and immediately move on to my other goals and activities for the day.

But listening is active and it requires that I seek to understand. In the home and in business, unless you listen carefully and understand what your spouse, child, or boss is saying, you will not truly know what to do. Why did the nation of Israel suffer at the hand of its enemies, when God was eager to turn His hand against their enemies (verses 13-14)? It was because the people were stubborn in their own ways and would not listen to God.

Today, take an extra 15 minutes of just quiet listening to God. With pen in hand, ask God to reveal to you where the stubbornness of your heart is keeping you from obeying what you have heard Him saying to you through His Word, or through a sermon you heard recently.

—Mark Upton

Prayer Starter: *Lord, today I want to listen and hear Your voice in these quiet moments. Cause me to hear You in a fresh and powerful way.*

SIGNED, SEALED, DELIVERED

In Him you also trusted, after you heard the Word of Truth, the Gospel of your salvation; in whom also having believed, you were sealed with the Holy Spirit of promise. (Ephesians 1:13)

In all our past wars and present actions in foreign countries, great effort goes into getting soldiers, sailors, and airmen their mail from home. Mail time means opening up a letter or package that has traveled thousands of miles and carried with it a message of "home:" love, hope and encouragement (and even cookies sometimes!).

This passage you read from Ephesians carries with it the idea that like a letter, moving safely and "unopened" between the sender and receiver, we carry Almighty God's "seal." Meaning that even though we can't see it, we carry God's "stamp of approval" until we get safely home to Heaven.

What a picture of commitment and security! And what a word picture of what we need to do in our marriage as well. From the ring we wear that shows the world our commitment, to the actions we do each day in the privacy of our homes to increase commitment and caring, we can model God's love for us in our marriage.

— John and Cindy Trent

Prayer Starter: *Lord Jesus, Your "seal" carries with it the certainty that we need to "rest" in You. We can't "wander off" or get lost. We can't "unseal" Your seal. You take us from where we met You for the first time to the day we'll be with You in Heaven. Help us, Lord, to "seal" our commitment to each other by trusting You and loving each other each day.*

HUMBLE SERVANT

We give thanks to God always for all of you, making mention of you in our prayers; constantly bearing in mind your work of faith and labor of love and steadfastness of hope in our Lord Jesus Christ in the presence of our God and Father. (I Thessalonians 1:2-3)

I remember when Scottsdale Bible was still located on the McDonald site. The parking lot was unpaved. After services, many cars exited the lot onto a side street, causing dust to swirl onto neighbors' homes, and causing ill-will toward the church.

During an elder meeting, we asked Joe, the elder overseeing facilities, what it would take to create a "tank trap" (an earth-berm barrier), so that cars couldn't exit onto the side street, but would instead have to use the McDonald driveway. I expected Joe, an IBM executive, to say something like, "I'll look into the cost of hiring a bulldozer." Instead, his answer was, "About half a Saturday of my time with a shovel."

I sat in silence, marveling at the grace of God that would produce such a humble spirit of service in someone the world would probably think was above such menial labor. I was reminded of what David once wrote, "As for the saints who are in the earth, they are the majestic ones, in whom is all my delight" (Psalm 16:3).

—Don Sunukjian

Prayer Starter: *Lord, may I never become so self-important that I am unwilling to humbly serve Your people.*

LIFE: EASIER SAID THAN DONE

Do not merely listen to the Word, and so deceive yourselves. Do what it says.
(James 1:22)

Things in life are easier said than done. I mean that in a broad, general, overarching sense. It's easier to talk about going on a diet than it is to go on one. It's easier to dream with a friend about taking a vacation together than it is to book the plane ticket. It's easier to say, "Let's do coffee soon!" than it is to actually "do coffee." That's just reality. But do we transfer our everyday lackadaisical approach to life to how we respond when the Lord specifically calls or asks us to do something?

You know the moment. You can't deny it. It's when the Holy Spirit tugs on your heart and asks you to do something that's out of your comfort zone (but, of course, it's for His glory and for your growth as His child). Example? Maybe He wants you to stop and talk to the homeless man on the street. Or maybe He would like you to open up your home so the cousin of your sister-in-law's best friend will have a place to stay while passing through town. Maybe He is asking you to give above and beyond your typical tithe to help someone in need.

Of course you can say, "Yeah, sure, no problem!" But then…do you follow through? Do you actually DO what the Holy Spirit prompts you to do? Don't take the easy way; follow through!

—Kristin Beasley

Prayer Starter: *Lord, please help me to follow through when You ask me to do something.*

SALT

You are the salt of the earth; but if the salt has become tasteless, how can it be made salty again? It is no longer good for anything, except to be thrown out and trampled under foot by men. (Matthew 5:13)

Jesus tells us that we are like salt in this world which becomes a brilliant illustration for us as to how to live our lives. People in biblical times were well aware of the value and importance of salt. Salt has been used for over 6,000 years for the preserving of food and it is probably the most popular seasoning for food. We know that sodium chloride or common salt is an essential element for living beings, but it is deadly to most plant life. The sodium and chloride ions are used in our bodies to regulate the water balance.

Jesus uses this illustration to indicate the importance Christians play in flavoring this world. Imagine shaking out salt onto our food and it making no difference to the taste—it would be worthless. In the same way Christians living in this world, but not flavoring it, should be repulsive to us. Our lives, as they touch others, should change them. People should be different because they have come into contact with us. God expects it and others need it. "Please pass the salt."

—Paul Wegner

Prayer Starter: *Lord, I pray that today someone's life will be changed because they came into contact with me.*

TRUTH AND FREEDOM

Jesus therefore was saying to those Jews who had believed Him, "If you abide in My Word, then you are truly disciples of Mine; and you shall know the truth, and the truth shall make you free." (John 8: 31-32)

Ever since the serpent deceived Eve, deception has wreaked havoc in our lives. And it all began with a snake.

I'm not a fan of snakes. Recently while hiking Shaw Butte, there was a snake beside the trail looking straight at me…as hard as he could. He didn't move toward me, but you can bet I was moving backwards, screaming like a girl and doing my snake dance (you know the one, where you dance in place on tip toes?). Got the picture?

This event reminded me of the subtlety and unexpected nature of deception. We may not have a negative reaction to deception. For instance, sometimes I'm tempted to run a yellow light. I think: "I can make it." Believe it or not, I did that once and was hit by a car. Lesson learned? Deception hurts us; and when we believe lies, we slip into spiritual bondage.

Over the next months in my devotionals, I'll explain nine common ways we experience spiritual deception.

—Nonie Maupin

Prayer Starter: *Precious Father, thank You for Your truth that sets me free.*

COMFORT

Blessed be the God and Father of our Lord Jesus Christ, the Father of mercies and God of all comfort, who comforts us in all our affliction, so that we may be able to comfort those who are in any affliction, with the comfort with which we ourselves are comforted by God. (2 Corinthians 1:3-4)

The apostle Paul certainly knew a thing or two about suffering and affliction. The trials he experienced during his ministry would put most of our daily hardships to shame. He was beaten on multiple occasions, subjected to stoning, was shipwrecked, and endured conditions while in prison that were undoubtedly less than humane (2 Corinthians 11:23-27). Paul is quick to point out in his second letter to the church at Corinth that God was faithful in comforting him through all of these afflictions, which serves as a reminder that God is faithful to us today in our afflictions.

It is easy for us to miss the importance of the second part of Paul's message however; that we are to use our affliction as a witness and a source of encouragement to those around us. Experiencing God's faithfulness while suffering through life's trials can only draw us nearer to Him. We can steward this blessing by being careful to give God the glory for allowing us to walk with Him through our trials, and to be diligent in sharing our experiences with those whom He places in our path. Don't waste this opportunity! God can and does use our trials to draw others to Himself. While suffering through life's trials is never easy, our obedient response should always be to glorify the King by telling others of His goodness and provision.

—Scott Edwards

Prayer Starter: *Father, I thank You that You are always with me as I walk through life's trials. I pray that I am a good steward of Your faithfulness as I share my story with others.*

UNCONDITIONAL FAITH

Five times I received from the Jews thirty-nine lashes. Three times I was beaten with rods, once I was stoned, three times I was shipwrecked, a night and a day I have spent in the deep. I have been on frequent journeys, in dangers from rivers, dangers from robbers, dangers from my countrymen, dangers from the Gentiles, dangers in the city, dangers in the wilderness, dangers on the sea, dangers among false brethren. I have been in labor and hardship, through many sleepless nights, in hunger and thirst, often without food, in cold and exposure.
(2 Corinthians 11:24–27)

The apostle Paul certainly didn't have it easy. As you read the Pauline letters, you discover that Paul didn't sound down or discouraged, which is something that very few of us can consistently say today. Do you suppose it could be because Paul walked so intimately with Christ and was continually in that "happy state" that George Muller wrote about?

Paul's faith and trust in God was based upon God's unconditional love for him. He knew, and we can know also with that kind of faith, that no matter the circumstances we find ourselves in, God is with us, for us, and will bring us through to the conclusion He knows is best for us.

—Donald Farr

Prayer Starter: *Thank You for Your unconditional love. Help me to give You unconditional trust.*

SOURCE OF OUR REJOICING

Hallelujah! For our Lord God Almighty reigns. Let us rejoice and be glad and give Him the glory. (Revelation 19:7)

The seventy-two returned with joy and said "Lord, even the demons submit to us in Your name." He replied, "Do not rejoice that the spirits submit to you, but rejoice that your names are written in Heaven" (Luke 10:17-21).

There is a temptation every Christian worker faces all the time. This temptation is to rejoice in our work, in seeing how God has used us and how effective we have been in His service.

Don't get me wrong. It is perfectly all right to feel and express joy over witnessing the wonders of God's grace working in the lives of those we have been called to serve. When I see our national leadership growing in maturity as they fulfill their God-given vision for their communities and countries, I am full of joy and I thank the Lord for His work in each one of them.

And yet…my rejoicing must go further than the people I work with; those which I have had the privilege of serving for many years. My rejoicing is not conditional on what happens or does not happen. My rejoicing is in the Lord (Philippians 3:1).

I remember meeting a wonderful man of God, Dr. Ralph Freed. My wife, Renata, and I served under his leadership with Trans World Radio in Monte-Carlo for three years. He was the father of TWR's founder, Dr. Paul Freed. Dr. Ralph Freed worked as a missionary among the Muslims of North Africa for 25 years – and he never saw one of them saved.

Do we rejoice only when we see the fruit of our labors? Or do we rejoice regardless, because the source of our rejoicing is the Lord Jesus Christ Himself?

—Ota Vozeh

Prayer Starter: *Lord, I rejoice in Your saving grace. I give You the glory and praise.*

IN OVER OUR HEADS

Uzziel… one of the goldsmiths, repaired the next section, and Hananiah, one of the perfume-makers, made repairs next to that… Shallum… repaired the next section with the help of his daughters. (Nehemiah 3:8, 12)

The Lord isn't above expecting us to serve Him while operating completely out of our league. Just ask Uzziel. Uzi who? He's part of the remnant that returned from the Babylonian captivity to find Jerusalem little more than a pile of rubble.

For 70 years, Zion lay in ruins; the sad consequence of a nation's prolonged disobedience. Now, these ragtag refugees were expected to turn this heap of scattered rocks and broken dreams into the spiritual heart of a nation again. There was only one major problem. None of them were wall builders. They were perfumers, jewelers or able men with only their daughters as a work crew.

But God doesn't need sophisticated talent to do His heavy lifting. All He needs is a willing heart. When we're in over our heads, it's great to know that if God is all we have, God is all we need.

Fifty-two days after they started, they finished their work. As Nehemiah reports, "When all our enemies heard about this…(they) were afraid and lost their self-confidence, because they realized that this work had been done with the help of our God" (Nehemiah 6:16).

—Tim Kimmel

Prayer Starter: *Lord, when I'm in over my head, help me trust in Your unlimited strength and Your unwavering love.*

CALEB'S COMMITMENT

But my servant Caleb, because he has a different spirit and has followed me fully, I will bring into the land into which he went (as a spy) and his descendants shall possess it. (Numbers 14:24)

Numbers 14 and Joshua 14 contain a wonderful story of a man called Caleb. His name actually means "all heart." What a fitting name it was! He truly had a great heart! Caleb is one of my favorite Biblical heroes. How deep and yet how simple is the secret of his greatness. Great people are not complicated; they usually are simplicity itself. In all of my devotionals I would like to share with you some of the reasons of his greatness.

The first clue to his greatness was Caleb's Commitment (Joshua 14:8, 9, 14).

The phrase, "wholly followed the Lord" (used six times in these two chapters) meant "closing the gap." This was a phrase used by hunters to refer to closing the gap between themselves and their prey. Caleb was committed to keeping the distance between himself and the Lord at a minimum. Every inch, every ounce, every nerve, and every fiber of Caleb belonged to the Lord. You see half-hearted Christians are faint-hearted Christians, and they never learn to conquer the giants in their lives. Caleb's commitment was total!

The man who kneels before God can stand before anybody or anything because he is committed. How about you? Are you totally sold out to Jesus as your Lord?

—Wayne Lehsten

Prayer Starter: *Lord I desire to wholly follow You all the days of my life.*

ALL-IN TO YOUR CALLING

Therefore I, the prisoner of the Lord, implore you to walk in a manner worthy of the calling with which you have been called. (Ephesians 4:1)

What is the call of Christ to those He intends to make His disciples? The call of Christ to disciples is, "Come, follow Me." It is a call to pursue holiness (1 Peter 1:15-16) and it means commitment to Christ above all things, even to the point of renouncing all that one has, including even one's own life. The call is to deny oneself and take up one's cross daily and follow Christ. This is a "C-A-L-L-I-N-G" to be ALL-IN (Luke 9:23; Luke 14:26, 33) whereby our Commitment and Attitude will direct our Living, our Labor, our Integrity, love for our Neighbor and Glory to God. In chapter four of Paul's epistle to the Ephesians, he urges us to live worthy of our Christian calling. Believers are called and thus chosen to represent Christ. In fact, the Greek word for "church" is *ekklesia,* which means the "called-out ones." Christ is the Caller and His sheep are the called ones. Paul presents specific characteristics of the worthy life that disciples are called to walk verses 2-3:

Christians must not be proud or arrogant. The promise of humility is exaltation (James 4:10). "God opposes the proud, but gives grace to the humble" (James 4:6).

Some older versions of the Bible may use the word "meekness" in verse 2. Rather, meekness is gentleness where one's strength is under control. Jesus told His disciples, "Blessed are the meek, for they will inherit the earth" (Matthew 5:5).

Patience is a virtue that takes time to learn. Almost always in learning patience, one of the chief ways we learn it is through suffering. Those who suffer will either learn to be patient or bitter. Nevertheless, we are called to bear fruit with patience (Luke 8:15).

—Darien Bennett

Prayer Starter: *Lord, help me be all-in for You. Help me be humble, patient and gentle.*

OFFERING MYSELF

I appeal to you therefore brothers, by the mercies of God, to present your bodies as a living sacrifice, holy and acceptable to God, which is your spiritual worship. (Romans 12:1)

Not long after my wife and I committed our lives to Christ, we began praying fervently for our son to accept Christ. He was away at college. We prayed this way for over a year. Then one day I had a great idea. I prayed that God would bring our son to his knees in order to break his resistance to God. I was so proud of my deepening spirituality. I was willing to surrender our son, a la Abraham and Isaac. I prayed like this for another year or more. One morning, I was reading Romans 12 and in verse 1 I saw that I was to present my body as a sacrifice. That is a big difference than presenting my son's body!

So, I changed my prayer to offer myself that my son would see Christ in me. In short order thereafter, I was devastated to lose a very lucrative job after seventeen years. Ironically, our son was due to arrive at our home the very same day for a short visit from out of state.

A year or so later, he attended a church in another city with his girlfriend and committed his life to Christ. He has testified that a significant factor in opening his eyes to Christ was the day he observed how his mother and father reacted to extreme adversity. What a great "coincidence" that God orchestrated my firing on the very same day our son was in town!

Do you need to sacrifice your best interest for the benefit of someone else's best interest?

—Bob Cain

Prayer Starter: *Lord, use me today that others may see Christ in me.*

USING A MEMORY TO BLESS OTHERS

*Blessed be the God and Father of our Lord Jesus Christ, who has blessed us with every spiritual blessing in the Heavenly places in Christ. (**Ephesians 1:3**)*

Did you know that the word "blessing" in Scripture carries with it the idea of "adding" weight and value to another's life? Think back to a picture in your past that blessed you. Perhaps it's a teacher who encouraged you, a parent who believed in you, a friend who accepted you.

Now think about the people in your own life—a parent, a child, a friend, a mate, a teacher, a co-worker. How can you pass on to them that kind of blessing that was passed to you?

Perhaps you can smile a little more. Make a phone call. Write a thank-you note. Take a walk with them during your lunch break and just listen to their story and pray for them.

There are lots of ways to get started. The place you start is not nearly as important as the time. Which is now. And when you do, you'll be modeling what Jesus has done for you.

—John and Cindy Trent

Prayer Starter: *Thank You Jesus. You have done everything for me. Help me to be a blessing to others in Your name.*

PERSEVERANCE

Count it all joy, my brothers, when you meet trials of various kinds, for you know that the testing of your faith produces steadfastness. And let steadfastness have its full effect, that you may be perfect and complete, lacking in nothing. (James 1:2-4)

In the summer of 1983, I took a job as a stock boy at a local hardware store. I had been a Christian for less than a year, and I was fired up and sold out for Jesus. One of my bosses there did not like me at all, primarily because of my outward expressions of faith in Christ. He made it his mission to persecute me – he assigned me the nastiest jobs and continually had me unloading trucks with the crudest, rudest drivers. He berated and degraded me at any opportunity. Remembering Scripture that encouraged me, I persevered and trusted God to bless me to endure that summer of adversity.

God used my perseverance through my boss's persecution as a witness to everyone else who saw what he was doing. And God used those trials to shape me and strengthen me for challenges I'd face later in life. By faith, I refused to give up; today I continue to reap blessings.

Right now you might not see the point in sticking with what God has begun in you. Your life might be harder now than it was before you were a Christian. You might be worn down, tired out, or ready to quit. God wants you to rest in Him, trust in His guidance, and take your next step by faith. Someday you too will look back and see the unexpected harvest of perseverance.

—Jamie Rasmussen

Prayer Starter: *Whatever trial I'm in Lord, give me strength to persevere for You.*

GOD OF THE IMPOSSIBLE

If you have faith like a grain of mustard seed, you will say to this mountain, "Move from here to there," and it will move, and nothing will be impossible for you. (Matthew 17:20)

We arrived in Russia to lead Moscow Bible College only to learn the college was $50,000 in debt with no operating funds. School was to start in two weeks. In my devotions, I had just read how God used Nehemiah to rebuild Jerusalem's walls in 52 days. With the college staff I shared, "God did not bring me here to close the college, but to keep it going. By faith we are going to ask Him for $50,000 in 52 days." If He could rebuild Jerusalem's walls in 52 days, surely He could provide $50,000 for us! We did not know who on earth to ask, so we bombarded Heaven asking God for this miracle.

By the end of the week we had $20,000 to begin the semester. In 52 days we had received $50,000. By the end of the school year we had covered all costs, paid our debts and had $20,000 left to start the next school year! That same year, more than 2,000 Russians professed faith in Christ with our students!

When our requests harmonize with God's will, He delights to answer our prayers of faith. Trust God to move your mountains today. It only takes mustard-seed faith.

—Tom and Deborah Nite

Prayer Starter: *God, may I have faith as a mustard seed and help me to apply it in this particular area of my life…*

GOD'S PLACEMENT

For if you remain completely silent at this time, relief and deliverance will arise for the Jews from another place... who knows whether you have come to the kingdom for such a time as this? (Esther 4:14–15)

Esther was a young Jewish orphan, an unlikely candidate to be queen to the influential King Ahasuerus. The powerful Haman, second in command to the king, commanded all the kings' servants to bow down and pay homage to himself. Mordecai would not bow down to any man but only to the one true God. This enraged Haman so he devised a plan to kill not only Mordecai but also all the Jews, the people of Mordecai. But, God had placed Esther in the kings' court to protect His people. She knew that she was risking much – perhaps even her life. As she and her friends fasted and prayed, God guided her in accomplishing His plans and delivered His people.

Do you find yourself in a place you didn't anticipate? Has God placed you there to join Him in His plans? Or will His plans be accomplished through another?

—Deb Pirtle

Prayer Starter: *Oh, Father in Heaven we praise You as the Great I AM. We thank You for the privilege of joining You in Your plans. May we hear Your voice. May we respond to Your call. May we follow You all the days of our lives.*

CHOICES

Trust in the Lord with all your heart and do not lean on your own under-standing. In all your ways acknowledge Him, And He will make your paths straight. (Proverbs 3:5–6)

As my sons were growing up there were three choices I often reminded them of:

1. Choose achievement over activity.

2. Choose impact over position.

3. Choose discipline over talent.

These three choices are critical to maturity and often overlooked. We fill our calendars with so many things. We are busier than ever, but being busy was never intended to be a goal. We must choose to give ourselves to things that matter.

The world loves to measure people by title and position. But that is not how life is really measured. Life is fullest when we are where we make the greatest impact. Choosing impact over position may cut across the grain of our culture, but it will result in a life with real meaning.

There are many talented people in the world. But every person reaches a point where their talent will no longer carry them. They must discipline themselves to maximize the gifts God has given them.

These choices are important, but none of them compare to the big one. Choose to pursue Christ. Pursue Christ above all else. Be relentless in your commitment and desire to know Him and serve Him. What are you choosing?

—Larry Anderson

Prayer Starter: *Dear God, I choose You. Help my choices to be Your choices.*

CONFLICTING PRIORITIES

Martha, you are worried and bothered about so many things, but only one thing is necessary, for Mary has chosen the good part, which shall not be taken away from her. (Luke 10:41-42)

When priorities converge and conflict results, "splitting" occurs. I am speaking here of intense emotional pain – a deep piercing – caused by being divided within myself over what my priorities should be in a particular situation.

As I sort out what to do in my "splitting" times, I often think of the story of Mary and Martha found in Luke. Jesus came to Martha's home for dinner. As was His custom, wherever He went, Jesus began to teach and entertain questions from the group who gathered to share the occasion with Him.

Mary, Martha's sister, chose to sit at Jesus' feet listening to His words instead of assuming the normal role of a female in that culture which was to help with the meal preparations. Because Mary was not helping, Martha was extra busy and overburdened. Finally, when her frustrations reached the boiling point, she complained to Jesus, asking Him to "tell her then to help me."

Jesus responded to Martha with wonderful tenderness because He recognized her emotional state. He used her name and gently instructed her on how to lower her anxiety by shifting her priorities. This is where I relate to Martha and her plight.

Jesus continues on with His lesson in restructuring priorities by saying only "one thing is necessary" or absolutely needed. Only one thing has eternal value, only one thing brings peace – even though, at times, it may ever be at odds with the expectations of polite society.

What is that one necessary thing? Nothing is more important than communing with Jesus and letting Him speak to me. And so, when my distraction level hits high alert – when I'm tempted to move FASTER and work HARDER, that is my cue to SIT DOWN at Jesus' feet and simply listen. Because in quietly listening to His instruction and wisdom – I am pleasing Him – first.

—Holly DelHousaye

Prayer Starter: *Lord, help me to always listen to You and put You first.*

ALL THINGS THROUGH CHRIST

I can do all things through Him who strengthens me. (Philippians 4:13)

There was a young Christian who once stood at the pulpit, preaching to a small church as a lay leader of that church. His sermon message is not the important part of this story.

Being a very immature worshiper of Jesus, he had yet to fully understand that all things should be done to glorify God. He was very full of himself and confident that he could do all things now that he had received his salvation.

After finishing his sermon message, he puffed up his chest and loudly announced that he "could take on anything the world had to offer." Taking his seat he felt good about what he had said.

Apparently Satan also heard these words and openly attacked this young Christian for several years. Almost all the battles were won by Satan. I encourage all who have their hearts open, to read Philippians 4:13 in its entirety, "...through Him who strengthens me."

Yes, with Jesus all things can be accomplished. Without Him you can do nothing on your own. Today, let's all lean on Jesus and have a great day!

—Gary Phipps

Prayer Starter: *Lord Jesus, strengthen me today to do Your will.*

LIFE SAVERS

Do not work for the food which perishes, but for the food which endures to eternal life. (John 6:27)

Sitting next to me on the plane was a man who was obviously a professional; nicely attired, though why he was in economy class was a mystery. I engaged him in conversation and discovered that he was a heart surgeon.

Immediately my esteem for the man leapt. My mind began racing through its own picture of the man's years of schooling, academic competition, training, internship, untold hours of sacrificial devotion and lost sleep. All this directed toward preparation to perform surgery that could extend the life span of a person—perhaps a few years or even a number of decades.

And then it hit me. We Christians and this surgeon are in the same line of work. He labors to give people life and hope while they inhabit their earthly bodies. We labor to give people life and hope that lasts for billions and billions of years—for eternity! The surgeon's work is valuable but always ultimately temporary, while ours is infinite. Who does the greater good?

We who follow Jesus Christ have been given the privilege and the power to bring people to the Life Giver, not just for temporal relief, but for joyous communion forever with our awesome, loving God. Whether you are a plumber, a cashier, a pilot, a student, a housewife, a fisherman, or a tax-collector, you can be a life saver by introducing people to the One who gave His life so that we could truly live.

—Dave Cottrell

Prayer Starter: *Lord, give me fresh eyes to see the needy, spiritually dead people all around me, a tender heart to truly care about their desperate need, and a renewed mind that understands the life-saving power You have given me.*

STUDYING THE BIBLE

But he answered them, "It is written, 'man shall not live by bread alone, but by every word that comes from the mouth of God.'" (Matthew 4: 4)

All Study Bibles contain two kinds of words. The first kind is the actual words of the Bible which are the very words of God to us. These are usually printed in larger font at the top of each page. The difference in font sizes serves to remind readers that the words of the Bible itself are infinitely more valuable than the words of the notes. The words of the Bible are the words of our Creator speaking to us. They are completely truthful, they are pure, they are powerful, they are wise and righteous. Through these words God gives us eternal life and He daily nourishes our spiritual lives in this present world.

The best way to use a Study Bible is always to begin and end with the actual words of the Bible, seeking to understand them and to hear God's voice speaking to your heart. After beginning with the actual words, read the study notes to gain additional information about the background and meanings. Finally return to the Bible itself, reading it with enriched understanding.

—Wayne Grudem

Prayer Starter: *God, speak to me through Your words.*

THE TEMPTATION OF CHRIST

Again, the devil took Him to a very high mountain and showed Him all the kingdoms of the world and their glory; and he said to Him, "All these things I will give you, if you fall down and worship me." Then Jesus said to him, "Go, Satan! For it is written, 'You shall worship the Lord your God, and serve Him only.'" Then the devil left Him; and behold, angels came and began to minister to Him.
(Matthew 4:8-11)

Before Jesus began His earthly ministry, the Spirit led Him into the desert for 40 days of focused prayer and fasting. When the 40 days came to an end, Satan himself tempted Jesus to fulfill His own needs in His own timing, defend His own authority, and worship Satan in exchange for power and wealth (Matthew 4:1-11).

Though each temptation is different, there's a common thread in all three—self-reliance. In each case, Christ is given the opportunity to take the reins rather than rely upon the Father. It might seem strange, but even Jesus was subject to the Father's will (Philippians 2:5-8, Luke 22:42) and dependent on the Father's plan (John 17:8). Hence, Christ uses Scripture to answer and, ultimately, resist each of Satan's temptations.

We face the same questions Christ did, don't we? When tempted to rely on myself (when the things of the world look more attractive than the things of God), who do I rely upon? Do I count on my own strength to resist, or do I seek the Father's help?

— Lucas Cooper

Prayer Starter: *Father, teach me to recognize when I'm being tempted, and then to rely on Your strength and Your strength alone.*

LIVES OF INTEGRITY

But above all, my brethren, do not swear, either by Heaven or by earth or with any other oath; but your yes is to be yes, and your no, no, so that you may not fall under judgment. (James 5:12)

Toward the end of James' letter to the dispersed tribes of Israel, James makes an emphatic statement, "But above all," or "Most importantly," or "Pay attention to this," my brothers and sisters, do not swear.

This is not a prohibition about uttering profanities, but James is speaking of swearing oaths. Why is James so emphatic about this? What is wrong with swearing oaths? The importance of oaths is documented throughout the Old Testament.

James' concern here is one of integrity. Christians must have a solid reputation for speaking truth. There should be no insincerity or falsehood between one's inner disposition and their words as they lovingly obey Jesus. There will be no need of oaths or swearing according to Heaven or earth, or his or hers' mother's grave or anything else, because they are blameless by reputation and behavior.

Such are those called by God, focused on Jesus and empowered by the Holy Spirit. Such is our call and a one-day-at-a-time pursuit to live lives reflective of the One who loved us first and gave his life for us. May we live faithfully in obedience to Him.

—David Walther

Prayer Starter: *Lord, thank You for the gift of your Son. Thank You for sending your Holy Spirit. Through Your power, give us the desire and courage to walk in Your ways. May we above all live lives of integrity today.*

FADE AWAY

Let the lowly brother boast in his exaltation, and the rich in his humiliation, because like a flower of the grass, he will pass away. For the sun rises with its scorching heat and withers the grass; its flower falls, and its beauty perishes. So also will the rich man fade away in the midst of his pursuits. (James 1:9–11)

Was the Egyptian Pharaoh the exception to this verse? Was King Solomon? The Shah of Iran? Of course not.

Have you ever wanted to be rich? Surely you and I are not the exceptions for wishing for wealth. Is there a possibility we dodged a bullet when God's sovereignty said, "Money is not your problem." The desire to be rich could lead to temptation and be the root of all kinds of evils. But, richness in love, peace, wisdom and service is the secret of living and overcoming life's difficulties. Then we can say, "I can do all things through Him who strengthens me."

—Barry Asmus

Prayer Starter: *Dear Father, both wealth and poverty bring enormous pressure to focus on the world rather than Christ Jesus. Material possessions tend to reinforce my self-sufficiency and independence from You. Give me just what You think I need.*

HIS MOST VIOLATED WORDS

If your brother sins against you, go and show him his fault, just between the two of you. (Matthew 18:15)

"Just between the two of you"—literally, "Between you and him alone."
It's no one else's business!

These are the most violated words of Jesus Christ, among those who call Him Lord. Why do we so often "go public" first when our brother sins against us?

Is it because we are hurt, so we call in the troops to feel sorry for us? If so, then let's allow God—"The Father of mercies and God of all comfort"—to comfort us instead.

Is it because we are angry, so we call in the troops to help us hurt the one who offended us? If this is true, let's remember: "Never take your own revenge, beloved, but leave room for the wrath of God, for it is written, 'vengeance is mine, I will repay, says the Lord'" (Romans 12:9).

Is it because we are fearful of rejection, so we call in the troops for reinforcements? Then let's instead believe with David, "The Lord is the defense of my life" (Psalm 27:1).

Our relationships are always targeted by Satan. Why? Because to the world our unity is the verification of Christ. If Jesus prayed that His followers, "May all be one...that the world may believe that Thou didst send me"—then if you were Satan, what would you target? Satan will never let our relationships flow naturally. That's why the "peace" must be preserved by the peacemakers...and why peacemakers are called "Sons of God" (Matthew 5:9).

—Darryl DelHousaye

Prayer Starter: *Lord help me to be a peacemaker and work things out individually.*

JUDGE NOT

*Do not judge so that you will not be judged. For in the way you judge, you
will be judged; and by your standard of measure, it will be measured to you.
(Matthew 7:1–2)*

Having grown up with Jesus, I know that we are not to judge. Over the years I have learned to practice grace, to give someone the benefit of the doubt, and to focus on the positive. I was surprised when God challenged me about a new pattern of judgment that had taken hold in my heart. Recently I was faced with two situations in my life where friends had stepped away from God and pursued sin. Both were professed believers even though their actions indicated they were choosing to live outside of His will.

When asked to come alongside them, my first thought was, "Will my support condone their sin? Will I communicate to others that I approve of their sin?" My inclination was to withhold love and even my support. Then God quietly spoke. This is a call to love: judge not so that you will not be judged.

I realized how "un-Christian" it looks to stay away by withholding love and was convicted that I should step forward, following Christ and live the call to love in grace. The old saying "hate the sin, love the sinner" sums it up best. Jesus modeled loving us all in our sin, and He never participated or condoned our sin; He died for it. As my grandmother would say, "I stand corrected," and will strive to remember that I have a call to love.

—Jessica Neill

Prayer Starter: *Lord, please forgive me for the times I have withheld love from others when I could step out to love them the way You love.*

FOR SUCH A TIME AS THIS

Who knows whether you have come to the kingdom for such a time as this?
(Esther 4:14b)

I count it a privilege to have just studied the Book of Esther with a precious group of mighty women who seek that very question in verse 14. There are days recently when I think all believers have wished they had not been appointed for "such a time as this" whatever their "this" may be. For all of us the recession has caused some trouble; a painful marriage, a hurtful family situation, deteriorating health, and the list goes on as long as we walk the earth, all bring difficulties we would rather not face.

The conclusion we have wrestled with is this: yes, Christ has appointed me for this time and circumstance to be in His kingdom! Nothing at all surprises Him or slips through His fingers, He knows what His purposes are and how He surprisingly has prepared us if we will trust Him wholly. The good news is that He promises, "In whom we have boldness and access with confidence through our faith in Him" (Ephesians 3:12a).

I need boldness, I need confidence, and I am promised complete access to Him as I bravely accept the time and position He gives me no matter what it looks like. The incredible wisdom of a teenage girl turned queen many years ago is still relevant for me. Queen Esther's faith gave her the courage she needed to face her challenge.

I love how timeless God is and how we all are called exactly for the time in history in which He has placed us. Perhaps you are in your position for "such a time as this?"

—Brooke Hellestrae

Prayer Starter: *Thank You Lord for keeping me brave as I boldly seek You to move me through difficult times. Help me never forget the rich blessing of access I have with You. I love You Lord.*

GUARD MY EYES

Do not be deceived: God is not mocked, for whatever one sows, that will he also reap. (Galatians 6:7)

When you sow seed, there is no instant harvest. It takes time for things to grow, but one day the fruit of what you sow will show itself; and that is what you reap.

The same goes for sensual images and sounds. You may not think that these images matter now, but one day or month or year later, you will reap the consequences from that sensuality. The things you struggle with today were sown yesterday. Be watchful with what you take in with your eyes.

—Joe Gordon

Prayer Starter: *Lord, guard my eyes this day. Lead me by Your Spirit whenever I wander.*

THE GREATEST GIFT

This is how we know what love is: Jesus Christ laid down His life for us.
(I John 3:16)

I have prayed many prayers for which the answer was "no." Each time this happens, the temptation is to feel that God doesn't love me. It's so easy to feel good when I get a gift I have been longing for, when I hear good news about something I have been worrying about, or when I am watching something great unfold before my eyes. But when the answer is "wait" or the situation just keeps getting worse, I start feeling bad.

How do I counteract this temptation? I remember one thing. Jesus already gave me the ultimate, greatest gift He could give. He gave me His life. This one gift tells me powerfully and for all time that He loves me. If He never gives me another thing, it is enough. "Three times I pleaded with the Lord to take it away from me. But He said to me, 'My love *(kharis)* is enough for you…'"(2 Cor. 12:9). The one gift so overshadows all else that everything else pales into insignificance.

Knowing He loves me enables me to accept the "no" and start looking for the reason. Jesus said, "For My power is made perfect in weakness."

—Ronald Moe

Prayer Starter: *Dear God, I know You love me. Thank You for the greatest gift of all…Jesus.*

STEPPING OUT IN FAITH

…For we walk by faith, not by sight… (2 Corinthians 5:7)

When you're new in town, it's easier and more comfortable to stay put in your house. "After all, I don't really know anyone," you tell yourself, "and it takes so much effort to walk into a room of strangers at a Bible study, or go anywhere unfamiliar. It's easier and not as scary to just stay where I feel comfortable," you think.

Yes, that would be the safest place to stay. Peter probably thought the same thing, too (Matthew 14:22-32). You can imagine him saying, "It's scary to get out of the boat in unfamiliar waters. I'd rather stay right here!" Peter's focus was on the wind and the waves, not on Jesus his Savior. Your focus might be on the circumstances around you and all the unknowns that come with being new in town.

"Take courage! Don't be afraid," Jesus said to the disciples. "It is I…come," He said.

Why not step out in faith right now? Join that Bible Study, take that class you've always wanted, or invite someone over for coffee. Get out of the boat one step at a time. You can do it. Just keep your focus on Jesus and begin to walk towards Him.

—Susan Miller

Prayer Starter: *Lord, today I choose to step out in faith and keep my focus on You!*

DOUBTLESS FAITH

If you have faith, and do not doubt... (Matthew 21:21)

Doubtless faith moves mountains. C.S. Lewis said, "You never know how much you really believe until its truth or falsehood becomes a matter of life and death to you. It is easy to say you believe a rope to be strong and sound as long as you are merely using it to cord a box. But suppose you had to hang by that rope over a precipice. Wouldn't you then first discover how much you really trusted it? Only a real risk tests the reality of a belief."

Take a moment and reflect upon that time when you believed God wanted you to step out in faith, but doubt and fear came to the surface and kept you from moving forward? What about today? Is there a precipice that God wants you to step over and trust Him to hold you up?

The great heroes of past and present generations are people who heard a call from God and then moved forward in doubtless faith. Jesus said, "All things you ask in prayer, believing, you shall receive." Whether big or small, if we believe God's leading without doubt, it is not only possible, it will happen. God-sized outcomes are based on faith (Matthew 21:21-22).

If you feel like you missed an opportunity because you failed to act in faith, it is not too late. Believe now and act upon your faith (Matthew 21:28-32).

—Mark Upton

Prayer Starter: *Lord, my heart is saying that You want me to step out in faith to …*

THE "WEAKEST" LINK

Bless the Lord, O my soul, and forget none of His benefits. (Psalm 103:2)

During the span of years allotted to each of us, we often say, "I will never forget this!" But in reality, we do forget! The joys and sorrows, the experiences, good and bad, tend to fade away. In this verse in Psalms, we're told not to forget the ways God has encouraged, blessed, and benefited us.

One couple, married over fifty years, started doing something after 30 years of marriage that they never regretted (and wished they had started earlier). They bought a small, green notebook with a blank page for each day of the year. The husband always wrote in the temperature measured by an outside thermometer they could see from their back porch. And the wife would write down anything special that day. And together, at the end of the day, they'd write down something large or small that had happened, something they'd learned from God's Word or even a struggle they'd had.

Those green books became a picture of God's faithfulness in their lives. And now that they're gone, their children treasure these books to keep their memories alive.

—John and Cindy Trent

Prayer Starter: *Lord, it's so easy to forget. You do things that amaze us. But with so much packed into our lives, it's so easy to let all the daily things crowd out our memories of your faithfulness. Help us, Lord, capture memories of answered prayer and of other ways You've worked in our lives so that we "forget not all Your benefits."*

I BELONG TO CHRIST!

In love He predestined us for adoption as sons through Jesus Christ, according to the purpose of His will, to the praise of His glorious grace, with which He has blessed us in the Beloved. (Ephesians 1:5-6)

This past year our daughter and son-in-law decided to expand their family of four to five by adopting a baby girl. I have watched our daughter with fascination as she has responded to some who have made innocent but thoughtless comments like, "It's nice that you decided to adopt after having children of your own." My daughter's reaction is swift, fierce, passionate and loyal: "She is my own and I am her mother!"

Her concern is not so much for the one making the comment, but for her daughter. She will never miss a chance to declare to any and everyone that her daughter is her own, is loved, and belongs to her.

I sense the same swift, fierce, passionate loyalty coming from the Holy Spirit through Paul as he writes to the Ephesians. God has declared that we Gentiles have been loved from the beginning and that we belong to Him. I think of how the angelic hosts must have glorified God the day they found out the mystery hidden from ages past, that in God's manifold wisdom, His plan has always been to extend salvation to humanity through Christ by adopting Gentiles into His family.

—Kory Schuknecht

Prayer Starter: *Father, Thank You for reaching out and making it possible for me to be in relationship with You. Thank You for adopting me into Your family and giving me the Holy Spirit as a guarantee of my future inheritance. Father, may my everyday life be different because of what You have done.*

LIVE IN RESPONSE TO GOD

Do not merely listen to the Word, and so deceive yourselves. Do what it says.
(James 1:22)

James is a hard-hitting book. When I read it I often feel I'm being plopped in the center of a boxing ring and the punches that come at me are the realizations that I have a long way to go on this journey of becoming more like Christ. I believe the most succinct of these reminders is James 1:22. Did you know that "the Word" is not only the Bible, but it is God Himself? John 1:1 says, "In the beginning was the Word, and the Word was with God, and the Word was God."

Are you merely listening to the Word, or are you actively responding to Him? What is the Lord asking you to do? Is it a small thing that you can do in the next minute? Or is it a bigger request that will alter your life's course as you know it? Perhaps He's asking you to step out in faith. Perhaps He's asking you to "Go into all the world" (Mark 16:15). Or maybe He's asking you to "stay," but to increase your support for others who are "going."

A life lived in response to God's calling and promptings is a glorious, light-filled life and produces beautiful, precious fruit. And it is fruit that remains, that lasts for eternity. May you be encouraged today to not only tune in to God, but to also tune up your actions in response. Hear, hear! And do, do!

—Kristin Beasley

Prayer Starter: *God, please help me to hear You and do what You want me to do.*

DISASTROUS LEADER

King Saul got the nation of Israel into disaster because he chose to disobey God rather than follow His guidance. One of the clearest areas of disobedience is found in 1 Samuel 15 where God tells Saul to totally wipe out the Amalekites, and instead Saul spared King Agag and the best of their things. The prophet's classic response still rings in our ears today:

And Samuel said, "Has the Lord as great delight in burnt offerings and sacrifices, as in obeying the voice of the Lord. Behold, to obey is better than sacrifice, and to listen than the fat of rams." (1 Samuel 15:22)

Of course, we know that we are supposed to obey God but there are times we falter. But God's command is no different today, "To obey is better than sacrifice." Saul teaches us four principles:

1. We must be fully committed to God.

2. We must admit our sins.

3. We must care more about what God thinks than what people think.

4. We must follow through God's instructions.

See if you can find these principles in 1 Samuel 15. That should give us plenty to think about today.

—Paul Wegner

Prayer Starter: *God, we pray You will make us more obedient people. We pray You can trust us and use us.*

GOD IS GOD

For from Him and through Him and to Him are all things. To Him be the glory forever. Amen. (Romans 11:36)

The lies we believe, the ways we are deceived by the Evil One, probably outnumber the stars. Realize deception is designed to deceive…it's a cover up. Hitler had a chilling saying: "If you repeat a lie often enough, it becomes truth." Realize, I am usually unaware that I am operating out of a downright, bald-faced lie. But I can assure you, I will live my life in a way that lines up with the lies I believe. One such lie is that I am the God of myself. I am the captain of my soul.

Being the daughter of an alcoholic I believed this. Of course as a Christian I would never have articulated that, but my actions reflected my belief. For instance, when I taught Bible studies, I was not a good delegator. I wore myself out doing everything myself. I had a not-so-healthy sense that I was better than others because I thought I was the God of myself. My healing began as I acknowledged the lies I was believing and asked God to teach me the truth.

—Nonie Maupin

Prayer Starter: *Dear Lord, thank You that the burden for living my life is truly not on my shoulders but on Yours. Teach me that You are God and I am not. Reveal to me the lies that I think are truth, and help me repent.*

WHAT WE KNOW

And we know that all things work together for good for those who love God, who are called according to His purpose. (Romans 8:28)

Emotions are a wonderful thing. Like all parts of the human fabric, God created emotions to allow us to more fully experience the life that He has designed for us. Imagine going through life without being able to feel compassion, sorrow, empathy, affection, or gratitude for the people that God has placed around you. Sounds pretty boring, right? However, we often allow our emotions to dictate our decision-making process, which can lead to disaster. As followers of Christ, it is imperative for us to make daily decisions based upon what we know – the truth of Scripture – rather than what we are feeling in the moment. Reconciling our emotional state with what God tells us in His Word can help navigate us through life's turbulent waters.

- Feeling alone or separated from God?
  Know that He will never leave you or forsake you (Deuteronomy 31:6).

- Feeling unsure about your future?
  Know that He has a perfect plan for your life (Jeremiah 29:11).

- Feeling insecure about your appearance?
  Know that He is more concerned about the condition of your heart (1Samuel 16:7).

- Feeling anxious about the condition of our world and leaders?
  Know that He is sovereign (Colossians 1:16).

What we know to be true about God and His perfect will for our lives should always overcome our emotional state. By leaning into Him through prayer, and refreshing our mind with Scripture during times when our emotions are running high, we can experience His peace and wisdom to make better decisions.

—Scott Edwards

Prayer Starter: *Lord, help me to trust in what I know to be true about You and Your will for my life when my emotions try to overtake me.*

SEEK THINGS ABOVE

If then you have been raised up with Christ, keep seeking the things above, where Christ is, seated at the right hand of God. Set your mind on the things above, not on the things that are on earth. (Colossians 3:1-2)

It is clear that God's plan for our lives includes our continual seeking of Him. We are to put our minds on the things of Heaven, not the things of the here and now that so often crowd our day.

What a beautiful concept – to keep our focus on things above; on Christ at the right hand of God. But it is so easy to be distracted.

Remember the four "P's"– prayer, persistence, perseverance and a humble posture.

They are just as important in keeping our focus on things above as they are in dying to self. As you go through your day, or lie in bed before going to sleep tonight, talk to God about your desire for persistence in seeking those things above. If you don't hunger for that today – boldly ask Him to help you make it a priority in your desires.

—Donald Farr

Prayer Starter: *Lord, help me to keep focused on You. Keep my eyes on things from above.*

UNDERSTANDING GOD

Praise be to the name of God forever and ever. Wisdom and power are His. He changes times and seasons. He sets up kings and deposes them. He gives wisdom to the wise and knowledge to the discerning. (Daniel 2: 20-21)

We must understand the character of God in order to worship Him. All worship is based on comprehension of God. Understanding God is impossible without a maximum understanding of the Word, for it is the Word that reveals who God is. God is in control of human history. He makes and unmakes kings. God is in control of all human events. He is absolutely, totally sovereign. He is the Lord above all and above everything.

A far more important documented history of human affairs than any that have been written so far, would be one which shows the purpose and objective of God in regard to placing a ruler "on the throne." Of some rulers, like Cyrus, Sennacherib, and Pilate, we can see the reason they lived and reigned when they did. Of others, like Nero, Hitler or Stalin, it would be more difficult to say. Yet doubtless God has had some important end to accomplish in the development of His great plans in the case of every person who has ever occupied a position of power.

The year of 1989 will always be remembered as the year when godless Communism went down in former eastern Europe. It happened suddenly, quickly, and it has showed us that no matter what the politics of man are at the time, the politics of God trumps them all. It's good to remember because it will happen again and again whether anyone likes it or not.

—Ota Vozeh

Prayer Starter: *God, You are all-powerful and have a purpose for all. Thank you.*

REMINDERS OF HIS GRACE

Then Solomon began to build the temple of the Lord in Jerusalem on Mount Moriah, where the Lord had appeared to his father David. It was on the threshing floor…the place provided by David. (2 Chronicles 3:1)

It was in the twilight of his life, the waning hours of his reign as King of Israel, that David allowed his foolishness to overwhelm his faith. Perhaps he was wondering how his son, Solomon, would fare once he was gone. Would Solomon be able to stand up to his enemies and overwhelm his competition? Regardless of the reasons, David decided to do a head count of his available warriors.

This is David the giant killer, the one who told Goliath that he was coming against him "in the name of the Lord Almighty" (1 Samuel 17:45). Now, late in life, when he should know better, he was turning to man-made solutions for his worries. This faithless act cost 70,000 people their lives. But in his repentance, God gave him forgiveness. David bought the land where God's judgment came to a halt (2 Samuel 24:17-25). It seemed a fitting place for David's son Solomon to build the Temple.

God is still turning heartache to hope. He has a way of transforming the wounds of our foolishness into the healed reminders of His mighty grace.

—Tim Kimmel

Prayer Starter: *Lord, I Thank You for my sacred scars. Use them as on-going reminders of Your forgiveness and mighty love.*

CALEB'S CONFIDENCE

So now give me this hill country, of which the Lord spoke on that day for you heard on that day how the Anikim were there with great fortified cities. It may be that the Lord may be with me, and I shall drive them out just as the Lord said. (Joshua 14:12)

Caleb's confidence was in God's Word. This is another clue to Caleb's greatness.

What was it that gave this eighty-five year old warrior the idea that he could be a giant killer? Caleb's confidence was grounded firmly on the bed-rock of God's Word. Caleb had seen the Promised Land. He had walked in it for forty days as one of the spies. He had tasted the figs and pomegranates and the delicious grapes that were so large they had to carry them on a pole between two of them.

He and Joshua came back with the good report, "If the Lord delights in us, He will bring us into this land and give it to us, a land that flows with milk and honey. Only do not rebel against the Lord. And do not fear the people of the land, for they are bread for us" (Numbers 14:8,9). Literally, Caleb said, "We can eat their lunch"–"...their protection is removed from them and the Lord is with us; do not fear them!"

Caleb had seen the Promised Land and now for 45 years that vision had burned in his heart as he wandered through the wilderness! While others whined and complained, Caleb looked for a mountain where milk and honey flowed and where the grapes of Eschol grew. His faith never weakened.

—Wayne Lehsten

Prayer Starter: *Father I know that faith (confidence) comes by hearing Your Word. Help me to feed on it deeply today.*

CALL FOR THE ELDERS

Is anyone among you sick? Then he must call for the elders of the church and they are to pray over him, anointing him with oil in the name of the Lord; and the prayer offered in faith will restore the one who is sick, and the Lord will raise him up, and if he has committed sins, they will be forgiven him. (James 5:14-15)

As an elder, I have been called on numerous times to pray for those who are sick. At the beginning of our elder meetings, people come and share their story of suffering, and we take time to lay hands on them, anoint them with oil and pray for them. We have visited hospitals and sickbeds to pray for those who are ill. And we have conducted times of fasting and prayer for people suffering from spiritual attack.

Each time I have the honor of entering into prayer before the throne room of God Himself to bring brothers and sisters before Him, I am in awe of what God has done. For example, during the 1990's two men we prayed for were suffering from stage 4 cancer and were not expected to live much longer. Both were completely healed and served later on our elder board. We have seen depression lifted, eating disorders healed, chronic pain relieved, comfort received and lives extended. We have also seen God heal by taking the suffering person home to be with Him in complete wholeness.

I encourage you, brothers and sisters, to obey this command. For some reason, many feel their suffering isn't important enough to ask for elder prayer. For some, pride keeps them from asking. And according to this passage, sin may be the reason some are suffering and need to seek help to be healed.

Whatever the reason, James tells the body of Christ in no uncertain terms to ask the elders to pray for them. It is a mystery we will not completely understand until Heaven, but God directs us to do it. And we need to obey and receive His blessing.

— Jeff Goble

Prayer Starter: *Father, please give me the courage to ask the elders to pray for me when I am sick.*

FOR OUR GOOD

Count it all joy, my brothers, when you meet trials of various kinds, for you know that the testing of your faith produces steadfastness. And let steadfastness have its full effect, that you may be perfect and complete, lacking in nothing. (James 1:2-4)

The first day that an eighteen or nineteen year-old young man or woman enters the hallowed gates of West Point as a new cadet is a life-changing experience. So it was for me in the summer of 1957. From the moment my foot stepped over the threshold, upper classmen descended on me as if they thought I was going to destroy the Academy! What's your name, mister? Drop that bag! Pick up that bag! Stand up straight! Why are you looking around? Are you thinking about buying this place? Why are you smirking? Wipe that look off your face!

And so it went as one upper classman would pass me off to another for more instruction on how to become another Eisenhower, or Macarthur, or Patton. By the end of the day, after double-timing here and double-timing there from one formation to another, I was in shock. We all were.

That evening all of the new cadets in my company were assembled for a talk by our tactical officer. There were no upper class cadets; just us plebes and an army officer. He started by saying, "You men are probably asking, 'Why are they doing this to me?' A better question you should ask is, 'Why are they doing this for me?' " He went on to explain how a life of instant and unquestioned obedience would serve us well in serving our country in the years to come.

That thought has stuck with me all these years. As I have matured in my Christian walk in the last several years, I have encountered various trials. I found myself asking, "God, why are you doing this to me?" Then I remember the lesson from 50-plus years ago and marvel that God loves me enough to be doing this for me!

What is God doing for you in your trials right now?

—Bob Cain

Prayer Starter: *God, Thank You for the blessings and for all the trials, too, that You are using to shape me into Your child.*

THERE IS A WAY OUT OF THE TUNNEL

If I say, "Surely the darkness will overwhelm me, and the light around me will be night," even the darkness is not dark to you, and the night is as bright as the day. (Psalm 139:11–12)

There is a popular black-and-white photograph that shows a little boy and girl from the back, holding hands as they are walking out of a dark, leafy tunnel and into the shimmering light. If you think a minute, I'm sure you'll remember seeing it somewhere. The father of the children, W. Eugene Smith, took the picture. For him, it was all about the bright, shining "future" that he hoped for his children. However, we all know that sometimes it seems like life is always a tunnel, with no light. But what this picture reminds us is that even in the darkest of times, God's light can lead us safely out of those dark places.

King David spent dark days where life seemed like a tunnel. But he knew something hugely important: "Even the darkness is not dark to You, and the night is as bright as the day."

We may think that the "tunnel" times we are in will never end. But God's love and light will be with you in the tunnel, and into His "light" when you walk with Him to a place of warmth and love.

—John and Cindy Trent

Prayer Starter: *God, help me feel Your love and light as I walk today.*

HOLD YOU IN MY HEART

I hold you in my heart, for you are all partakers with me of grace.
(Philippians 1:7)

One of the priceless benefits of being a pastor is the unmatched joy of how God fills my heart with so many of you. As the days add into years and our time together increases, God has a way of placing you in my heart. I thank God for you, that He allows me to pastor you. I remember you fondly when I think of the amazing things that God accomplishes through Scottsdale Bible. I care for you and I want God's best for you.

This language of "holding you in my heart" is no accident, because it's an emotional matter being allowed to shepherd you as you follow Christ. I hurt when you hurt and I rejoice when you rejoice. I hold incredible hopes for you that you will discover God's great love for you.

The reason why my heart is filled with you is because we are partakers of His grace. Alone and together we have received God's undeserved goodness. He has blessed us with forgiveness and filled us with His Spirit. He has knit us together as a family of faith. He has given us unity in purpose, agreement in direction, and focus for our future. He has brought us together to live together as a community of faith and to impact eternity together.

You are precious to me, and we are all precious to God. I am doubly humbled – to be drawn into fellowship with Jesus by His edeeming love; and to be your pastor, heart-filled with gratitude to guide you as a partaker of God's endless grace.

—Jamie Rasmussen

Prayer Starter: *Thank You for letting us be a part of Your family.*
Fill us with Your love and Your Holy Spirit.

ENDURANCE

...Fixing our eyes on Jesus, the author and perfecter of faith, who for the joy set before Him endured the cross, despising the shame, and has sat down at the right hand of the throne of God. (Hebrews 12:2)

In 1963, Barbara and I, with our four children, drove to Costa Rica to language school. Those first months were peppered with discouragement. As we traveled south we learned that Barbara's brother, a college senior, had been killed in a boating accident. We grieved and sensed how difficult it is to be far away from family.

In Costa Rica, our shipment was delayed in customs for weeks until we could pay the unexpected fees. A teenager ran out in front of our vehicle and his ankle was injured. With little Spanish we were challenged as we helped him and dealt with police and the legal system.

Several times baby Jenny stopped breathing with no medical explanation. Volcano Irazu began showering ash over San José making Duane's asthma critical. Barbara flew with him to the U.S. Seeking medical help. We were struggling with the language to combine the correct gender, number and verb tense and to say it with a semblance of Spanish phonetics. Early on, a veteran missionary asked us "Have you come to stay?" Sometimes we wondered.

But God reminded us: "Faithful is He who calls you, and He will also bring it to pass" (1 Thessalonians 5:24). We reviewed how He had led us and provided for our needs. We remembered that Paul suffered much more and still traveled on: "We are afflicted in every way, but not crushed; perplexed, but not despairing...struck down, but not destroyed" (2 Corinthians 4:8-9). We praise God who sustained us and blessed us during many years of ministry in Guatemala.

Identify the problem that discourages you and then read these verses. "Pray" them into your heart and express your trust in God.

—Stan and Barbara Orth

Prayer Starter: *God, help me to trust You always.*

LIFT UP YOUR EYES ON HIGH

Do you not know?
Have you not heard?
Has it not been declared to you from the beginning?
Have you not understood from the foundations of the earth?
It is He who sits above the circle of the earth,
And its inhabitants are like grasshoppers,
Who stretches out the Heavens like a curtain
And spreads them out like a tent to dwell in.
He it is who reduces rules to nothing.
Who makes the judges of the earth meaningless.
Scarcely have they been planted,
Scarcely have they been sown,
Scarcely has their stock taken root in the earth
But, He merely blows on them, and they wither.
And the storm carries them away like stubble.
"To whom then will you liken me
That I would be his equal?" Says the Holy One
Lift up your eyes on high
And see who has created these stars
The one who leads forth their host by number
He calls them all by name
Because of the greatness of His might and the strength of His power
not one of them is missing....
Do not fear, for I am with you;
Do not anxiously look about you, for I am your God.
I will strengthen you, surely I will help you, surely I will uphold you with my righteous right
hand. (Isaiah 40:21–26, 41:10)

—Deb Pirtle

Prayer Starter: *O Lord, our Lord, how majestic is Your name in all the earth. Lord, help us to see You. Help us to run to You. Help us to rest in You. Lord, help us believe.*

GOD'S LOVE AND FAITHFULNESS

Do not let kindness and truth leave you; bind them around your neck, write them on the tablet of our heart. (Proverbs 3:3)

Your Heavenly Father wants to remind you of something important. Three words: steadfast love and faithfulness.

Steadfast love. The Hebrew word is sometimes translated "kindness" and in other contexts "mercy." This word is used in the Old Testament to refer to God's faithful love to His children. We call it a covenantal word. God made a covenant with us and He keeps it in spite of us.

Sounds like marriage doesn't it? No wonder marriage is the metaphor for our relationship with Christ. He is the Bridegroom who has made His covenant with His bride, the church, and He is faithful and consistent, never wavering in His love.

Faithfulness. This is a person you can count on no matter what. This is a person with a reputation for stability and kindness through thick and thin over a long period of time.

And what are we to do? We are to bind this steadfast love and faithfulness to our lives. We have to remind ourselves all the time.

Our worldview includes the reality that God loves us unconditionally. He keeps His covenant with us. His love is steadfast and faithful and because He is faithful, we can be faithful.

—Larry Anderson

Prayer Starter: *Lord, Thank You for always being faithful. Help me to be faithful to You.*

THE MOMENT OF TRUTH – LITERALLY!

And I will ask the Father, and He will give you another Helper, to be with you forever, even the Spirit of Truth, whom the world cannot receive, but it neither sees Him nor knows Him. You know Him, for He dwells with you and will be in you. (John 14:16)

Because I have been contemplating transformational change, thoughts about how this happens have been rolling around in my head for several months.

Discovering what motivates the heart of an individual is a tricky challenge. But, I believe God knows the key to motivation for each of His children and He is the expert at revealing, to those of us who are watching, what it will take to stir someone up!

My role in assisting with transformational change over the years has been to be a prepared and available vessel for God to use to connect to this deep pool of motivation in whatever way He deems necessary.

Is it hope? Is it possibility? Is it being believed in? Is it compassion? Is it removing obstacles? Is it confrontation? Is it a dose of reality? Is it shocking them? Is it knowledge? Is it freedom from distortion? Is it revealing lies? Is it patient, on-going repetition of the truth?

It is evident when the connection or heart spark (where God's heart is revealed and an individual's heart is exposed – a combustion of both hearts colliding over the same truth at the same time) has occurred because it is like witnessing a lightning strike. It is the mysterious work of the Spirit that confirms a truth so deeply that it rocks an individual down to their soul!

Romans 8:16 says, "The Spirit Himself bears witness with our spirit that we are children of God." In the moment of truth, the heart spark shocks the heart into motion or back into rhythm and the light reveals the source of the power so that there is no misunderstanding that it is the work of God!

I live to participate in this process of transformational change and the pure exhilaration keeps me coming back for more!

—Holly DelHousaye

Prayer Starter: *Lord, prepare me to be available for a moment of truth when it comes.*

CREATOR GOD

In the beginning, God created the Heavens and the earth. (Genesis 1: 1)

Scripture simply assumes God exists. The first verse of the Bible, "In the beginning, God created the Heavens and the earth," matter-of-factly presents God as Creator. God always was. He was not created; He never came into being. He is from "everlasting to everlasting" (Psalm 90:2).

Scripture also tells us that all persons everywhere have a deep, inner sense that God exists, that they are His creatures and that He is their Creator. In Romans 1:19, Paul writes that even for the wicked, this sense is "plain to them, because God has shown it to them." The knowledge of God that Paul refers to can be "clearly perceived...in the things that have been made" (Romans 1:20).

Every created thing gives evidence of God and His character. But human beings created in the image of God give the most evidence of God's existence and character.

Therefore, belief in God is not some "blind faith;" it is based on evidence found both in the Bible and in the natural world.

—Wayne Grudem

Prayer Starter: *Lord, Thank You that we can see You in the Bible, ourselves, and the world around us.*

KEEP ON DOING GOOD

Let us not grow weary in doing good, for in due season we will reap, if we do not give up. (Galatians 6:9)

In one of my favorite episodes of the television show M.A.S.H., Father Mulcahey struggles as he questions the effectiveness of his ministry. He laments how he, unlike the doctors in the medical camp, never knows whether or not he does any good in people's lives. He rarely sees the tangible effects of his efforts.

Isn't it frustrating to do good things and not immediately see positive results? You labor away at something you know to be right and pleasing to the Lord but you just don't see the "fruits" of your labor. Sometimes it's hard to keep doing good.

Paul has some encouragement for those who feel like giving up. Keep doing good, he says, because you will reap blessings. He appeals to a universal law of agriculture – "You reap whatever you sow." Paul knows that if we sow good things, we will reap good as well.

Now there is a catch. Paul says we will reap these blessings "in due season." That may or may not be while we are living on this earth. This isn't a promise of wealth or health for us. It is a promise that the Sovereign God of the universe rewards His children who persevere in doing good and He does so in His timing.

—Steve Eriksson

Prayer Starter: *Lord, help me persevere in doing good. Remind me of Your promised blessings to those who trust and obey You.*

WALK WITH INTEGRITY

O Lord, who may abide in your tent? Who may dwell on your holy hill? (Psalm 15:1)

David asked the Lord who may be a welcomed guest in His home and who may live where God lives. The answer is provided in verse 2: He who walks with integrity, and works righteousness, and speaks truth in His heart may abide in God's home.

The Hebrew word, *tamim* translated "integrity," has a range of meaning including "sound," "wholesome," "unimpaired," or "innocent." As we consider one who walks with integrity, we think of he or she who does not have any incongruence between his or her "internal" world and "external" world. What is just—what is right—is working inside the person's thoughts, emotions, and will and the results are visible in action and behavior. There is no distortion, no twisting of the form of what is in the heart and what is spoken with the mouth. A clear, unaltered speech flows from the seat of emotions. This type of person is welcome in the Lord's home; he or she is invited to reside with the Maker of Heaven and earth.

Praise be to God that He calls us not just to sojourn, but to live with Him permanently. We do not earn it by our own perfection, which is impossible, or in self-righteousness, but through the righteousness of our Savior King, the perfect One in integrity, righteousness and truth. Our hearts are changed, and we are becoming like our King!

—David Walther

Prayer Starter: *Thank You, Lord, for welcoming us to Your home. Strengthen us in Your Holy Spirit to walk with integrity in who You say we are.*

HUMILITY AND SERVANTHOOD

God opposes the proud, but gives grace to the humble. (James 4:6)

When Jesus says in the Beatitudes, "Blessed are the poor in spirit, the meek, the merciful and the pure in heart," His message is humility. We should live to be servants with humble hearts. We should pray empty-handed, or as Saint Augustine said, "The best disposition for praying is that of being desolate, forsaken, stripped of everything." God is holy, we are not. His holiness is incorruptible, we are not. His words are unalterable, His thoughts are unsearchable and His knowledge is immutable. Ours is not.

God is the great I AM. We are the little I am nots. I am not always gracious. I am not always humble, kind and patient, forgiving, merciful and gentle. But there is one thing I am: a sinner saved by the sacrifice of God's Son. Throw yourself totally on Him. Give up. When we repent and admit our weakness, we are really saying, "I am Yours, oh Lord!"

—Barry Asmus

Prayer Starter: *Dear God, I know I am filled with the Holy Spirit. Help my commitment to mercy and justice and loving my neighbor become more walk than talk. Humility and servanthood are loved by You because they describe You. Make me the humble servant You desire.*

NO GREATER MOTIVATION

If we confess our sins, He is faithful and righteous to forgive us our sins and to cleanse us from all unrighteousness. (1 John 1:9)

What is this confession of sins all about? The Greek tense of the word translated "confess" speaks of "continuing confession." It's all about our spiritual growth – sometimes called our sanctification. God is faithful and righteous "to forgive us our sins" and even "to cleanse us from all unrighteousness." God continues to forgive each of us our offenses, and by doing so He is cleansing us from them. How so?

There's no greater motivation for doing good than knowing we've been completely forgiven for doing bad. My guilt would push me to just give up and sin again; but my continual forgiveness pushes me to try again to please Him.

As I seriously look at my sins and let the light of God's Word expose them for what they are, I turn away from them, for I know of their evil. It comes down to learning to discern—becoming one of the mature ones "who because of practice have their senses trained to discern good and evil" (Hebrews 5:14).

But "if we say that we have not sinned" – if our response is to deny both our sin nature and our specific sins – "we make Him a liar, and His Word is not in us" (1 John 1: 10). We choke off our growth, and forfeit the joy of our fellowship with God.

There is a mystery in the confession of our sins. In that confession there is a release from them, from the guilt and from bondage to them. And because this is so important to our spiritual health, God commands us to do it.

—Darryl DelHousaye

Prayer Starter: *God, forgive me…*

LOVE BOUNDARIES

[Love] does not rejoice in unrighteousness, but rejoices in the truth.
(1 Corinthians 13:6)

When we think of love, we think of being patient and kind, how to believe and hope and endure, and how to let go of an offense. But, what do we do when situations get tough? I was faced with this in my own life and needed to have balance in my love approach.

One day as I was seeking the Lord to help me love well, I stumbled upon the middle of 1 Corinthians 13 where clearly stated were these words: "Love does not rejoice in unrighteousness, but rejoices in the truth." I smiled at the Lord as He restated this to my heart. "Love does not support sin or deny truth." I had spent years being patient and kind and had sacrificed more than Christ had ever asked me to sacrifice, not knowing how and when to draw a good boundary. This particular day God showed me that when my love started to support someone in sin or deny the truth in the situation, I was no longer loving.

This new truth confirmed why we lovingly discipline our children and why we set boundaries in our lives with others. I now look a bit deeper, ask God if I am walking in His love to support the person, or if I have crossed the line to support sin. It is a balance statement that has made my love stronger.

—Jessica Neill

Prayer Starter: *Lord, help me love in balance, with patience and kindness, but also in truth.*

GOD'S PURPOSES

When He had received the drink, Jesus said, "It is finished." With that, He bowed His head and gave up His Spirit. (John 19:30)

While Jesus was on earth, His life was a reflection of the fruit of the Spirit at all times, even when He was nailed to the cross.

Among the characteristics of the fruit of the Spirit is joy, and this attitude is one of the most difficult to achieve. In fact, we always ask ourselves: "How do we have joy in difficult life situations such as pain, disease, and death?"

Often, in situations of pain, we strive to smile, to be happy, when what we want to express is our pain.

However, we can see through the experiences of Jesus on the cross and in Gethsemane that joy is not the absence of distress or the lack of pain, nor is joy synonymous with laughter.

Joy is a state of mind due to the satisfaction of a goal accomplished.

Jesus joyfully gave up His Spirit even though He was still in pain when He said, "It is finished."

Joy comes when we look down on the circumstances around us and we seek (or achieve) a higher goal set by God.

—Adrian, Sandra and Agustina Azzati

Prayer Starter: *Lord, help me understand Your purpose in my life so I can give it the priority it deserves over the circumstances surrounding me.*

SIMPLE SACRIFICES

There is a boy here who has five barley loaves and two fish, but what are they for so many? And when they had eaten their fill, He told His disciples, "Gather up the leftover fragments, that nothing may be lost." So they gathered them up and filled twelve baskets with fragments from the five barley loaves left by those who had eaten. (John 6:9–13)

In John 6:9, Jesus took a kid's lunch and multiplied it to feed five thousand people; not to mention that twelve baskets of it were left over. Have you ever considered the size of this kid's sacrifice? It was miniscule!

The Bible tells us that he had two dishes – bread and fish. Bread at this time was baked flat like a tortilla and approximately the size of a hand. The two fish he had were literally sardines! Thus, Jesus took a sardine and made it into a whale! He took a meager sacrifice and made it accomplish a lofty goal with more to spare. God can take your simple sacrifice and make it accomplish big things!

—Joe Gordon

Prayer Starter: *Lord, here is my meager sacrifice. Please multiply it for Your glory.*

THE GREATNESS OF GOD

For by [Jesus Christ] all things were created, both in the Heavens and on earth, visible and invisible, whether thrones or dominions or rulers or authorities—all things have been created through Him and for Him.
(Colossians 1:16)

At my home here in North Africa, I was recently reading a science article on the growing body of evidence pointing to the existence of mysterious dark matter in the cosmos, and the implications sent me to my knees in worship. Perhaps 85% of all substance is invisible, dark matter, flexing its gravitational muscle on massive groups of galaxies, bending light and warping orbits. Some suppose that dark matter is merely some great sterile counterbalance keeping the galaxies in their orbital precision, like the lead weights on the clumsy scales of a Moroccan fruit vendor. But I doubt it.

Without exception, what science initially has thought to be simple and mechanically noncomplex—whether miniscule subatomic elements or astrobodies of galactic proportions—have later proven to be unimaginably complex worlds within worlds. Such sophistication and symmetry consistently reveal the fingerprint of an astonishingly intelligent and powerful Designer.

What fodder for the contemplative Christian imagination! One cannot help but be reminded of the doxology in Romans 11:

Oh, the depth of the riches and wisdom and knowledge of God! How unsearchable are His judgments and how inscrutable His ways! For who has known the mind of the Lord, or who has been His counselor? Or who has given a gift to Him that He might be repaid? For from Him and through Him and to Him are all things. To Him be glory forever. Amen

Open your eyes and your imagination today to the created order all around you.

—Steve and Jean McLurg

Prayer Starter: *Oh, Father! Give to me a clear mind to discover and eyes to see that You are infinitely greater than all You have made!*

WHEN THERE ARE NO ANSWERS

And after you have suffered for a little while, the God of all grace, who called you to His eternal glory in Christ, will Himself perfect, confirm, strengthen and establish you. (1 Peter 5:10)

When you hurt physically or emotionally, you can lose perspective and forget God's faithfulness. Take the life of Job for example. He lost everything – possessions, home, even his children. He also suffered from a horrible disease. Job asked "why" many times. It is not always easy to answer "why" to our suffering, pain, or hurt. Sometiwes we simply have to rely on God's promises instead of explanations.

Job learned God's faithfulness through being faithful to God. His faith did not lie in outward circumstances, nor in speculative explanations, but in the encounter of faith in an all-powerful and all-knowing God. Job wanted to reason with God but he learned to rest in God. His faith kept him going. In spite of his suffering – his life, faith, and hope were in God.

Wait on the Lord. Trust Him. You cannot measure the greatness of God (Job 11:7-9), but you can immerse yourself in the measureless love and power of God. (Ephesians 3:14-21)

—Susan Miller

Prayer Starter: *Oh Lord, give me Your strength, Your grace, and Your mercy at this time in my life. Help me to rely on Your promises, and remember Your faithfulness.*

CELEBRATION

Seven days you shall celebrate a feast to the Lord your God in the place which the Lord chooses, because the Lord your God will bless you in all your produce and in all the work of your hands, so that you shall be altogether joyful.
(Deuteronomy 16:15)

How are you at celebrating God's goodness? I tend to be one of those people who celebrate quickly and then move on to the next project or objective to achieve. However, as a leader I have learned that celebration is an important aspect of motivating others to move forward to the next challenge.

Celebration provides energy and confidence, giving hope for the future. In America, we celebrate Independence Day, Memorial Day, and many other holidays to remind us of our heritage. In today's reading which celebrates the Passover, the Lord commands Israel to remember the day the Lord delivered them from the land of Egypt. They were to celebrate what God had done for them and for what He was continuing to do for them. The Lord commanded them to celebrate not for the moment, not even for the day, but for seven days and then to celebrate this event every year so that all generations would remember God's goodness.

Think about initiating a week of celebration for the next seven days. Individually, as a family, or in your small group or company, choose to celebrate God's goodness.

—Mark Upton

Prayer Starter: *Lord I want to celebrate Your goodness to me. Thank You for...*

A SALUTE TO COMPASSION

And He remembered His covenant for their sake, and relented according to the greatness of His loving-kindness. He also made them objects of compassion in the presence of all their captors. (Psalm 106:45-46)

One of the most highly decorated soldiers of the Civil War was the North's General Joshua Chamberlain. He was a college professor, teaching history and theology, who became a captain in the 1st Maine. On a hill named "Little Round Top," it was Chamberlain who charged downhill, broke a Confederate advance, and won the Medal of Honor. He was a key reason the North won that terrible battle.

Chamberlain was wounded eight times and had nine horses shot out from under him before the war ended. He was so respected by President Lincoln, General Grant, and all the Union soldiers that his unit was designated the "Honor Guard" when General Lee surrendered at Appomattox Courthouse.

When the surrender was completed and General Lee began to ride down the road flanked on both sides by Union soldiers, some of the Northerners began to laugh and jeer at their defeated enemy. But General Chamberlain rode down the line silencing the men. He then ordered every man to stand at attention, present arms, and salute in honor of their greatest foe.

In today's verse, Chamberlain shares a trait with the God he loved – compassion. Adding compassion to our love, particularly when our spouse or friend or child needs it, is a mark of God's love.

—John and Cindy Trent

Prayer Starter: *We are so grateful, Lord Jesus, that You chose to have compassion on us. Help us to extend that mark of Your love to our loved ones and all we meet.*

MUSIC ROCKS!

So these stones shall become a memorial to the sons of Israel forever.
(Joshua 4:7b)

To commemorate crossing the Jordan River into the land that Israel had been promised, Joshua instructed that twelve stones be set up – a "memorial" to what God had done for them. These rocks were called *Ebenezers* - stones of remembrance. I keep a handful of rocks on my office shelf to remind me of special times – including a small piece of sandstone, picked up on the then-future school property in Kondoa, Tanzania.

Music, in its wonderful and powerful way, also provides memorials in our lives such as a song remembered from childhood or a favorite family song. More importantly, music can serve as a memorial of who God is and what He has done for us. We sing of the Triune God, repeating the theological truth that He is Father, Son, and Spirit.

In the middle of a sleepless night, a song may be a reminder that God will take care of us. Sometimes, we discover that a song is the best expression of our prayer to God. Further, Scripture is often learned best by singing a song – a musical rock of remembrance, an Ebenezer. Bono, the lead singer of U2, said, "Words and music did for me what solid, even rigorous, religious argument could never do, they introduced me to God."

So when we sing in worship, let's not be thoughtless or casual. After all, we're stacking rocks of memorial to God's presence and work in our world – rock music!

—Ed Willmington

Prayer Starter: *Dear Lord..."Here I raise my Ebenezer, hither by Thy help I'm come." Amen.*

ON A DONKEY

Behold, your king is coming to you; righteous and having salvation is he,
humble and mounted on a donkey, on a colt, the foal of a donkey.
(Zechariah 9:9)

Why the donkey?

The long awaited Messiah had come. The King was ready to ascend his throne and over-throw the yolk of Roman oppression.

The people cried *"Hosanna"* quoting Psalm 118:25 – "Save us, (hosanna) we pray, O Lord! O Lord, we pray, give us success!"

Hosanna means "save now."

The Jews wanted a king, and they wanted him now. They looked to the fulfillment of the prophecy: "I will establish the throne of His kingdom forever" (2 Samuel 7:13b).

But, when He rode into Jerusalem, Jesus fulfilled another prophecy: "Behold, your king is coming to you; righteous and having salvation is He, humble and mounted on a donkey, on a colt, the foal of a donkey" (Zechariah 9:9).

The people were correct as they proclaimed Jesus as King, but they didn't understand God's timing. That's where the donkey comes in.

In the Hebrew tradition, the animal the king rode on was highly significant. Conquering kings rode a horse; humble, peaceful kings symbolized their intent by riding a donkey. Yes, Jesus came as King, but not the conquering king the people expected. He came as the sacrificial King. A conquering warrior could not become the sacrifice for the sins of all humankind. What was required was a Lamb. But, the next time our King appears, He will not be riding a donkey: "Then I saw Heaven opened, and behold, a white horse! The one sitting on it is called faithful and true, and in righteousness He judges" (Revelation 19:11).

—Bill Epley

Prayer Starter: *Jesus, You are my King. Thank You for coming and saving me.*

CHANGE OF HEART

Blessed are the pure in heart for they will see God. (Matthew 5:8)

To people steeped in the Old Testament, those listening to Jesus' words would have been amazed to think that anyone could have a "pure heart." Even after the "Day of Atonement" you would only be pure until you sinned again and for most of us that would not be too long.

Jesus' offer was truly amazing. I believe that what Jesus was offering was a totally new answer and one that could never have been offered until Jesus paid the ultimate sacrifice for sin. He was offering a way to change their heart and this could only happen after Jesus died for sins and the Holy Spirit was sent into their hearts to help them live a pure life.

This does not mean you will never sin, but that when you sin those sins have already been pardoned. You still need to ask God for forgiveness for them, but it is for a different purpose. It is because sin hinders your relationship with God and we want all the barriers between Him and us removed.

Based upon Jesus' sacrificial death on the cross, we can have a pure heart before God. What an amazing possibility and one that the Old Testament saints could not even have fathomed.

—Paul Wegner

Prayer Starter: *Thank You, God, that we can have a pure heart before You. God, make us more useful to You.*

RUN THE RACE

…Let us run with endurance the race that is set before us, fixing our eyes on Jesus, the Author and Perfecter of faith… (Hebrews 12:1-2)

Lie: life is too hard. I can't do it.

You're partially correct. Life is hard…sometimes. Life was hard for Perry Edinger, a previous athletic trainer at Arizona State University. He lost his beloved wife to cancer and he lost a good friend, Pat Tillman, who was killed in Afghanistan. Perry could have given up after such devastating losses.

But instead, he continued to do something that gave him joy: he loved to run. He ran marathons and ultra-marathons. He finished 9th in the world's toughest footrace during July's Badwater Ultra-marathon that begins in Death Valley. But the run was not without tremendous challenges…the heat, blisters, and an 8,000 foot altitude change, to mention a few. I don't know about you, but I'm exhausted just thinking about it. Quitting, however, was not an option for Edinger. He said, "It's a matter of what you choose."

As you run your race today, will you give up, or will you choose to run it in the power and strength of the Lord? Will you choose the truth that Jesus is perfecting your faith each day, or will you believe the lie that life is just too hard?

—Nonie Maupin

Prayer Starter: *Dear Lord, help me to choose to cling to You; to fix my eyes on You when life is hard.*

THE FORGOTTEN DISCIPLES

These are the names of the twelve apostles: first, Simon (who is called Peter) and his brother Andrew, James son of Zebedee, and his brother John; Philip and Bartholomew; Thomas and Matthew the tax collector; James son of Alphaeus, and Thaddaeus; Simon the Zealot and Judas Iscariot, who betrayed Him.
(Matthew 10:2-4)

Recently, I had occasion to reexamine the lives of the disciples of Jesus. Most of people can name the big three – Peter, James and John. And with a little thought some can recall Thomas, Judas Iscariot of course, then Matthew, perhaps Andrew and Philip. But then it gets a little tougher. Bartholomew (or Nathanael) may surface because John's Gospel records that Nathanael was a devout Jew who was skeptical of Jesus at first but quickly became convinced of His Deity. Simon the Zealot might be recalled if we really scratch our heads, but that still leaves two unnamed.

Only the most devoted Sunday School and Vacation Bible School veterans will recall James son of Alphaeus and Thaddeus (or Judas son of James). These two are the forgotten disciples of Jesus. Little is known about them other than their names. Tradition suggests something about where they traveled as they preached the Gospel of Jesus Christ and how they may have died, but there are no written records. What we do know is that they were chosen by Jesus, just as Peter, James and John. They accompanied Jesus during His three-year ministry. They heard His teaching, viewed His miracles and were witnesses to His resurrection. And we know that they were part of God's plan to make disciples of all nations.

As I reflect on these apostles, I believe these two are more representative of us as Christ-followers. We, too, have been chosen by Christ. We have read His teaching, perhaps know something of His miraculous power and bear witness to His resurrection. But the world will not mark our life or when the time comes our death, except in passing. And yet, like James the Less and Thaddeus, we play an important part in carrying out the mission of making disciples of all nations, teaching them to observe all that He commanded us.

—Dave Zehring

Prayer Starter: *Lord, thank You for choosing me. May I be faithful in Your sight this day.*

PASSING IT ON

You therefore, my son, be strong in the grace that is Christ Jesus. The things which you have heard from me in the presence of many witnesses, entrust these to faithful men who will be able to teach others also. (2 Timothy 2:1-2)

This is the theme verse for our Timothy leadership training program at Scottsdale Bible Church. We desire to pass on what we have learned to younger men so that they will also be able to pass it on to others.

This is a leadership characteristic that is easy to see in the letters of Paul. Just the fact that he was writing to those whom he had instructed and modeled the love of Christ, communicates that he had left the ministry in the hands of others after he left.

Paul had led Timothy to Christ during his first missionary journey (1 Corinthians 4:17; 1 Timothy 1:2, 18). Here is the main admonition in the first part of the letter. Paul is calling for Timothy to overcome his apparent drift toward weakness and renew his commitment to his ministry. Are you drifting toward weakness? Ask God to help you renew your commitment to Him and your ministry today.

—Patrick Sullivan

Prayer Starter: *Heavenly Father, may we be faithful to pass on to others what we have learned from You.*

DON'T LOSE HEART

Therefore we do not lose heart. Though outwardly we are wasting away, yet inwardly we are being renewed day by day. (2 Corinthians 4:16)

My father-in-law, who was a world-class tennis player and also pastor of a church in Prague, used to say, "Young people in our church don't get old until they are 120." And he was like that himself. The Lord took him home when he was 96 years old just as he was returning from a Sunday morning church service. He was young until his death.

At the time of writing this short devotional in Baden, Austria, I am 67 and I am wasting away. I know because I climbed a 1,900 meter-high mountain last week (probably the lowest mountain in the Austrian alps), and I thought I would die in the process! No legs, no breath: I am an old guy. My wife was way ahead of me.

"Teach us to number our days aright, that we may gain a heart of wisdom," God tells us through Moses (Psalm 90:12*)*. Wise people know that they are wasting away regardless of all the vitamin pills and fitness programs. However, Christian faith is much more about "there and then" than "here and now," despite what we so often hear these days from the pulpit.

Why was Paul able to say what he did in the leading quote? The answer is in the verses preceding: "We know that the one who raised the Lord Jesus from the dead will also raise us with Jesus and present us with you in His presence" (2 Corinthians 4:14*)*.

Therefore…don't lose heart! He keeps renewing you by His Spirit for now and He will raise you even when the "now" is gone.

—Ota Vozeh

Prayer Starter: *Lord, thank You for renewing me day by day.*

LIKE A BRIDGE

Since my youth, O God, you have taught me, and to this day I declare your marvelous deeds. Even when I am old and gray, do not forsake me, O God, till I declare your power to the next generation, your might to all who are to come. (Psalm 71:17-18)

It was Easter Sunday. Darcy and I were bringing our granddaughter to church because her mother and father were involved in the worship service. I'd dropped Darcy off to secure us a seat while I parked the car.

But as I was pulling in, two things happened simultaneously. Our granddaughter fell asleep in her car seat, and Simon and Garfunkel's classic ballad "Bridge Over Troubled Waters" came on the radio. I decided to sit there a bit longer to savor the song and let my granddaughter get a few more minutes of sleep, but the Holy Spirit had other plans.

As I sat there in the car with my granddaughter asleep in her car seat, I couldn't get over how much the words to that familiar song define our role as grandparents (and parents). When our children and grandchildren are worn out and feeling overwhelmed, we will help dry their tears. When they feel all alone in difficult times, we'll be there to give them support. We want to promise them that no matter what, "Like a bridge over troubled water, I will lay me down."

—Tim Kimmel

Prayer Starter: *Dear Lord, thank You that I can lay my life down for my children because You first laid Your life down for me.*

CALEB'S STRENGTH

I am this day eighty-five years old. I am still as strong today as I was in the day that Moses sent me; my strength is now as my strength was then for war and for coming and going. So now give me this hill country. (Joshua 14:10-11)

Caleb's strength never weakened. At age 85 he declared that he was as strong as ever. A faith that never wavered had enabled him to lay hold on a strength that never weakened-the very power of God Himself. He would agree with Paul that, "Though the outward man may perish, yet the inward man is renewed day by day." This man knew how to toil and fight and exhaust himself and still be full of the strength of God.

Caleb at 85 still had to face three formidable giants- the three sons of Anak. May I suggest that we too must face three giants?

The grasshopper mentality: there will always be someone saying that it can't be done. It's never been done before; we can't afford it. We can't do it.

The giants mentality: all of us have giants in our lives. Giants of discouragement, finances, sickness, family distress, doubt etc. We can't defeat them ourselves any more than Caleb could. We have two options: fear or faith.

The gray hair mentality: when God makes a promise, he will give us the strength to see its fulfillment. Never count God or yourself out. True faith looks beyond the present circumstance and sees the provision of the Almighty.

—Wayne Lehsten

Prayer Starter: *Lord I need courage today. Turn my unbelief into Your strength.*

THE TRUE HEALER

So we do not lose heart. Though our outer self is wasting away, our inner self is being renewed day by day. For this light momentary affliction is preparing for us an eternal weight of glory beyond all comparison, as we look not to the things that are seen but to the things that are unseen. For the things that are seen are transient, but the things that are unseen are eternal. (2 Corinthians 4:16-18)

As a Christian physician, I am at peace knowing that our Lord is an all-powerful, yet all-loving healer who will touch the sick person at his or her greatest point of need. Confronting the frailty of one's physical body, even in the context of a minor illness, brings up the God-ordained longing we have for the eternal. Though I have been trained as a physician to focus on healing the physical body, I must also conduct my work in a uniquely spiritual context. It is therefore highly relevant for us to turn to Scripture and study the divine attributes of the true healer, Jesus.

As the ultimate physician role model, and the source of our life and strength, Jesus perfectly blends authority over all things with compassion for the lost and suffering. As God and man, He has a unique understanding of the human condition that propels Him with the intense purpose of saving souls and pointing people to God. He consistently connects word and deed, healing in the context of teaching truth (Mark 1:39). As He preached the Word, people were drawn to Him and brought Him their sick (Mark 2:2-3).

Jesus' compassion and focus on the whole person is beautifully recorded in the Gospels, and serves as a high standard for Christians in the healthcare field, and frankly to all believers as they serve in the name of Christ. Jesus knew and understood the whole person's needs, connecting both the heart and health in a compelling and personal manner.

Reflect on the ways in which your behaviors mirror those of Jesus as recorded in the Scriptures. Am I serving others with compassion and understanding the way our Lord would?

—Keith Frey

Prayer Starter: *Jesus, teach me to have compassion for people they way You do. Help me to serve others and not lose heart.*

TRUSTING GOD'S WORD

Do not be anxious about anything, but in everything by prayer and supplication with thanksgiving let your requests be made known to God. (Philippians 4:6)

And my God will supply every need of yours according to His riches in glory in Christ Jesus. (Philippians 4:19)

During the big real estate downturn of the mid-1980's, I was engaged in land investing. I had what to me was a rather large annual land payment that was coming due in a few months. There was no foreseeable way I could make the payment given the economy at the time. My wife was not aware of the situation and I did not want to alarm her or make her anxious about finances. So I kept putting off telling her, waiting for just the right moment. I anguished for many, many weeks about how to tell her. I knew she would be distraught.

One morning I came out ready to leave for work and my wife was sitting in the living room, quietly doing her Bible study. She greeted me cheerily. I thought that this might be the moment to drop the bombshell. I gingerly broached the subject, eventually giving her the full details. She listened patiently for the full explanation and then asked me when the payment was due. I told her it was due in about a month.

She looked up from her Bible and asked gently, "Why do you think God would give us the money before we need it?" After all of my anxiety about telling her, I was speechless.

A week or so later a man called me. Several years earlier he bought land from us and was making annual payments over a long time. He was calling to see if I would discount the balance if he paid it off in full now. His proposed payment was within a few hundred dollars of the amount I owed in less than a month!

Are you trusting your instincts or are you going to trust God's Word?

—Bob Cain

Prayer Starter: *God, help me to trust Your Word with all my heart.*

ALWAYS AND FOREVER

And Jesus came and spoke to them saying, "…lo, I am with you always, even to the end of the age." (Matthew 28:18-20)

"That does it!" A seminary student said in a loud voice to his friend as they both sat in the school library studying for a Bible test on the book of Matthew. "I'm never getting in an airplane again!"

Confused, his friend asked him what he was talking about and he said, "It's right here! Look!" And he showed him Matthew 28:20, "It says, 'Lo, I am with you always.' Not high! I'm never getting on another plane!"

Obviously, this (bad) attempt at "Bible humor" misses the point that Jesus made sure His disciples understood. Namely, "high or low," good times or bad, struggling at work or a relationship, or as happy as we've ever been, we have Jesus' word that He'll be there for us.

For those of us who may have come from difficult backgrounds, the security we have in Jesus' love and presence is no small thing. In a world with so many broken promises and relationships, it's a tremendous gift to know that Jesus "always" being there for us means… "always!"

—John and Cindy Trent

Prayer Starter: *Thank You, Lord, that You're with us day in and day out, high or low! And thank You as we go through life that You'll be with us each and every step of the way.*

EASTER

But if there is no resurrection of the dead, then not even Christ has been raised. And if Christ has not been raised, then our preaching is in vain and your faith is in vain. (1 Corinthians 15:13–14)

Without a resurrection there would be no Christianity. As C.S. Lewis noted it is the one miracle on which all the other ones rest. If Jesus was truly raised from the dead then it proves He was who He said He was and that all He did was certainly possible.

When you get right down to it, the resurrection of Jesus means three very practical things for those who believe. It means eternal life with God; it means victory over sin now; and it means hope for the future. The resurrection of Jesus brings a power to our spiritual lives that defeats sin and its consequences and gives hope for a God-centered, God-infused future.

The resurrection of Jesus means that there is nothing this side of Heaven (or the next) that can separate us from God and His love. As the great reformer Martin Luther says so well, "O death, where is thy sting? O grave, where is thy victory? This is so true that even Satan cannot deny it. Christ's resurrection and victory over sin, death and hell is greater than all Heaven and earth."

— Jamie Rasmussen

Prayer Starter: *May the power of Jesus' resurrection flow in and through me today O God.*

PASSION WEEK

Rejoice greatly, O daughter of Zion! Shout, O daughter of Jerusalem! Behold, your King is coming to you; He is just and having salvation, lowly and riding on a donkey, a colt, the foal of a donkey. (Zechariah 9:9)

"Passion" week unfolds in the pages of Scripture. Are we aware of the tensions that are set before us in God's Word? Do we realize the massive contrasts in God's plan of redemption? We as believers walking through this week, grieve the death of our Savior, while celebrating the victory of His resurrection!

Jesus rode triumphantly into Jerusalem before His death. As the cross loomed before Him, Jesus was hailed as King. The King rode humbly on an unbroken, untamed foal of a donkey. Please read again the last three sentences. Did you catch those contrasts? We read about a lowly King, humbly riding through a crowd on an untamed animal. Is that even possible? And, He is honored by those in the crowd as His execution is fast approaching. As there are no contradictions in Scripture, we are reading God's truth.

Many of those who hailed Jesus as King, cried, "Crucify Him" several days later. Why? What did they miss? Of course, we know that Jesus' death was God's plan – for God's glory! We read in Isaiah 53:10, "…it pleased the Father to bruise the Son." How are we to live within the light of God's glorious plan of redemption? What might we be missing?

—Cathy Wilson

Prayer Starter: *Lord, as we prepare for Easter, please don't let us miss Your glory – all that You are in Your splendor and majesty. Cause us to worship and exalt You – our suffering servant who is the victorious, eternal King!*

GOD'S PLANS

"For My thoughts are not your thoughts, nor are your ways My ways," says the Lord. "For as the Heavens are higher than the earth, so are My ways higher than your ways, and My thoughts than your thoughts." (Isaiah 55:8–9)

Rather than getting consumed in our disappointments, let's look at God's plans as ones that outshine our own. Our anticipation of an outcome may fall short of His glorious plans for us to have the abundant life He speaks about in John 10:10.

Ruth, of the Old Testament, was barren and then her husband died. Ruth could have become despondent due to her ties to social norms, and could have rejected God because her plans failed. But Ruth chose to seek the Lord. He revealed His plans for her were to go to Bethlehem with her mother-in-law, marry Boaz and as a result, be in the lineage of Jesus!

Today, unemployment may seem like a huge disappointment and challenge, but maybe that unemployment is a gift, allowing you and your spouse to grow spiritually as a couple—to trust God together for His plans for your future. In your vulnerability, you may get to model how to really trust God in front of your children or others. In our "'disappointments" in life, may we look for God's plans. In what area of your life might God have a "higher" way for you?

—Deb Pirtle

Prayer Starter: *Oh, Father in Heaven, help us to recognize Your ways. Guide us in aligning our hearts with Your heart, embracing Your thoughts and plans for our lives.*

MY PURPOSE IN LIFE

I will give thanks to you, O Lord my God, with all my heart, and will glorify your name forever. (Psalm 86:12)

I had been taught that we are supposed to glorify God, but nobody ever told me what that meant. What is "glory" and how do we "glorify" God? 1 Corinthians 15:41 begins, "There is one glory of the sun, and another glory of the moon..." Each of these gives a different light because of their different attributes. The sun is a giant nuclear reactor, its elements producing light and heat that give life to our planet millions of miles away. The moon is a big dead rock that cannot produce even 1 watt of its own light, but may reflect the sun's light.

God is like the sun, full of light and power for life. I am like the moon, unable to produce any light of my own, but able to reflect God's light to others as I walk in the power of His Spirit. Those who do not know God walk in darkness, just as at night people cannot see the sun, but they can see the moon brightly reflecting sunlight. Jesus said we are the light of the world. Our job is to shine noticeably with God's love so that when people want to know how we have so much light, we can introduce them to our Lord and bring them to the Father.

—Dave Cottrell

Prayer Starter: *Remind me daily, Lord, as I look up to the sun or to the moon, that You have given me a special job to do.*

LIGHT AND MUSIC

For at one time you were darkness, but now you are light in the Lord. Walk as children of light (for the fruit of light is found in all that is good and right and true), and try to discern what is pleasing to the Lord. (Ephesians 5:8-10)

I made up a phrase for people who bless instead of curse as they pass by. I call them "The light and music" people. These people are the pleasant, agreeable people who bring good energy to our lives – leaving a lingering memory behind that uplifts and elevates. We feel better after interacting with them and when we check our emotional gas tank – we find that we have received a free fill-up!

I am using the term "light" in regard to how little energy someone requires from me because they are easily endured with little difficulty or discomfort. I am using the term "music" in regard to the energy that flows into me when I hear an agreeable sound that is pleasing to my mind and my senses. Both of these things become profitable deposits into my own spirit.

It is interesting to note that the law of conservation of energy states that energy cannot be created or destroyed. It can only be converted into matter and vice versa because energy cannot create energy.

I guess the only hope for those of us who don't necessarily carry around with us an abundance of energy is to stay connected to the only true power source – God. His energy flows into us when we access His resources and then we have the amazing privilege of allowing His energy to flow through us into the lives of people we meet.

It has been said that there is a generous supply of Heavenly light and music for those who are tuned in. Is it time to change your dial?

—Holly DelHousaye

Prayer Starter: *Lord, help Your power to flow through me to those around me and help me to be "light and music" to all I meet.*

PASTORS

To the angel of the church in… (Revelation 2:1,8,12,18; 3:1,7,14)

Over the past fifty years, tens of thousands of people have come together at Scottsdale Bible Church to hear a message from the Lord. What began as a small gathering has developed into a large assembly in the heartbeat of Scottsdale.

In that time, God has faithfully spoken through dozens of messengers to share timely, timeless messages to bring life, provide hope, and rescue souls. Specifically, God has graciously appointed six men over Scottsdale Bible Church's fifty years to serve as chief messengers as the senior pastor. Despite distinct personalities and individual qualities that make each of these pastors special, they have in common a deep love for Jesus, a commitment to communicating God's messages with integrity, and a pastor's shepherding heart for the congregation.

When Jesus delivered the timely and timeless messages to the seven churches in Revelation 2 and 3, He first instructed His beloved disciple John to deliver these important messages to the churches' pastors.

This intentionality was not a matter of formal protocol or of honoring a dogmatic hierarchy. Rather, God loves His church so much that He made sure His messages would be communicated through their loving, caring, shepherding pastor. Each church receives an important message. Each church would be surprised, encouraged, or challenged by the message that God had for them. Every church had a promise from God to consider through the message. The magnitude of the message was so important that God determined to deliver it through a protective, thoughtful, servant-minded messenger.

So it is today. God continues to deliver messages of significance and magnitude to the assemblies of His children, using His chief messengers. Many times weekly, pastors stand before crowds and deliver messages from Heaven's King. Sometimes those messages are surprising, usually encouraging, and often challenging. The faithfulness of Scottsdale Bible's chief messengers, and of countless pastors in countless churches across the world over the years, points to the loving initiative of Jesus Christ to continually maintain vital communication with you, His church.

—Bryan McAnally

Prayer Starter: *Thank You Lord for our godly pastors. This is Your church. Work through us.*

HOLY, HOLY, HOLY

And the four living creatures, each one of them having six wings, are full of eyes around and within; and day and night they do not cease to say, "HOLY, HOLY, HOLY is THE LORD GOD, THE ALMIGHTY, WHO WAS AND WHO IS AND WHO IS TO COME." And when the living creatures give glory and honor and thanks to Him who sits on the throne, to Him who lives forever and ever, the twenty-four elders will fall down before Him who sits on the throne, and will worship Him who lives forever and ever, and will cast their crowns before the throne, saying, "Worthy are You, our Lord and our God, to receive glory and honor and power; for You created all things, and because of Your will they existed, and were created."
(Revelation 4:8-11)

One of my all-time favorite songs is the timeless hymn, "Holy, Holy, Holy". It's among many great songs that originate from the text of this Scripture. It's that Heavenly worship that we read about that causes me to long for a worship experience that is not complicated by our human interventions here on earth.

There are certain Sundays where it seems as though the "windows of Heaven" open and we experience something unique and special. There are still other Sundays where it might seem that those windows are tightly shut. It's certainly not that God is fickle in His posture towards us, it is that we complicate it with our own desires and expectations.

I love each and every opportunity I have to lead people into His presence, yet I'll be quite satisfied to be released of that calling and responsibility when we pass from this life to eternity and join with the Heavenly hosts and cry, "Holy, Holy, Holy!"

—Troy Peterson

Prayer Starter: *Father, forgive me for the complications and expectations I have created...*

GLORIFY GOD

Let the words of my mouth and the meditation of my heart be acceptable in Your sight, O Lord, my Rock and my Redeemer. (Psalm 19:14)

In every aspect of business activity, God knows our hearts and we must glorify Him by having attitudes of heart in which He delights. Therefore, in all our ownership of property and in all our stewardship, if we want to glorify God in business, we should seek to avoid pride and to have hearts full of love and humility toward others and toward God.

In producing goods and services for others and in using them for our own enjoyment, we should have hearts of thanksgiving to God for His goodness in providing these things to us.

If we work for someone else, we should work as if we were working "For the Lord and not for men, knowing that from the Lord you will receive the inheritance as your reward" (Colossians 3:23-24).

And if others work for us, we need to think of them as equal in value as human beings made in the image of God, and our heart's desire should be that their job brings them good and not harm. We should be thankful to God for money and profit, but we should never love money or profit.

—Wayne Grudem

Prayer Starter: *God, help me love You and others with all my heart.*

THE DIVINE GARDENER

I planted, Apollos watered, but God gave the growth. So neither he who plants nor he who waters is anything, but only God who gives the growth. (I Corinthians 3:6-7)

One of the great fears that many Christians have today involves sharing their faith with others. We tense up sometimes just imagining walking up to a friend or family member in order to share the Gospel with them. What if they don't receive the message? What if I can't get them to believe? What if I don't know enough to convert them? In our results-based culture, these thoughts and the fear of failure can prevent us from taking even that initial step.

Fortunately, Paul puts this thinking into the proper perspective. God is the one who causes the growth. He is the one who "converts." He is the only one who can truly change a heart. Not the one who plants, seeds or waters them – they can't cause the growth. The Holy Spirit alone bears this responsibility for spiritual growth.

Now the beautiful thing is that we get to participate in this process of saving people. We get to preach the Gospel. We get to model Christ-likeness to our friends and neighbors. We get to share our testimonies. He only holds us responsible for these things – not the result of these efforts. Whew! It kind of takes the pressure off, huh?

—Steve Eriksson

Prayer Starter: *Lord, use me to bring the Gospel to people. Remove from me the fear of failure and the pressure to "succeed." May You alone receive the glory for a changed life.*

ASK FOR WISDOM

But if any of you lacks wisdom, let him ask of God, who gives to all gener-
ously and without reproach, and it will be given to him. (James 1:5)

Going through trials is never easy. Many times we feel like we don't know which way to turn. If we lack wisdom and the ability to have our faith tested, we should ask, we should pray to our loving Heavenly Father for it.

Joy comes to the believer during times of testing not because the immediate experience of the test is necessarily pleasant or cheerful, but if experienced with the proper perspective, it brings us closer to Christ-likeness, the reason the believer exists—to have Christ formed in us.

God gives wisdom from above in His grace; its results produce those thoughts, emotions and behaviors to walk this life faithfully in Christ. This wisdom indwells us not "in an it," but "in a who:" the Holy Spirit. Humbly ask Him for wisdom; for the Holy Spirit to fill you. He wants to give to you generously and without reprimand, as you trust in Him fully.

—David Walther

Prayer Starter: *Heavenly Father, I love You! Thank You that You give the gift of wisdom,*
Your Holy Spirit as a gift of grace. Fill me with Your wisdom that I may
grow in Your Son's likeness and have Your perspective on all things.

COME AND SEE

"Can anything good come out of Nazareth?" Nathaniel asked. "Come and see," replied Philip. (John 1:46)

Every human being will ask sooner or later, "Who am I? What am I living for? How did I get so far off track, so far from the place I know God wants me to be?" Those are important questions, even eternal ones. The Bible tells us that life is full of dark tunnels, but there is hope. Look at any person's life and you will find both adversity and abundance.

In the tunnel you find loneliness, despair and weakness. In the light you see faith, hope and love. In the wilderness, despair abounds. But then a dawning – I would rather be God's failure than someone else's success.

Faith can do things we think impossible. Hope is a reality being constructed by God that is not yet visible. The Bible promises us that God will complete the work He has begun. Love prays this: create in me a pure heart, O God, and renew a steadfast spirit within me (Psalm 51:10). Satan might shake his fingers and say, "Look what I have done." But God says, "Come and see what I can do."

—Barry Asmus

Prayer Starter: *Dear Lord, cynics may raise their theories, doubters may raise their questions, but all their musings fade in the bright light of easter morning. He is risen!*

HIS GREATEST WORK

If Christ has not been raised, then our preaching is in vain, your faith also is vain.
(1 Corinthians 15:14)

If Christianity isn't based on truth, it shouldn't be too difficult to destroy. All you have to do is knock out its foundation. The Bible itself even tells you how.

But there's proof that what Jesus said about Himself was true.

Jesus said, "The works I do in My Father's name, these bear witness of Me." The greatest work was His resurrection from the dead. That's why His resurrection is at the core of the Gospel ever since it was first proclaimed (Acts 2:24).

Paul says Christian preaching and faith are in vain—meaningless, empty, only air—if Christ was not raised. Destroy the truth of the resurrection and you have destroyed the faith! And you will not only have destroyed it; you will also have exposed the real evil of it all. Paul says we are "found to be false witnesses of God" if we preach the resurrection if there was no resurrection. The Gospel is not good news if it's all a lie. And look at the fool you've been! "If Christ has not been raised, your faith is worthless" (1 Corinthians 15:17). Your faith would be aimless, leading to nothing, having no object of truth.

Our faith cannot be "in faith." Sincerity isn't the issue. Faith must have an object, and its object must have reality to give credibility to the faith. The Christian faith is true because it is faith in truth. The Christian faith is not an enigma of history, but a fact of reality; the truth upon which all of Christianity stands. Because of it, you and I have not a religion, but a personal relationship with the living Lord.*

—Darryl DelHousaye

Prayer Starter: *God, help me have absolute faith in Your truth.*

SIGNS OF A BELIEVER

Now the works of the flesh are evident: sexual immorality, impurity, sensuality, idolatry, sorcery, enmity, strife, jealousy, fits of anger, rivalries, dissensions, divisions, envy, drunkenness, orgies, and things like these. I warn you, as I warned you before, that those who do such things will not inherit the kingdom of God. But the fruit of the Spirit is love, joy, peace, patience, kindness, goodness, faithfulness, gentleness, self-control; against such things there is no law. (Galatians 5:19-23)

Meditate on this list. Read through it again and ask the Lord to show you the sin He wants to not only take out of your life, but also the good things He wants everyone around you to see exhibited in your life. Are you envious of your friend's new car? Is pornography something you think is just a secret sin that doesn't hurt anyone? Are you yelling at your kids? Are you competing with a business associate or your sister-in-law? Are you holding a grudge…still? Are you practicing sexual purity all the time?

God is not a killjoy making you give up your fun. Our loving Father wants us to have a full, abundant life in which we are useful to Him everyday. If He hands us a list of behaviors that He Himself says will mark the one who will not inherit the kingdom of God, we better take notice. We better surrender the sin we are holding onto and ask Him for the power to change.

God is so wise. He knows if we try to get rid of a sinful behavior, we need a positive behavior to substitute in its place. He shows us in the next verses what we are aiming for in the power of the Holy Spirit! Instead of fighting, be loving and forgiving. Instead of being envious, be peaceful, gentle and self-controlled. Instead of stirring the pot with gossip and divisions, bring peace, joy and kindness. These are signs of a believer in Jesus Christ.

So look again at the list. What do you need to surrender today?

—Tracy Goble

Prayer Starter: *Lord, convict me of my sin and fill me with the power of Your Holy Spirit so I can exhibit these Christ-like qualities to the world.*

HEAVENWARD

I saw the Lord sitting on a throne, lofty and exalted, with the train of His robe filling the temple. Seraphim stood above Him, each having six wings: with two he covered his face, and with two he covered his feet, and with two he flew. And one called out to another and said, "Holy, holy, holy, is the Lord of hosts, the whole earth is full of His glory." And the foundations of the thresholds trembled at the voice of Him who called out... (Isaiah 6:1-4)

In Isaiah's time, it seemed the earth was filled with darkness where fear and evil reigned. Yet the Lord lifted Isaiah's sights Heavenward to let Him know that despite the apparent triumph of wickedness, Christ was still on His throne. From a new perspective, Isaiah saw that all Heavenly activity still surrounded Him who is high and exalted. He envisioned countless six-winged seraphim (literally "fiery ones"), burning with zeal to serve and praise the Lord. With two wings their faces were covered in reverence and humility, another two covered their feet in humble service and two wings carried them in tireless worship proclaiming Christ's holiness.

Like Isaiah, though our days may seem dim, we can lift our sights to the omnipotent Christ, whose dazzling robe fills His temple. With newfound zeal, let each activity surround your Lord. Let every word, action or intension of the heart towards your spouse, children, family, friends and stranger, glorify Him so "the whole earth is filled with His glory."

—Christy Osborn

Prayer Starter: *Dear Lord, as I go throughout my day, may You ignite my thoughts and activities with such zeal that the foundation of the temple within me trembles with praise for You.*

AUTHORITY

Is it lawful to pay taxes to Caesar, or not? But Jesus…said, "…show me the coin for the tax." And they brought Him a denarius, and Jesus said to them, "Whose likeness and inscription is this?" They said, "Caesar's." Then He said to them, "Therefore render to Caesar the things that are Caesar's, and to God the things that are God's." (Matthew 22:17–21)

Image implies ownership. This is why God says in the second commandment, "You shall not make for yourself a carved image (of me)." He wanted to teach the people that his people will not have authority over him, like a false God that can be placated by paying homage to an image.

The denarius is a coin with Caesar's image. Therefore, he owns it and he has authority to do with it however he wishes. If he demands it back, then we should give it to him. It's his.

In the same way, we're made in God's image. He owns us. he has authority to do with us however he wishes. If he demands our lives, we should give them to him.

—Joe Gordon

Prayer Starter: *Lord, forgive me when I have kept what is not rightfully mine.*

THE GREAT COMMISSION

He [Jesus] said to them, "Thus it is written, that the Christ would suffer and rise again from the dead the third day, and that repentance for forgiveness of sins would be proclaimed in His name to all the nations, beginning from Jerusalem." (Luke 24:46-47)

These verses changed my life. I was a pastor at Scottsdale Bible in 1981 when the Lord used these verses to bring about a total paradigm shift in my life goals and values. The truth of Luke 24:46-47, in turn, "opened my eyes" to the rest of the Scriptures.

In this passage, Jesus reveals to His disciples the two mega-themes of the Old Testament (OT). The first mega-theme is "Messiah" – there are hundreds of OT passages about the coming Messiah.

The second mega-theme of the OT is the "Great Commission" – God's plan to take salvation to every people group on earth. This was new to me. Previously I had thought that the Great Commission was only revealed in the New Testament (NT), but I was wrong. The Great Commission is a mega-theme of both the NT and the OT.

The fact that the Great Commission is one of the two mega-themes of the whole Bible reveals God's heart for reaching the nations with the message of salvation. This is God's big goal in human history (Matthew 28:18-20; 24:14).

Upon realizing this, I decided that I wanted to take part in God's big goal. Whether as a "sender" or a "sent one," I wanted to be a pro-active participant in this major goal of God in human history.

—Walt Edman

Prayer Starter: *Lord, I want to commit myself anew to Your Great Commission. Empower me to be faithful as a sender (or as a sent one).*

YOU ARE NEVER ALONE

Never will I leave you; never will I forsake you. (Hebrews 13:5)

I wonder if Jesus ever felt lonely when He was moving around from place to place preaching, teaching, healing, and doing what only Jesus could do. I'm sure there were times He felt isolated and alone when He was in unfamiliar surroundings or in a new town. Probably a lot like the same feelings you have when you move to a new place.

Although you might feel lonely, you are never truly alone! Jesus is with you wherever you go. His presence accompanies you from place to place. He has felt your loneliness, your pain, your despair, and your desire to be known. When you really think about it, He wanted the same thing as you do when He moved from place to place – for people to know Him, love Him, and accept Him.

May the presence of Jesus bring you comfort in your loneliness. And may you discover a new friend in Jesus as you get to know Him, love Him and accept Him all the more!

—Susan Miller

Prayer Starter: *Lord, it is comforting to know that I am never alone, and that Your presence is with me always. Thank You for being the friend I so desperately need, and the reminder that You understand how I feel.*

CARING FOR CHILDREN

Vindicate the weak and the fatherless; do justice to the afflicted and destitute. Rescue the weak and needy; deliver them out of the hand of the wicked. (Psalm 82:3-4)

Children: 3,000,000 reports of child abuse or neglect are made every year in the United States. 510,000 children in the United States are in foster care. Annually 600 teenage foster children in Arizona turn 18 and "age out" of foster care with limited support. 3 in 10 of the nation's adult homeless are former foster youth. These are the effects of the hand of the wicked upon children just in America, and worldwide there are 143-210 million orphans.

The Psalmist calls out to God and asks Him to reach down with His hand and deliver these children out of the hand of the wicked. In James 1:27 we read, "Pure religion is to care for the widows and orphans."

King David was called a man after God's heart. Where is your heart? Does it beat at all with the things that concern God? Today, pray for the children in the streets of our city, nation, and world who are affected by the hand of the wicked. Ask God how you can demonstrate His love by reaching out your hand to help rescue these children.

—Mark Upton

Prayer Starter: *Lord, You have said to me that to love You is to love others and that means to care for children who are in the hands of the wicked. Show me today how I can demonstrate my love to You by caring for a child in need.*

FROM LOW TO HIGH

For He Himself knows our frame, and He is mindful that we are but dust.
(Psalm 103:14)

Far from being "discouraging," it's actually encouraging to know that our God knows our strengths and our weaknesses. He knows our humanness and our propensity to fall short (even though we don't want to). Instead of looking down on our weakness, He accepts it – and us – and offers love, healing and hope for a better day.

When Diane was born and her parents were handed their precious newborn daughter, they saw that her left arm had never developed below the elbow. The doctors rushed in, and within a few weeks, they were told there were no other serious problems – but still there was that missing arm. Diane's parents however had made a decision long before the doctors made their report. They had decided they would love her and do everything they could to encourage diane to become all that God would allow. That "all" has taken her through college, through a master's degree, into a wonderful marriage, and to being the mother of two precious children. Because of her parents love and God's love, in her words, she isn't "missing a thing."

God's love can do the same for us. None of us "have it all." We all fall short. We're all "limited" in some way. Gratefully and thankfully, Almighty God's love can "complete" us and help us value and appreciate our loved ones' limitations as well.

—John and Cindy Trent

Prayer Starter: *Lord, it's comforting to know that we don't have to be perfect. We don't have to always be "put together." You know we're limited, weak and imperfect. But Your love can make all the difference in completing us, and making us — each of us – all we can be.*

PASSING THE MESSAGE STICK

Only be careful, and watch yourselves closely so that you do not forget the things your eyes have seen or let them slip from your heart as long as you live. Teach them to your children and to their children after them.
(Deuteronomy 4:9)

The winning or losing of an Olympic relay race is not always determined by the team that has the fastest runners because the successful passing of the baton is vital to the outcome of the race. The history of the relay race dates back many centuries when messages were carried by a series of couriers over a long distance and delivered safely to a specific destination. Today the "message sticks" the runners carry are called batons which are passed from runner to runner during the relay race. The race is only successful if each runner carries the baton and successfully passes it to the next runner within a set distance in which the baton must be passed or the whole team is disqualified. One bad segment in the race can result in a loss for the entire team.

In reviewing the great historical legacy of many continuous generations of Christians, I was reminded of the similarities involved in a winning relay team. Successfully raising children in our generation is only one segment in the relaying of spiritual wisdom from generation to generation.

We, as fathers and mothers, with God's help, must train our children to understand the importance of their spiritual walk as they go through the race of life. We must prepare them to receive the truth of the Scriptures; to carry this truth carefully throughout their lives and to be prepared when it is their turn to pass the spiritual baton to another generation. Like the passing of the baton, we have a limited number of years to accomplish our responsibility.

It only takes one generation to drop the "message stick" that carries the message of the Gospel of Jesus Christ and if that happens several generations could be lost.

—Ron Goble

Prayer Starter: *Lord, help us to pass the baton of Jesus to all children.*

BELONGING TO JESUS

Behold, I have inscribed you on the palms of my hands… *(Isaiah 49:16a)*

Wow – you know how you can read a verse many times and then all of a sudden it jumps out at you? To think my name is inscribed on the palms of Jesus' hands is truly amazing!

I thought of all the times you see names carved on booths, trees or at special vacation sights. Everyone wants everyone else to know they were there. But, to be carved on Jesus' palms – there's no better place to be!

In church we listened to Barry Asmus say that people have lots of wants, and when we got home my husband asked me what my wants were? That was so easy to answer. I have one want.

I want my family to all be in the protection, guidance and safety of Jesus Christ.

There is no better place to be on this earth. There is no place else you can receive such joy, peace or love than in the arms of God and His Son.

Will they have problems? Absolutely, but the Lord will deliver them out of them all *(Psalm 34:19b)*. In a way, it's a selfish want because then I can be at peace about them, too. I'll know they have their ticket marked Jesus and their names are carved in the palms of Jesus' hands.

—Sue Phipps

Prayer Starter: *Jesus, fill the hearts of my children and grandchildren and all in my family with Your love and truth.*

GOING WITH GOD

"I will send an angel before you and I will drive out the Canaanites, the Amorite, the Hittite, the Perizzite, the Hivite and the Jebusite. Go up to the land flowing with milk and honey, for I will not go up in your midst."
(Exodus 33:2-3)

Following the golden calf incident in Exodus, God told Moses to take the Israelites on to the Promised Land without His presence. Later Moses says to God, "If your presence does not go with us, do not lead us up from here." (Exodus 33:15)

I believe Moses made the right decision, even though it cost him dearly. Moses could have looked very successful, and I wonder how many people would have even known that God's presence was not with Moses? But Moses would have known.

As it works out, Moses never made it to the Promised Land, something that Moses had set his heart on. But at least he knew that God's presence was with him. I believe that was better then anything the Promised Land could have offered him.

—Paul Wegner

Prayer Starter: *Father, I pray we will follow Your leading no matter what the cost. Your presence is better than anything this world could ever offer. Anything that hinders Your presence in our lives is a cost that is far too dear.*

I AM A ROCK

…And let us consider how to stimulate one another to love and good deeds… (Hebrews 10:24)

Lie: people hurt me, so I just won't trust anyone.

Someone once said: "No man is an island." There's even a song by Simon and Garfunkel entitled "I am a Rock" (1965). "I am a rock, I am an island, I've built walls that none can penetrate." This song describes an emotional armor designed to keep me from the one-anothering that is described in Scripture. Yes, this lie seems to protect me from being hurt. But, it also prevents me from experiencing emotional and spiritual connection to God's people.

Indeed, I just received a call telling me that a dear friend of thirty years died. Her friendship sustained and enriched both our lives in ways that only God knows. We loved each other through thick and thin. She loved and mentored me through some difficult times.

I confess however, that there were times I didn't want to visit her in those last difficult days. That way I wouldn't have to feel sad, or hurt, or grief, but that's not God's kind of thinking. Simon and Garfunkel's song closes with the words: "And a rock feels no pain; and an island never cries." Don't let this happen to you.

—Nonie Maupin

Prayer Starter: *Lord God, remind me that I am neither a rock nor an island and that I need people.*

SCRIPTURAL BUTTERFLIES

For I am confident of this very thing, that He who began a good work in you will perfect it until the day of Christ Jesus. (Philippians1:6)

Some years ago I read an article about Monarch butterflies. According to the article, the Monarch butterfly migrates from as far north as Canada to their winter nesting grounds in the mountains northwest of Mexico City, a distance of over 2500 miles!

When I think about migration I usually think about geese. I have seen the ordered "V" formations in the sky as those birds course toward their destination in a determined fashion. But have you ever watched a butterfly fly? There hardly appears to be a pattern to their flight. They flit and flutter from leaf to flower, seemingly without any apparent direction. Their fragile frames don't seem capable of a long extended journey. And yet, they cover thousands of miles just as geese and many other migratory birds.

I am encouraged by Monarch butterflies. Their pilgrimage resembles my own spiritual journey much more closely than that of geese or ducks. As much as I would like my spiritual pilgrimage to be one of steady and determined progress toward the ultimate spiritual destination that God has planned for me, it has not been that way. Rather my movements toward Heaven as a new creature in Christ appear, at times, to be quite random – like those of the butterfly. Nevertheless, as I look back I can see that there has been progress in my life. And though my spiritual frame is quite fragile, I am confident that God will sustain me and guide me to the ultimate haven for my soul.

—Dave Zehring

Prayer Starter: *Father, thank You for Your promise to complete the work You began in my life. I confess that I am inconsistent at times in my journey of faith. Strengthen and sustain me this day as I seek to live for You.*

PASSING IT ON

You therefore, my son, be strong in the grace that is in Christ Jesus. The things which you have heard from me in the presence of many witnesses, entrust these to faithful men who will be able to teach others also.
(2 Timothy 2:1-2)

During Timothy's many years of close association with Paul, he had heard divine truth which God had revealed through the apostle. Silas, Barnabas, and Luke, and many others in the church could attest to the divine authenticity of Paul's teaching. Timothy was to take the divine Revelation he had learned from Paul and teach it to other faithful men – men with proven, spiritual character and giftedness, who would in turn pass on those truths to another generation. From Paul to Timothy to faithful men to others encompasses four generations of godly leaders. That process of spiritual reproduction, which began in the early church, is to continue until the Lord returns.

I have always appreciated Howard Hendrick's encouragement for all of us to have a Paul, Barnabas, and Timothy in our lives, and to also be each of these in the lives of others. Do you have a Paul (mentor), a Barnabas (encouraging friend) and a Timothy (disciple) in your life? Ask God to send people to fulfill these roles in your life.

—Patrick Sullivan

Prayer Starter: *Father, may we be faithful to pass on to others what we have learned from You.*

BE VULNERABLE

Don't copy the behaviour and customs of this world, but let God transform you into a new person by changing the way you think. Then you will know what God wants you to do, and you will know how good and pleasing and perfect His will really is. (Romans 12:2)

I was too focused on my ministry. My marriage went into crisis. My relationship with my three children suffered. I sought God in the pain, and he taught me three important truths:

1) Be with me

2) Become more like Jesus

3) Serve me

It was like Jesus was telling me these words: be with me, my child. Practice telling me the whole truth about yourself. It builds intimacy in your relationship with me, your spouse, your children and also with anybody you work with or you serve. I called you, my disciple, in the first place to be with me! (Mark 3:14).

A friend of mine once said, "Become more and more like Jesus and ministry will follow." I prayed for God to transform me into a new person by changing the way I think. I began to learn transparency and vulnerability in Al-Anon and AA groups my husband and I had started, and it was contagious. Watching how telling the whole truth was healing my friends Margit (an alcoholic), Suzanne and Eva (both adult children of alcoholics), led me to be vulnerable as well. And God started my recovery from being a people pleaser. God said, "When you are weak, I am strong." I no longer want to hide my weaknesses. There is so much freedom in being vulnerable!

When you serve within your weaknesses you show God's glory. God encouraged me from 2 Corinthians 12:10 that it is for Christ's good when I share openly. As a result, I began to share more openly about struggles within my marriage. I began to see fruit of my honesty and transparency! People in slovakia are now much more open to be vulnerable and that is why they are being healed.

—Ester Kriskova

Prayer Starter: *Lord, keep transforming us into a new person by changing the way we think. Start this work in us today.*

UNEXPLAINABLE ANXIETY

But if you will not listen to me and carry out all these commands… you will flee even when no one is pursuing you. (Leviticus 26:14,17b)

Sometimes it comes out of nowhere – that sinking feeling that you should be anxious about something when there's no clear and present danger. Other times it starts as a subtle second-guessing of issues that should be obvious, and then moves to full out, all-encompassing fear.

I've learned that unexplainable anxiety is often God's tipoff to me that there is something wrong in my life. Just like a fever points to an infection, paranoia tells me I've allowed something to supplant my confidence in God's faithfulness. It could be some debilitating sin I've allowed to get a grip on me, or perhaps i've neglected to lean on God's unflinching power through times of trouble.

In Leviticus 26, Moses builds a case for how God is going to provide for His children who choose to obey Him. They'll stand strong against overwhelming odds and enjoy bountiful lives that exceed their efforts and have opportunities tailored for success. But if they refuse to trust in God, among other things, they'll run from threats that don't exist. Don't let your fears run your life. If you're experiencing unexplainable anxiety, pray David's prayer from Psalm 139:23-24.

—Tim Kimmel

Prayer Starter: *Search me, O God, and know my heart; test me and know my anxious thoughts. See if there is any offensive way in me, and lead me in the way everlasting.*

CALEB'S VICTORY

Then Joshua blessed him and he gave Hebron to Caleb...for an inheritance. Therefore hebron became the inheritance of Caleb...because he wholly followed the Lord, the God of Israel. (Joshua 14:13-14)

Caleb's conquest was complete. Caleb was the only one who succeeded in expelling the enemy. The others made poor headway as we see in the last part of the book of Joshua. Over and over again we read, "They were not able to drive them out."

Caleb experienced what God had promised! He climbed the mountain with a sword in one hand and a property deed in the other. He claimed the mountains, he defeated the giants and he claimed his possession. The name of the place Caleb inherited was Hebron. The word "Hebron" conveys within itself the meaning of fellowship, love, and communion. That was the place that Caleb cherished and longed for. It is a place all of us must seek and find.

Caleb refused to quit until he had everything the Lord had for him! He refused to stop until he had obtained that place of fellowship with God. We all ought not to settle for anything less than the place of perfect fellowship with the Lord our God.

God has a place of peace and power and victory for you, but you must be willing to claim your possession.

—Wayne Lehsten

Prayer Starter: *Lord, help me to press on to possess all of Your promises for my life of love and fellowship with You.*

MOST MISUNDERSTOOD COMMANDMENT

You shall not take the name of the Lord your God in vain, for the Lord will not leave him unpunished who takes His name in vain. (Exodus 20:7)

Most of us have been taught that the third commandment prohibits cursing and swearing, especially including "God" (which is not a name, but a description) or "Jesus Christ." But when have you ever used the verb "take" when you really meant "speak?"

The Hebrew verb *nasa* means to take up or to carry. This commandment warns those who take His name unto themselves—who identify themselves as the people of Yhwh (or of Jesus)—that this must not be "in vain": empty or fruitless. It's like putting on a nametag that says, "Hi, my name is Dave, and I represent Yhwh." What kind of life should I live before people who will judge my God based upon the conduct of His representatives? How many have rejected Christ because of the misdeeds of people who call themselves Christians without living holy lives?

Jesus reiterated this commandment more than any other. When He taught about four soils, talents, wheat and tares, branches of the vine, a barren fig tree, the rented vineyard, minas, hidden leaven, etc., He was telling them again that God's people are required to bear fruit that brings glory to His name. "My Father is glorified by this, that you bear much fruit, and so prove to be My disciples" (John 15:8).

No, we should not curse or swear, but more importantly, we should be diligent, in the power of the Spirit, to take up His name and produce a good return for the glory of Yhwh.

—Dave Cottrell

Prayer Starter: *Fill me afresh with Your Spirit that I may produce abundant fruit for Your glory, Lord!*

WATERING SEEDS

I planted, Apollos watered, but God gave the growth. (1 Corinthians 3:6)

In the 1940s, in preparation for World War II, General George Patton's army troops trained in the desert in western Arizona. The men set up their pup tents of about twenty in a row opposite another row of twenty. Between the two rows there was a "Company street." At the end of the street, there hung a "Lyster bag" which was made of canvas and held about thirty gallons of water. Evaporation of the water seeping through the canvas cooled the water in the bag. The troops would fill their canteens from the Lyster bag. The ground under the bags was moist from the spillage and seepage.

One day not long ago, I was flying over that area and noticed the outline of hundreds of the company streets. Yet today, at the end of the "streets," there is a clump of desert vegetation that rooted as a result of the water from more than sixty years ago. No one knows how long the seeds had been there. No one knows how many more seeds would germinate if they were watered.

Have you ever thought of the "seeds" of the Word of God that have been planted in the hearts of your friends, acquaintances, or family? It might be that all they need is a little bit of water to bloom into what God intends them to be…something even more beautiful than a clump of desert vegetation!

—Bob Cain

Prayer Starter: *Lord, use me as water today for all the seeds You have planted in the people I meet.*

HE PICKS UP THE PIECES

The Spirit of the Lord God is upon me, because the Lord has anointed me to bring good news to the afflicted; He has sent me to bind up the broken-hearted, to proclaim liberty to captives, and freedom to prisoners.
(Isaiah 61:1)

The first thing Nancy had to face when she came home each night was whether her mother would be at the door with her coat on or not. If she was, it meant that her father was in such an angry mood (driven by alcohol) that her mother, her brothers and Nancy would have to get in the car and drive around until her father was so drunk he'd pass out. Then it would be safe to go home.

Obviously, not everyone grows up in a home that's so challenging and you have to do your homework in the dim light of a car's backseat. But many people have come into marriage or relationships with heartaches and hurts from the past. And that's where this verse from Isaiah, a prophecy that describes Jesus, gives us so much help and hope.

Like a broken bottle, Nancy didn't even know where all the pieces of her broken heart lay. But when she came to know Jesus Christ, He gently began a healing process that continues today. In knowing and growing in her love for Jesus, she's experienced more security, love, and acceptance then she ever saw at home – and brings that, not just the brokenness, into her marriage.

Always remember that Jesus specialized in "binding up the brokenhearted." Knowing Him more and more brings His love and healing to our hearts – no matter the pictures of our past.

—John and Cindy Trent

Prayer Starter: *Thank You, Lord Jesus, that You can restore what was lost and broken in my past. All those missing, broken pieces You can piece together as I grow close to You. Thank You that I bring both my brokenness, and Your healing into my life.*

POWER TO INFLUENCE

But you will receive power when the Holy Spirit has come upon you, and you will be my witnesses in Jerusalem and in all Judea and Samaria, and to the end of the earth. (Acts 1:8)

God has set it up that everyone is given some portion of power in life. Whether you are a parent or a boss or a supervisor, you have power that is to be used for leadership, guidance, or direction. Maybe you are a friend, a neighbor, a coworker, or trusted advisor. You have power to influence, to encourage, or to exhort people in your life. Power can be an incredible asset or an easily mismanaged liability.

When we talk about the Great Commission, it is often spoken of in the context of reaching our "Jerusalem, Judea, and Samaria, and to the ends of the earth." While it is important to embrace an "Acts 1:8 mindset" that tries to reach all people groups in every missions region, we better not neglect the first part of this important verse.

Reaching the world with the Gospel of Jesus is only possible because the Holy Spirit has come upon His followers – His church – and filled them with His power to accomplish this task. The power of God's Holy Spirit provides the courage, the selflessness, the compassion, the commitment, and the follow-through that leads people to the "pockets of lostness" in the world, whether nearby or far away.

Because of the indwelling power of God's Holy Spirit, "you will be" God's witnesses. God doesn't invest His Spirit in you just to be a power-packed person who idles away in isolation. He has determined to fill you with His powerful presence so you can represent Him and share Him with others as He leads you through life.

—Jamie Rasmussen

Prayer Starter: *Fill us with Your Holy Spirit. Lead us to be witnesses for You wherever we are.*

REMEMBERING

…That their hearts may be encouraged, having been knit together in love…
(Colossians 2:2)

As a recent seminary graduate who had decided to go back to my own people in Guatemala as a missionary, I was facing the big dilemma of raising my monthly support. For me, this was an overwhelming task due to the fact that I did not have a family or a home church in the USA. In fact, I had no idea how to go about contacting people to become part of my supporting team. However, God had a plan for my support and that plan included Scottsdale Bible Church.

During this same time, the members of the Scottsdale Bible Missions Committee realized they did not have a national missionary family on their support roster so they decided to contact a missionary agency that could help them find someone to support. It just so happened that they contacted my missionary agency! The next thing I knew, I was on my way to Scottsdale.

When we met, the Scottsdale Bible Mission's Committee's members prayerfully decided to support the work God was doing through me in Guatemala. It was decided that I should move to Scottsdale for eight months to do an internship at the church and to live with different families for three weeks at a time. It was during those weeks that many friendships were made, which greatly encouraged and blessed me. Our hearts were knit together in love. Some of these families became part of my financial supporting team and, to this day, our relationships are still going strong.

Our work in Guatemala has been greatly blessed by the Lord and I praise God for Scottsdale Bible Church's involvement in it since 1986. Scottsdale Bible commitment not only to the Word and work of God, but also to the workers of God has been a model for me, so I try to teach Guatemalan church leaders to do the same. May God continue to use sbc for the enhancement of the kingdom of God in the whole world just as He used it mightily in my own life!

—Isaias Colop XEC

Prayer Starter: *Lord, help me to see how You are working in my life today.*

CONFIDENCE IN GOD

King Jehoshaphat appointed those who sang to the Lord and those who praised Him in holy attire, as they went out before the army and said, "Give thanks to the Lord, for His lovingkindness is everlasting." (2 Chronicles 20:21)

King Jehoshaphat had just been instructed by the prophet Jahaziel with a word from the Lord, saying, "Do not fear or be dismayed." He was told by the Lord, through the prophet, "The battle is not yours but God's." King Jehoshaphat was admonished to not fear or be dismayed; but to go out tomorrow remembering the Lord would be with him.

Jehoshaphat chose to walk in the instruction of the prophet's words. He led the people to face the battle brought on by his enemies. King Jehoshaphat's confidence in God caused them to begin with singing and praising as they went to war! This may seem like an unusual approach, but he believed the victory belonged to God. And it did. As their singing and praising began, the Lord set ambushes against his enemy and the enemy was routed! What is your current battle? And are you praising God and believing Him for the victory?

—Deb Pirtle

Prayer Starter: *Oh, Father in Heaven, we praise You as we acknowledge all victories belong to You. May we hear and follow Your instruction in our own battles. Let our March begin with singing and praises to You. Help us to see You, and bring Your victory in all our struggles.*

TRUST IN THE LORD

Trust in the Lord with all your heart and do not lean on your own understanding. In all your ways acknowledge Him, and He will make your paths straight. (Proverbs 3:5–6)

On old maps, back before the world was understood in modern terms, cartographers, (mapmakers) would put down what they knew, but at the edges of the map, beyond which they had no knowledge, they would often write, "Beyond here, there be dragons."

Most people are afraid of the unknown. Those things we have never seen or experienced can seem overwhelming. So what should we do when we don't know what to do?

These two verses in Proverbs remind us that we are to completely and totally place our trust in God. In contrast, we are not to lean on our own understanding. The root of this verb, lean, means to support yourself on something, placing all your weight upon it. This does not mean we don't use our common sense, but our lives are built on the truth and the promises of God's Word and His wisdom.

Verse six is built around the word "acknowledge." This word means to know God in a deep, experiential way. There is intimacy implied here. Our lives are built on our growing trust and intimacy with God.

The reward for this trust is more than guidance. The language here includes the removal of obstacles from the path of the wise and the surety of arriving at our destination. So today, trust in the Lord!

—Larry Anderson

Prayer Starter: *Lord, help me to completely and totally place my trust in You.*

INTERDEVELOPMENTAL PARTNERSHIP

Greater love has no one more than this, that someone lay down his life for his friends. (John 15:13)

Robert Browning and Elizabeth Barrett, married in 1846.
Frank Butler and Annie Oakley, married in 1882.
Pierre and Marie Curie, married in 1895.
George Burns and Gracie Allen, married in 1926.
Billy and Ruth Bell Graham, married in 1943.

Why are these names familiar? They represent couples whose names are linked together forever because they experienced a special kind of relationship – an interdevelopmental partnership. This is a relationship in which both partners bring out the best in each other by encouraging personal development and growth.

An interdevelopmental partnership demonstrates that along with supporting and bringing out the best in each other, there are many opportunities to lay down our lives for each other.

A great example of this is found when the comedy team of George Burns and Gracie Allen started their partnership. Burns wrote all of the funny punch lines for himself and wrote Allen's character as the "straight man." When they performed, however, the audience rewarded Allen with laughter for her supposed straight questions and responded to Burns' funny answers with silence.

Individual egos can really mess up a great partnership and this was a true test of George's ego. As Burns put it, "It broke my heart, but I was young, hungry and not a dope." From then on, he wrote routines to take advantage of Allen's natural gift for comedic delivery. This was the beginning of over four decades of fame and success for Burns and Allen. In later years, both attributed their success to each other.

During the course of our marriage, we can provide what great partners have always provided for each other - encouragement and sacrifice bathed in love and friendship.

Because friendship is at the heart of a good creative partnership, the whole is much greater and stronger than the individual parts. Together we are better!

—Holly DelHousaye

Prayer Starter: *Lord, help me to offer love, friendship, encouragement and sacrifice to those I love today.*

UNIQUELY AUTHORIZED

Write: the words of... (Revelation 2:1, 8, 12, 18; 3:1, 7,14)

Even in this electronic age of digital communication, it is still a noteworthy event to open up the mailbox and see a letter in it.

With most personal communication now being handled by social networks or email, about the only items showing up in your mailbox are official, authoritative letters demanding your attention. Sometimes that mail is good, such as news of your child being named to the Dean's List. Sometimes the mail is bad, like when your HOA wants you to know your new fence is in violation of code.

Whether the news is good, bad, or somewhere in between, it's typical to check the name and title of the person sending the message. Doing so confirms the authenticity of the message and the authority of the messenger.

The same is true with Jesus in His messages to the seven churches in Revelation 2 and 3:

- To the Ephesian church, He is the Judge of churches.
- To the Smyrnean church, He is the timeless God who was Resurrected from martyrdom.
- To the Pergamos church, He is the eternal Word of Truth.
- To the Thyatirean church, He is the Son of God, the judge of every person.
- To the Sardisian church, He is the Caretaker of the church; the judge of every human work.
- To the Philadelphian church, He is the holy, loving, sovereign God.
- To the Laodicean church, He is the Chief Authority, the faithful and true witness.

To every church, Jesus clearly identifies Himself to them in a way that is relevant to the message that follows. He does this so they will know He is uniquely authorized to speak truth into their lives and meet their needs. To the church today, Jesus remains uniquely authorized to speak to us. He alone is our judge, our timeless God, our caretaker and chief authority. He is faithful and true. He is Jesus and He is Lord God Almighty!

—Bryan McAnally

Prayer Starter: *I thank You that You are God Almighty, over all, faithful and true, with all authority and power.*

OUR RELATIONSHIP WITH GOD

Your Father knows what you need before you ask Him. (Matthew 6:8)

God wants us to pray so that our dependence on Him can increase. When we come to Him in prayer about something, we express a trust in Him; a trust that He will hear and answer our prayers. That is why Jesus compares our prayers to a child asking his father for a fish or an egg. As a child trusts and expects his father to provide for him, so we ought to expect in faith that God will provide for us. That is why Jesus said, "Whatever you ask in prayer you will receive, if you have faith" (Matthew 21:22).

God does not just desire that our trust in Him will grow through prayer; He also desires that our love for Him and our relationship with Him will deepen and grow. When we truly pray, we pray with the wholeness of our character relating to the wholeness of His character.

Therefore what we think and feel about God will come through in our prayers. This will, in turn, deepen our love and understanding of God, and in the end deepen our relationship with Him. This is something that God delights in and brings Him glory. Through prayer we are part of something with eternal significance.

—Wayne Grudem

Prayer Starter: *Father, help me to truly know You.*

COMPASSION

When He went ashore He saw a great crowd, and He had compassion on them and healed their sick. (Matthew 14:14)

We live in a world that is messed up and getting worse. Wars, disease, famine, and injustice plague our Globe. Widows, orphans and the oppressed cry out. You likely cannot find many people who wouldn't express some emotion of sympathy for the hurting, abandoned, poor, and abused people across the world.

Jesus showed that God's love is not limited to sympathy. When Jesus attracted a crowd, He didn't merely feel sorry for them. Jesus had compassion on them.

Compassion is the God-given compulsion to act when your heart is burdened or broken by the plight of someone else. Compassion demands that you do something to bring relief to their pain, cover to their nakedness, or nourishment to their hunger.

Jesus showed His followers what compassion looks like:

• It includes walking with them. He walked among them for three years.

• It includes meeting their needs. He healed them and He fed them.

• It includes loving them. He told them about the kingdom of God.

May we all be moved to follow Christ's example of compassion with the sick and hurting that God puts in our path. May we be kind enough to walk with them and share our lives with them. May we be faithful enough to meet their needs, feeding them and healing them as God enables us. And finally, may we always love them, telling them about Jesus and the kingdom of God that is available to them.

—Fred Beasley

Prayer Starter: *Jesus, help me show compassion to all You place in my path.*

WE MUST PRAY

Is anyone among you suffering? Then he must pray. Is anyone cheerful? He is to sing praises. (James 5:13)

Are you suffering, in trouble, or experiencing difficulties? Are you in the midst of an economic, physical or relational crisis? You must pray. This is the very first thing you must do. It is also the second thing to do and then it is the continual, ceaseless endeavor. Pray for patience, endurance, and His perspective. Be assured that He listens, cares, and will answer. Nothing can remove you from His grasp.

Are you joyful? Then you must sing. Lift your voice to Him accompanied by a musical instrument or a cappella. You must especially talk to Him. Why? Because during cheerful times, we are prone to forget Him. Praising Him is a most lovely, exquisite, and satisfying endeavor. Indeed, it is the reason we live—to worship Him!

Whether suffering evil or experiencing great joy, stay close to God, and tell Him about it. How will you respond to the Perfect Love today?

—David Walther

Prayer Starter: *Heavenly Father, You are perfect in love, draw me close to you, remind me of Your provision in every circumstance, and please increase my love for You.*

IN THE BEGINNING

In the beginning God created the Heavens and the earth. (Genesis 1:1)

For freedom to exist there has to be certain assumptions about the intrinsic worth of an individual. When God says that man is created in His image, He implies that every person has value, possesses an immortal soul and is on a journey that has eternal significance. He not only cares for you as the Lord of creation, but also as the Lord of salvation. "For God so loved the world that He gave His only Son, that whoever believes in Him shall not perish, but have eternal life" (John 3:16).

In just the first ten words of the Bible, God gives us spiritual direction. "In the beginning God" denies atheism with its doctrine of no God and it denies polytheism with its doctrine of many Gods. "God created" denies evolution and fatalism with its doctrine of chance. "God created the Heavens and the earth" denies materialism with its doctrine of matter being eternal, and denies pantheism with its doctrine of God in everything. Let it be restated: "In the beginning God created the Heavens, the earth—and you."

—Barry Asmus

Prayer Starter: *Thank You, Father, for such a majestic description of how You created the Heavens and the earth. You truly are an awesome God.*

WAGER EVERYTHING

How can a man be in the right before God? (Job 9:2)

Job asked a basic question: how can we be right with God? How can we know righteousness?

The answer is that righteousness is both a gift and a command. It is a gift because we can't achieve it without the intervention of God. "All our righteous deeds are like a filthy garment" (Isaiah 64: 6). The gift of righteousness is salvation through Jesus Christ. "He made Him who knew no sin to be sin on our behalf, that we might become the righteousness of God in Him" (2 Corinthians 5:21). The gift comes by our faith: Abraham "believed in the Lord; and He reckoned it to him as righteousness" (Genesis 15:6).

But righteousness is not just something you believe; it must be something you live out. Paul says, "The righteous man shall live by faith" (Romans 1:17). The evidence that we have received the gift of righteousness is in living out life in keeping with that righteousness. So there's a gift of righteousness, and there's a practice of righteousness, a passion to carry out the will of God. "The command," wrote Martin Luther, "is not to crawl into a corner or into the desert, but to run out…and to offer your hands and your feet and your whole body, and to wager everything you have and can do."

Today—are you looking to do God's will…to run out and do what is right?

What is more important to you: to do right, or to get others to treat you right?

— Darryl DelHousaye

Prayer Starter: *Lord, thank You for Your gift of righteousness. Help me to do right in Your sight.*

HE WILL SUPPLY

And my God will supply all your needs according to His glorious riches in Christ Jesus. (Philippians 4:19)

There was a large plaque hanging in our home when I was growing up with this verse on it. It was a family favorite. My mom taught us that we were under the leadership and hand of God and He was our source, our supplier.

Even though my parents had very little in material wealth, our family was rich in our faith and God was faithful to care for our needs. My mom taught us that we could never out give God. That message carried over into my life as an adult and into my own family.

So many times I can look back and see how God supplied our needs. I don't believe this verse is limited to financial needs. I believe that God knows us and is ready to meet our every need as we ask. What do you need God to do for you? Whatever it is, He will supply your needs!

—Margi Galloway

Prayer Starter: *Thank You God that You are the giver of all good gifts and You want us to ask in faith, believing that You know what is best for us—better than we know ourselves.*

FULFILLMENT

As the deer pants for the water brooks, so my soul pants for You, O God.
(Psalm 42:1)

Have you ever found yourself in a season where you've done everything right, but instead everything goes wrong, and you're exhausted by the battle? The enemy taunts you with thoughts that God isn't listening and soon despair threatens to close in. This is where David found himself in this Psalm. Chased into exile by his own son, he was forced to endure his mocking enemies. Yet, none of these troubles tormented his soul like the anguish of thirsting after a distant God. Like a bleating lost lamb, David would not be consoled until he reconnected with God. He mentions no regrets at being away from the privileges his kingship surely afforded him. It wasn't wealth or comfort he desired, it was the one thing that had become his heart's obsession—God Himself.

Once you've experienced the richness of the living God, not even the second best thing in life can quench your undying thirst. What are you longing for right now? Perhaps God has you thirsting to bring you to the real question…what exactly on your list of desires would you exchange for your relationship with God? "Whom have I in Heaven but you? And besides you I desire nothing on earth" (Psalm 73:25).

Don't make the mistake of thirsting after the gifts rather than the Giver. Only God can fulfill your deepest longings. He has reserved that place in your soul for Himself.

—Christy Osborn

Prayer Starter: *Heavenly Father, now that I have tasted the clear waters of Your love, I am no longer content to drink from less satisfying waters. You are the only refreshment for my parched soul.*

BRIDLE MY TONGUE

If anyone thinks he is religious and does not bridle his tongue but deceives his heart, this person's religion is worthless. (James 1:26)

Max Lucado tells a story about a courageous lady. She was courageous for several reasons. For one, she was on an uphill battle against alcoholism. For another, she was working hard to restore her relationship with God. It's tough to start over. It's particularly difficult when someone hinders the process.

She chose a small church to attend; a church where she knew many of the members. She thought she'd be received and welcomed there.

One Sunday she parked her car near the church building. She got out and walked toward the front door. Just then she overheard two women talking nearby. What they said was not intended for her to hear. But she heard it anyway. This is what she heard:

"How long is that alcoholic going to hang around here?"

She turned and went back to her car and she never entered another church building until she died.

The validity of our religion is determined by the way we speak about one another.

—Joe Gordon

Prayer Starter: *Lord, help me bridle my tongue.*

SEEK JESUS

"Good Teacher, what must I do to inherit eternal life?" (Luke 18:18) "Today salvation has come to this house." (Luke 19:9)

Two men.

Seeking two different ends.

Resulting in two different outcomes.

The rich young ruler comes to Jesus asking how to gain eternal life. After Jesus presses him about the law and sees that the young man has obeyed the law, He challenges him one last time. "Sell all that you have and distribute to the poor, and you will have treasure in Heaven; and come, follow me." But this is too difficult, so the young man walks away. He came seeking eternal life, and in the end walked away from Jesus.

Then there is Zacchaeus. He is also rich, for he is a tax collector. But he didn't seek eternal life...he sought Jesus. Little Zacchaeus, small in stature, climbed a tree just to catch a glimpse of Jesus! He wasn't trying to attain anything. He wasn't seeking for more. He just wanted to see Jesus.

But Jesus, seeing him in a tree and seeing his faith, called him down and dined with him. Zacchaeus responded by telling Jesus that he was going to give half of all he owned to the poor and give fourfold to those he had defrauded! Then Jesus said, "Today salvation has come to this house."

The rich young ruler sought salvation and was left with nothing.

Zacchaeus sought Jesus and was rewarded with salvation.

—Nate Hughes

Prayer Starter: *Jesus, today I seek You alone. Not what I can gain from You, but just You. May I find all that I need as I rest in You.*

NEW BEGINNINGS

Commit your way to the Lord. Trust also in Him, and He will do it.
(Psalm 37:5)

New beginnings force me to trust God all the more when I feel afraid and alone. Facing the unknown and the unfamiliar forces me to depend on Him for every step of the journey. The first place I want to run to is God's Word! How can I begin anything new without His promises to accompany me? Sometimes the very thing I fear is the thing God uses in my life to draw me closer to Him.

God will enable, encourage and equip you for a new beginning. He will embrace you as you start over. Do not be afraid to step out and begin again. You may even be surprised at the new, stronger and more confident you that emerges in the process!

Isaiah 43:18,19 -

Do not call to mind the former things,

Or ponder things of the past.

Behold, I will do something new,

Now it will spring forth;

Will you not be aware of it?

I will even make a roadway in the wilderness,

Rivers in the desert.

—Susan Miller

Prayer Starter: *Lord, walk with me as I face a new beginning. I release my fears and anxious thoughts to You. Give me peace for whatever lies ahead. Hold me close; never let me go.*

TAKE COURAGE

One of your men puts to flight a thousand for the Lord your God is He who fights for you, just as He promised you. (Joshua 23:10)

Winning when the odds are against you! Don't you love to read stories or watch movies where someone is out-numbered or facing what appears to be an unrealistic challenge – and wins? I certainly do. I think of the movies *Gladiator* and *Braveheart*, even *Jason Bourne,* or the conquest of David and Joshua in the Bible. What stories do you think about?

In today's reading, one man puts to flight a thousand. Men, can you imagine the excitement and adrenaline rush as you watch a thousand men flee from your wielding sword! These men, who became mighty warriors, had help. "For the Lord your God is He who has been fighting for you" (Joshua 23:3,10).

Knowing that the Lord is fighting the battle for us should give you and me confidence to face any challenge. It is also a warning – you don't want to go to battle without the Lord on your side! Verses 11-13 say, "So take diligent heed to yourselves to love the Lord your God" for if you ever go back and trust in someone or something else "Know for certain the Lord will not continue with you."

What challenge is laid before you today? Are the odds of victory overwhelming? Is your heart intent on doing all the Lord has commanded you to do? Then cling to the Lord and take courage, get an adrenaline rush, and go to battle with confidence that the Lord is fighting for you.

—Mark Upton

Prayer Starter: *Lord, today I need Your help and courage to face these challenges…*

DEEP, DEEP WATERING

He will be like a tree firmly planted by streams of water, which yields its fruit in its season and its leaf does not wither…(Psalm 1:3)

Back in the summer of 1992, something startling happened in the city of Seattle. Because of a record low snow pack, Seattle residents found themselves for the first time in a water crisis! States like California, Arizona and Nevada suffer through this kind of thing regularly but these Washingtonians weren't used to a "No lawn watering" mandate.

Many people were worried that one of the greenest places on the planet would turn brown! But it didn't happen and not because the rain finally began to fall. What people didn't realize was how much moisture from all the rain that had fallen for so long still remained in the soil!

The verse for today talks about a tree that grows next to not just one, but "streams" of water. And as such, it stayed green and yielded fruit season after season. That's a great principle to apply to our marriages. As we allow God's Word to pour into our lives, it builds up and provides deep reservoirs that can get us through the toughest times – full of green leaves and fruit for others!

—John and Cindy Trent

Prayer Starter: *Lord, it's so easy in our super-busy lives to forget what's important - reading Your Word and soaking up all You have to give us. We know there will be tough times, Lord, but thank You for the deep wells You fill in our lives.*

PASSING THE BATON

"Assemble the people before Me to hear My words so that they may learn to revere Me as long as they live in the land and may teach them to their children." (Deuteronomy 4:10)

Relay races have been lost due to either one runner not passing the baton correctly or another runner not receiving it correctly. Some runners receive the baton correctly, but while they are running their segment of the race, they fumble it before it is their turn to hand-off the baton to the next runner. Momentary loss of focus can bring devastating results. This is the reason that relay runners, even when they are not running, practice the handoff of the baton. The baton pass must be precise; there is no room for error. A fumbled baton means disqualification from the race.

The United States Women's 2004 Olympic 4x100 relay team dominated the preliminary races in their quest for an Olympic gold medal only to see their dreams quashed in the finals. This was due to the baton being fumbled during an exchange between two team members, as the baton was not passed within the allotted distance on the track. It's possible the team members who fumbled the baton will be haunted by this careless act and their being disqualified from the race for the rest of their lives. Before the fumble, they were on pace to establish a new Olympic record.

We cannot receive the spiritual baton for our children, but we have the responsibility to train each child regarding the importance of personally receiving and then passing this great spiritual legacy on to the next generation. The winner is rewarded with the greatest gift - the gift of knowing Jesus Christ as their personal Lord and Savior. We practice passing the baton each time we practice our faith in Christ in front of our children. Is your life a reflection of God's love to your children, or are you dropping the spiritual baton?

—Ron Goble

Prayer Starter: *Lord, help us model a love for Christ in our home.*

BE INCREDIBLE

"You will receive power when the Holy Spirit has come upon you…"
(Acts 1:8)

My favorite Pixar movie is "The Incredibles." We understand the anguish of Mr. Incredible. He has great power and knows instinctively that he has been given that power to help people. But the world around him says that his power must not be used; he should just be content to sit in his cubicle at work and push paper.

The world doesn't like our super power, either. We are told that we are "cramming our religion down people's throats" when we care enough to share the Word of Life with people who are dying. The world wants us to be quiet and keep to ourselves. Jesus instructed us to tell others about what we have personally experienced in relationship to Him. Which should we obey?

Ephesians 5:18 commands us to keep on being filled with the Holy Spirit. He is the source of our power. Without His power, I am a mere mortal, but in Him, I am Mr. Incredible, able to defeat the plans of the evil forces around me and to do works God has prepared for me (Ephesians 2:10*).*

Jesus said it was better for us to have the Spirit than to have Him with us in the flesh (John 16:7*).* He knew the impact the power of the Holy Spirit would have (read the book of Acts!*).* Don't be afraid of the Holy Spirit—He is God, He loves you and lives inside you to give you power to live the Christian life in victory and to share that life with people who are eternally dead without it. Keep on being filled with the Spirit and be incredible!

—Dave Cottrell

Prayer Starter: *Lord, empty me of self and fill me afresh with your Spirit to accomplish all the good works You have prepared for me to walk in today.*

A HOLY LIFE

As obedient children, do not be conformed to the passions of your former ignorance, but as He who called you is holy, you also be holy in all your conduct, since it is written, "You shall be Holy, for I am Holy." (1 Peter 1:14-16)

We are in a battle to live a holy life. It is not easy because we have a natural bent towards sin and going against that natural bent will be a battle. But people are watching us and they would like nothing better than to be able to say, "Yes, I know about those Christians and they are no different than me. I would never want to become one of them." By living a holy life, we are demonstrating to the watching world what our God is like. Eventually they will want to know why you are different and then you can share about your relationship with Christ.

In northern Europe and Asia lives a little animal called an ermine. In the winter his coat changes to a snow white fur which he will instinctively protect against anything that may soil it. Fur hunters take advantage of this unusual trait. They will find his home and smear the entrance and interior with grime. Then they set their dogs loose to find the ermine. The frightened animal flees toward home but doesn't enter because of the filth. Rather than soil his white coat, he is trapped by the dogs. For the ermine, purity is more precious than life.

—Paul Wegner

Prayer Starter: *God, we pray that You will give us this type of a desire for holiness.*

WORRY

In the world you have tribulation, but take courage; I have overcome the world. (John 17:33b)

A troublesome result of worry is my body's stress response. That's right! With only one worrisome thought, I can set in motion the sympathetic nervous system's fight or flight response that triggers a cascade of chemicals and hormones. Sometimes we need this if our child is running into the street in front of a car. However, worriers experience the stress response without an actual stressor.

In the early 1970s we lived in Idaho, near Yellowstone Park. It was a cold, snowy morning when my husband drove to the Idaho Falls airport to board a plane to Boise for business during a ground blizzard. A ground blizzard fills the air from the ground to about ten feet high with snow. You cannot see your hand in front of your face. When my husband arrived at the small airport, he couldn't see his plane and thought he'd missed it. But when he climbed to the second story of the airport, it was a clear day.

My worries are my own personal ground blizzard, but the Lord sees it all clearly, and asks me to take courage and trust Him.

—Nonie Maupin

Prayer Starter: *Lord, I confess the sin of worry and stress; and I ask You to be my strength & courage.*

THE LEGACY OF MY LIFE

Teach us to number our days aright, that we may gain a heart of wisdom.
(Psalm 90:12)

Alfred Nobel made a fortune by inventing powerful explosives and licensing the formulas to governments to make weapons. In 1888, Alfred's brother, Ludvig, died and a French newspaper mistakenly printed an obituary notice for Alfred instead. The paper said, "The merchant of death is dead." It went on to say, "Dr. Alfred Nobel, who became rich by finding ways to kill more people faster than ever before, died yesterday."

Alfred Nobel had the unique opportunity to read his own obituary and to see what he would be remembered for. As you can imagine, he was shocked to think that all he had worked for, his successes, his fortune and the totality of his life would be summed up as a merchant of death and destruction.

That unusual experience motivated Alfred Nobel to use the fortune he had acquired to establish special awards for accomplishments in various fields, which would benefit the world and all of humanity. And his efforts paid off! Because today, he's remembered not for his explosives, but for the Nobel Prizes.

—Dave Zehring

Prayer Starter: *Lord, give me wisdom to live today in light of eternity.*
May my life be a legacy of faithfulness to You. Guide me today.

CONTENTMENT

But I rejoiced in the Lord greatly, that now at least you have revived your concern for me; indeed, you were concerned before, but you lacked opportunity. Not that I speak from want, for I have learned to be content in whatever circumstances I am. I know how to get along with humble means, and I also know how to live in prosperity; in any and every circumstance I have learned the secret of being filled and going hungry, both of having abundance and suffering need. I can do all things through Him who strengthens me. (Philippians 4:10-13)

Two definitions that ring home to me on the subject of contentment are:
(1.) A state of mind in which one's desires are confined to his lot whatever it may be.
(2.) To be free from care because of satisfaction with what is already one's own.

Paul told Timothy how he was to deal with this matter of contentment, and his command is especially applicable to those of us living in affluent western cultures: "Instruct those who are rich in this present world not to be conceited or to fix their hope on the uncertainty of riches, but on God, who richly supplies us with all things to enjoy" (1 Timothy 6:17). Ask yourself today, "Am I placing my hope in my bank account, or is my hope in Jesus?"

—Patrick Sullivan

Prayer Starter: *Father, keep my eyes on you.*

REMEMBERING THE BEGINNING

I beseech you therefore, brethren, by the mercies of God, that ye present your bodies a living sacrifice, holy, acceptable unto God, which is your reasonable service. And be not conformed to this world: but be ye transformed by the renewing of your mind, that ye may prove what is that good, and acceptable and perfect, will of God. (Romans 12:1-2)

Prior to my first short-term mission trip, I had a long list of Bible verses to learn. As a young Christian, I wasn't familiar with a lot of "Christian-ese"—let alone old English. As I began memorizing Romans 12 verses 1 and 2 (In the King James version), I wondered what words like, "beseech" and "brethren" meant. And then came that part about the "living sacrifice." What could that possibly mean? I got out a dictionary, thesaurus, and other tools to help me understand what I was learning. As I learned what the words meant, the Lord began to work in my heart and teach me how to apply these verses. In fact, He's still teaching me!

The trouble with a living sacrifice is that it still has the ability to crawl off the altar. Each time I place myself on His altar and tell Him that I am available for Him to use me— whenever, wherever, however—I find myself trying to help Him decide when, where and how. Although I mean well, I gradually begin to climb off the altar. I may not jump off, but more likely I start with a foot, then one leg, then half of my body is off, and finally I'm running in the other direction. At that point I'm calling the shots and telling Him where I want to go and what I want to do. That's when I realize that I need to get back on the altar and let God be in charge.

—Jackie Benedict

Prayer Starter: *Dear Lord, although I mean well, I have put my plans above Your plans. Please forgive me for putting my ways above Your ways. Right now I come back to Your altar and I—once again—surrender myself to You. All that I have, all that I am, all that I hope to be and will be, are Yours. Please help me to stay focused and surrendered to You, and to not conform to the world and its standards. Help me to be a living sacrifice to You today.*

FREE TO LIVE

I know that my Redeemer lives, and that in the end He will stand upon the earth. And after my skin has been destroyed, yet in my flesh I will see God. (Job 19:25-26)

I don't know who said it first, but no matter how many times it's repeated, its truth never changes: "Until you're prepared to die, you're never really free to live." The statistics about our ultimate demise are sobering but unavoidable. 1 out of 1 dies. It's not a case of if we're going to end up the feature presentation at a funeral; just when.

Job was the poster child for a great life turned bad. First it was his financial empire, then his children, then his health, then his nay-saying wife, and finally his condescending "friends." Right in the middle of the book that could be sub-titled "Living Out the Worst-Case Scenario," Job lets loose with the only source of solid hope he has. He absolutely knew that the Redeemer of his pitiful life was eternally alive and divinely well. And even though there was nothing in his life worth smiling about, he knew he'd spend eternity in Heaven with God.

If you've put your faith in Christ's redeeming work for you on the cross, you can be convinced "That neither death nor life, neither angels nor demons, neither the present nor the future… will be able to separate you from the love of God that is in Christ Jesus" (Romans 8:38-39).

—Tim Kimmel

Prayer Starter: *Dear Lord, thank You for the unshakeable hope I have because of Your redeeming love.*

WHY DO WE DO WHAT WE DO IN MINISTRY?

...So in Christ we who are many form one body, and each member belongs to all the others. We have different gifts according to the grace given us. (Romans 12:5,6a)

A person's philosophy is his or her basic idea on how life should be lived or something should be done. So when preachers talk about a "philosophy of ministry," they are talking about "the general principles" (i.e., rules, convictions, laws, etc.) That determine their church's ministry. Presumably, these principles form the foundation for the church's work, providing an answer, in some form, to the crucial question, "Why do we do what we do in ministry?" A biblical philosophy of ministry would start with God, not man, as the ultimate source of the ministry (1 Corinthians 3:6).

A biblical philosophy of ministry understands that the Bible, not human wisdom, is the authority for our ministry (Isaiah 55:6-11). Please distinguish between absolutes and non-absolutes. Absolutes are the foundational biblical principles that do not vary with time or culture (e.g., Christians should gather together as stated in Hebrews 10:24-25). Non-absolutes are specific applications that may vary with time or culture (e.g., Christians should gather together at 11AM on Sunday and sit in pews).

This philosophy knows that people, not programs, are the focus of a ministry (1 Thessalonians 2:8; John 3:16). This ministry works toward mature believers, not simply converts, as the goal of ministry (Colossians 1:28-29). This is a ministry that sees the corporate body, not individualism, as the environment for ministry (Romans 12:3-8). This means that every member is a minister – the ministry is not just for the seminary trained professional. God has gifted every believer (1 Corinthians 12:7-11) so that they might have a part in building up the body of Christ. Everyone is essential and unique in this process.

—Jim Borror

Prayer Stater: *God, help me use the gifts You have given me.*

SURETY FOR OUR LIVES

For God so loved the world that He gave His only begotten Son to that world, that whom so ever believes in Him, shall have eternal life. (John 3:16)

God's plan for our lives goes far beyond a fire protection policy that takes us to Heaven when we die. Can you imagine a walk with God that is so transforming that living it will make even the toughest times worth the trials?

Consider Paul, imprisoned, beaten, and shipwrecked, and think about his consistent response until the end of his life. On the Damascus road, he caught the vision of living as a testimony to what we know today as Galatians 5:22 and 1 Corinthians 13 – and we can too! And in doing so, we can change our world.

Catch the vision by asking God to reveal it to you. It won't likely come in one day, but as you persist in asking God for it, it will come. He's promised it.

—Donald Farr

Prayer Starter: *Father God, bring into the light of Your love, those places in my day, my heart, that You would transform. Help me see the vision of my life as a whole life follower of Jesus.*

GOD IS ALWAYS THERE

Where shall I go from Your Spirit? Or where shall I flee from Your presence? If I ascend to Heaven, You are there! If I make my bed in Sheol, You are there! If I take the wings of the mourning and dwell in the uttermost parts of the sea, even there Your hand shall lead me, and Your right hand shall hold me. (Psalm 139:7-10)

The Santa Cruz River is one of three rivers in the United States that flows north. It flows up out of Mexico into Arizona crossing the U.S./Mexico border near Nogales. The second interesting thing about the Santa Cruz is that it intermittently flows underground. So, one can walk alongside the stream for a while, and then the water flows out of sight, only to re-appear further downstream.

As I reflect back on my life, I can recall times that I was vividly aware of God's presence in my life. However, at other times, I was oblivious to His presence. Some of those times that I was unaware of God, it was due to my indifference; other times it was because of the distractions that the world presents.

From the perspective of seventy-plus years, it occurs to me that as I walked along the riverbank of life, God was there all along. Just because there are times that the river cannot be seen, it does not mean that it is not flowing. And just because I am not aware of God it does not mean that He is not there. God is always there.

—Bob Cain

Prayer Starter: *God, I know that You are always with me because You told me in Your Word. Thank You.*

ENCOURAGING WORDS

For whatever was written in earlier times was written for our instruction, so that through perseverance and the encouragement of the Scriptures we might have hope. (Romans 15:4)

You spend two years in solitary confinement with leg irons shackled around your ankles fifteen hours a day. There is no light in your cell except for the light from that one, single bulb that comes on at dark and stays on all night until daybreak.

After more then 300 brutal interrogations, you have your already broken leg deliberately snapped and are beaten in the face with a fan belt until you go into convulsions. Repeatedly you are shown pictures of Jane Fonda in Hanoi, only a few miles away from where you're imprisoned, leading anti-war protestors. You are denied even a single letter from your wife back home and you're only halfway through your 2,714 days in captivity!

For almost anyone other then Captain James Stockdale, the most senior officer in the infamous "Hanoi Hilton," such a situation would have led to despair. But this incredible man of faith, and others imprisoned with him, had a "hope" like in today's verse that their captors couldn't crush. In fact, prisoners smuggled Bible verses to each other and used a special code of coughing and shuffling to send prayers and words of encouragement from cell to cell - including this verse from Romans.

Thankfully, most of us will never come close to facing the kind of challenges Stockdale did. But there are challenges in many life situations. We all begin life captive to sin and in need of a Savior. The same strengths and "hope" that helped the heroes of Hanoi stay strong can shelter us in God's care and free us from what chains us.

—John and Cindy Trent

Prayer Starter: *Lord, there are so many times when we seem "chained" to bad habits, held captive to a temper we can't seem to control, or often seem to fall short. Thank You that there is—in Jesus—a "hope" that can change our life even on the toughest of days.*

NEVER GIVE UP

And let us not grow weary of doing good, for in due season we will reap, if we do not give up. (Galatians 6:9)

One of the nice things that is often said about me is that I'm "the pastor of one of the largest and most influential churches in the country." And while this idea is nice to consider, it's not the most accurate way to reflect the church I have the honor to pastor. In reality, I am blessed to pastor a church that God has used to birth a multitude of influential ministries.

The distinction may be subtle, but it is important. We want to recognize that God has had His hand on our church in its first fifty years. He has seen fit to lead people to step out in faith, follow in obedience and take risks for His glory. As a result, Scottsdale Bible has been used as the starting point for ministries that have a regional, national, and even international reach. We have been blessed to be the sending point for missions and missionaries who God is using to change lives around the country and around the globe.

As wonderful as it is to celebrate how God has used Scottsdale Bible, the two worst things we could do are: *1)* sprain our shoulders patting ourselves on the back, or *2)* grow complacent and slow down or stop.

We believe by faith, that God has even greater plans and even more ministries to launch through Scottsdale Bible. He has more people to reach with the Gospel through you who He is preparing for your own faith adventure to begin soon. Let us never grow weary of doing good. Let us not give up, because God has promised we will reap His harvest in due season!

—Jamie Rasmussen

Prayer Starter: *God, continue to use us to bring spiritual and physical help to those in need.*

BIOGRAPHIES HELP US

Do your best to present yourself to God as one approved…(2 Timothy 2:15)

In the early seventies, I was challenged to read biographies of men and women who left family and fame to serve God in foreign lands.

I read about Hudson Taylor of China, C.T. Studd of Africa, Clarence Jones of HCJB Radio, Elisabeth Elliot of Ecuador, Helen Roseveare of Africa, and George Muller of England to name a few.

George Muller (1805-1898) is a particular hero. He read his Bible from end to end over 200 times, prayed for orphans daily, cared for over 10,000 in his lifetime alone (the orphanages continued 100 years after his death), raised millions of dollars and never asked for a cent. He never took a salary and God always provided. He lost two wives and three children to death. He traveled over 10,000 miles preaching three times a week for 60 years and daily for 17 years. He died in the night following the Wednesday prayer meeting he led.

His message was always the same: "God can be trusted." He claimed in every decision, "The Lord is good and doest good." Muller did not believe he had the gift of faith but rather the grace of faith, and encouraged all believers in development of the grace of faith.

Gift of faith: only a few have this spiritual gift (one of many spiritual gifts). Muller was not granted this spiritual gift.

Grace of faith: all who believe have faith by God's grace, e.g., Faith that God answers prayer, that His promises are true, that He is worthy, and that He can be trusted with all the affairs of life.

When Muller was asked the secret to his service, he replied, "There was a day when I died, died to George Muller…died to the world…and since then I have studied to show myself approved unto God."

—Donna Otto

Prayer Starter: *God, help me to trust You daily.*

GOD'S CALL

The Lord hurled a great wind on the sea and there was a great storm on the sea so that the ship was about to break up. Then the sailors became afraid and every man cried to his God, and they threw the cargo which was in the ship into the sea to lighten it for them. But Jonah had gone below into the hold of the ship, lain down and fallen sound asleep. (Jonah 1:4–5)

Later in the text Jonah admits he is trying to flee from the presence of the Lord, and that the Lord created this storm to get his attention. Many lost their livelihood in the Mediterranean sea. How many other ships on the Mediterranean that day suffered in this storm because of Jonah's disobedience? All the efforts of the sailors were to no avail, this storm was Jonah's storm, yet Jonah was found sleeping.

Are you in a storm? Are you embracing your storm or are you sleeping through it? Are others suffering because you are not willing to answer the call God has on your life? The Lord once told me that a crisis is a personal invitation to know Him better. Do you want to know the Lord better? Embrace your storm, answer His call. He loves you and will show to you His faithfulness.

—Deb Pirtle

Prayer Starter: *O Lord our Lord, how majestic is Your name in all the earth. Lord, help us to trust Your sovereign hand in our storm, believing You are gracious and faithful.*

HIS MERCIES ARE NEW EVERY MORNING

The Lord's lovingkindnesses indeed never cease, for His compassions never fail. They are new every morning; great is Your faithfulness. (Lamentations 3:22-23)

Volunteering on Tuesday mornings in women's ministry, I have had the privilege of mentoring young moms for many years. It forces me to think back on my years as a young mother and all the mistakes I made.

I remember feeling like I would never get it right as a mom. While pregnant, I thought motherhood would be filled with story times and trips to the park, and never-ending joy and hugs and tickles. And then I had kids.

What I found was my life went from clean clothes to spit-up-stained tops, make-up to dark circles under my eyes, career satisfaction to yearning for grown-up conversation, and a constant nagging that my children were doomed in life because they were stuck with me as a mother. I learned I could not be the mother I wanted to be by depending on my own strength. The Lord was teaching me how to depend on Him and His strength.

All along this verse in Lamentations brought me comfort. The Lord was not going to stop loving me because I made mistakes, because His lovingkindness never ceases! The Lord was not harsh toward me, because He had compassion for me and my situation. I could wake up every morning knowing it was a new day, and the Lord was going before me, so I could depend on Him to keep me patient and transform me into the mother He wanted me to be. As I was training my children's character for righteousness, God was training me.

I now remind the young moms they will fail, but if they confess their sins to the Lord and ask Him for help, He will have compassion on them and give them new mercies each morning to face each day. The Lord is able to make all things new because great is His faithfulness!

—Tracy Goble

Prayer Starter: *Father, I need a clean slate today. Thank You that Your mercies are new every morning! I confess…*

RESISTING A SHARK ATTACK

Be sober-minded; be watchful. Your adversary the devil prowls around like a roaring lion, seeking someone to devour. Resist him, firm in your faith, knowing that the same kinds of suffering are being experienced by your brotherhood throughout the world. (1 Peter 5:8,9)

Laura Hillenbrand, the author of *Seabiscuit*, has written a new book entitled *Unbroken* in which she tells an astonishing tale of survival, resilience, and redemption. During World War II, Louis Zamperini joined the Army air corps as a bombardier. After his B-24 Liberator crashed into the ocean, he survived 47 days on a raft at sea before his dehumanizing capture and torture by the Japanese.

While drifting at sea, Louie and two other surviving crew members experienced a fearful phenomenon – sharks!

"As the men sat together, exhausted and in shock, a shark lunged up over the wall of the raft, mouth open, trying to drag a man into the ocean. Someone grabbed an oar and hit the shark, and it slid off. Then another shark jumped on and, after it, another" *(p. 156-157)*.

During a strafing attack by a Japanese plane, Louie jumped overboard into the water and hid under the raft only to see the huge, gaping mouth of a shark emerge out of the darkness.

"Louie remembered the advice of the old man in Honolulu: make a threatening expression, then stiff-arm the shark's snout. As the shark lunged for his head, Louie bared his teeth, widened his eyes, and rammed his palm into the tip of the shark's nose. The shark flinched, circled away, then swam back for a second pass. Louie waited until the shark was inches from him, then struck it in the nose again. Again, the shark peeled away" *(p. 155)*.

Contemplating the horrific shark experiences, I can easily make a connection to what the Bible says about Satan and the tactics he employs. Hmm…bare my teeth, widen my eyes, and ram my palm into the devil's nose. This could well be another metaphor for resisting him and remaining firm in my faith. Certainly the threat is very real, but I would like my life to be a tale of survival, resilience, and redemption, just like Louis Zamperini.*

—Holly DelHousaye

Prayer Starter: *Lord, help me resist the devil strongly and securely, standing firm in faith.*

GOD KNOWS

I know… (Revelation 2:2, 3, 9, 13; 3:1, 8, 15)

Ken Jennings is perhaps the most famous contestant from the game show Jeopardy. He won 74 consecutive games and earned more than $3.5 Million from all his appearances. He eventually wrote the book Braniac about being a trivia "know-it-all."

Jennings and imitators like him don't really "know-it-all." They have considerable knowledge about a limited scope of information, but they really only know a small part of a small part of everything that is possibly known. In fact, there's only one "know-it-all," and His name is Jesus.

In His seven messages to the seven churches in Revelation 2 and 3, Jesus reveals that He really does know it all. Here is some of what He shares that He knows:

- I know your works,…toil, …patient endurance, how you cannot bear with those who are evil…
- I know you…are bearing up for my name's sake, and you have not grown weary.
- I know the distress you are suffering and your poverty…
- I know where you live.
- I know….your love, and faith, and service and patient endurance
- I know….you have the reputation…
- I know…that you have but little power…

This is by no means an exhaustive list of a mere manager or consultant who has come in and done a targeted evaluation. These are the insightful comments of the Lord God who knows every detail of every detail. He knows the first-hand, intimate experiential knowledge of every aspect of these churches. He knows their works, their motives for those works, the effects of those works, and the opposition and obstacles to those works. More than knowing the church's works, He also knows the churches…their heart, their faith, their hopes, their fears, their frustrations, their needs, their resources, and their destinies.

What an encouragement it is to us to know that God knows our church. He knows our history and our future. He knows our efforts and our motives behind them. He knows our needs and He knows our opportunities. Praise God that Jesus is our know-it-all! He knows it all.

—Bryan McAnally

Prayer Starter: *May the heart of our church be Your heart.*

A SHIELD ABOUT US

Blessed is the one who considers the poor…the Lord protects him and keeps him alive; he is called blessed in the land. (Psalm 41:1-2)

Standing at the edge of the broad landscape in front of me, I surveyed the opportunities. We needed to find a place for the foundation of the next classroom and school we were building in Tanzania. This required me to walk across the underbrush-covered surroundings and find a place suitable for the new construction. As I stepped forward to begin exploring, a young boy, probably no more than ten, called out to me.

"What are you doing?" he asked. I explained what I was planning on doing. "But you can't go out there!" he said. "There are snakes out there that will bite you and kill you!"

I told him that I must go out there because the work was important. The young boy then looked up at me and said, "Well then, let me go out with you. I will walk with you and protect you." This was a reminder to me of the ways the Lord surrounds me with His protection even when I am unaware of His presence.

A week later in this same location, a poisonous spitting cobra actually appeared and spit its venom on one of the local villagers.

God's great love for the poor promises blessings upon those who are moved by compassion to serve them. God desires to use you to bless others and to be blessed by serving others. Whether God takes you to the fields of Tanzania or the neighborhoods of Phoenix and Scottsdale, His hand of blessing and protection are upon you when you bless others in the name of Jesus. While you may be surprised by how He provides for your physical safety, His Holy Spirit safely guards your soul wherever He leads you.

—Fred Beasley

Prayer Starter: *Father, I pray for the compassion to see the needs of the poor and for the courage to go serve in some way to relieve their pain. Please be my shield as I go in faith.*

PRAYER

To those who believe in the name of the Son of God......if we ask anything according to His will He hears us. And if we know that He hears us in whatever we ask, we know that we have the requests that we have asked of Him.
(I John 5:13-15)

When we ask for things in prayer, God responds to those prayers. Our failure to ask God for things is often the reason we do not receive what He delights to give us. The Scriptures give many examples of God responding, even changing the way He acts, in response to the prayers of individuals. These many examples in the Bible should encourage us to pray more, boldly asking the Lord to work in ways only He can work.

If our faith is in Jesus, He is the reason our prayers are effective. Jesus is the only true Mediator between a holy God and sinful men. Our prayers should be prayed based on His authority as our Mediator. At all times we should pray in line with the general principles of Scripture. Praying according to God's will often requires humility on our part, for it requires that we pray not simply for what we deserve but instead for what God desires.

—Wayne Grudem

Prayer Starter: *Hear my prayer, oh God.*

JOY

You have turned my mourning into dancing; You have taken away my clothes of mourning and clothed me with joy. (Psalm 30:11)

There seems to be a low supply of joy in our world these days. There is so much to be mournful about, and yet as Christians, we are called to be joyful. At least nineteen times in the book of Philippians, Paul mentions joy, rejoicing or gladness. How could Paul rejoice in the midst of his circumstances? He was a Roman prisoner and could even lose his life. So how could he experience joy? It certainly did not depend on his circumstances. Are you allowing your circumstances to rob you of joy? When we receive Jesus, we receive our inheritance of joy. It is interesting that joy and grace are derived from the same root word. Joy is the natural response to the grace of God.

Our joy comes from abiding in Jesus for the joy of the Lord is our strength. It is independent of our circumstances. Paul did not look at Christ through his circumstances; rather he looked at his circumstances through Christ. That changed everything. Are you clothed in joy or are you burdened by your circumstances? Choose joy my friend and you will experience a peace that only Christ can give you.

—Margi Galloway

Prayer Starter: *Lord, when my circumstances are overwhelming, I choose to trust You and ask You to fill my heart with joy.*

MATURE IN FAITH

Is anyone among you sick? Then he must call for the elders of the church and they are to pray over him, anointing him with oil in the name of the Lord… (James 5:14)

As you read this, are you or someone close to you weak or suffering from an illness? You probably do not have to think long as the names and faces of family, friends, and neighbors come to mind. James calls the faithful to summon the elders, the *presbuteros* of the church, (those men who are mature in the faith, who guide, teach, and shepherd their flock in spiritual growth), that they may pray over you.

What great comfort to the ailing and afflicted to know that those who have charge over them are called to come to their side and pray. Those who are close to him and have the wisdom in their maturity in Christ not only guide from afar, but come near during times of weakness and frailty. Those who are advanced in the faith and have known Jesus intimately over time are well-suited to pray on other's behalf.

—David Walther

Prayer Starter: *Lord, thank You for Your care for me, and thank You for those who love me here on earth and desire my health, healing and spiritual growth in You.*

COUNT IT ALL JOY

Count it all joy, my brothers, when you meet trials of various kinds, for you know that the testing of your faith produces steadfastness, and let steadfastness have its full effect, that you may be perfect and complete, lacking in nothing. (James 1:2–4)

One of my best out-of-town friends says, "Count me out on all that trial stuff. It hasn't improved me one iota." Life's experiences, however, tell me that James is right. Trials, tribulations and adversities are often God's greatest benedictions in our lives—blessings in disguise—angels dressed in black but for a moment. The very thing that seems to break us is the thing that makes us. Re-doing cracked pots and straightening warped wood are always painful, but what circumstances in your life would make you perfect and complete?

God ensures that the person who remains steadfast under trial will receive the crown of life. God is putting the flesh to death so that you might be made alive in the Spirit. "Make every effort to supplement your faith with virtue, and virtue with knowledge, and knowledge with self-control, and self-control with steadfastness, and steadfastness with Godliness and Godliness with brotherly affections and brotherly affection with love" (2 Peter 1:8). The Bible promises that this process produces fruit and effectiveness.

—Barry Asmus

Prayer Starter: *Dear Father, help me to see that You are my shepherd and I lack in nothing. You are my provision, my protection, my peace, my courage and my hope.*

WHERE YOU ARE WHO YOU ARE

Who may ascend into the hill of the Lord? And who may stand in His holy place? He who has clean hands and a pure heart. (Psalm 24:3–4)

Jesus says it's "the pure in heart" who will see God (Matthew 5:8). But our hearts are pretty messed up in impurity and hypocrisy, as Jesus points out: "Out of the heart come evil thoughts, murders, adulteries, fornications, thefts, false witness, slanders" (Matthew 15:19). "The heart is more deceitful than all else," says the Lord in Jeremiah 17:9, "And is desperately sick; who can understand it?" Only God can purify a heart.

The heart is one's inner person, the center of personality, of intentions and will. Your heart is what makes you uniquely you. Your heart is who you are. That's why Solomon warns, "Watch over your heart with all diligence, for from it flow the springs of life."

God took the kingdom of Israel away from King Saul because of Saul's heart problems. And God gave it to David, not because he was younger, smarter, or stronger, but because the Lord "sought out for Himself a man after His own heart."

Today, if you will, speak to God the way David speaks in the Psalms: "Search me,O God, and know my heart;" (139:23) "Create in me a pure heart, O God;" (51:10) "Let the meditation of my heart be acceptable in thy sight, O Lord;" (19:14) and "My heart is steadfast, O God, my heart is steadfast" (Psalm 57: 7).

Paul tells us to present our bodies to God as a living sacrifice. Have you ever dedicated your heart to Him? Now would be a great time to do it.

—Darryl DelHousaye

Prayer Starter: *Lord, I want to dedicate my heart, my inner person to You.*

TRUSTING THE LORD

Trust in the Lord with all your heart and lean not on your own under-standing. In all your ways acknowledge Him and He will make your paths straight. (Proverbs 3:5-6)

I memorized this verse several years ago while moving through a very difficult time in my life. I knew God was always there for me. I thanked Him for all my many blessings; however, I relied on myself and my intellect when the going got tough.

As I repeated this verse, I came to realize God wanted a deeper relationship with me. He wanted one that would bring me to "trust in Him" completely; not just when everything was going well. He wanted me to know in my heart, not just in my head, that by trusting in Him completely, I would let go of my need to explain it all through my human insight. The burden of having to do that is heavy. Perhaps that is why in this Scripture we are directed to "trust in the Lord with all your heart" rather than all the power in our heads.

As I began to slowly but continually let go, my spirit lightened. It drew me closer to Him. I found myself saying, "Thank You Lord for this suffering, for it has caused me to glorify You." God can turn any suffering to serve a purpose if we "trust Him completely."

Once my trust shifted from myself to Him, I began to hunger more and more for His Word. For through His Word, we do come to know Him.

—Cathy Myers

Prayer Starter: *Dear Lord, thank You for always being there for us. Thank You for remind-ing us that suffering can serve a mighty purpose and bring us closer to You.*

RECONCILIATION AND RESTORATION

*…And through Him to reconcile all things unto Himself, having made
peace through the blood of His cross; through Him. (I say), whether things
upon the earth, or things in the Heavens. (Colossians 1:20)*

To be a useful disciple, one of the concepts with which we need to be familiar is the
biblical difference between "reconciliation" and "restoration." In the biblically cosmic sense,
reconciliation is bringing the broken creation – including our souls – back into a right relationship with God. In a sense, this means bringing it back into the relationships with God
that He intended in creation. The Bible speaks of this transaction clearly in Colossians 1: 20.

Scripture also speaks of this cosmic act as a one-time transaction that was done once and
was sufficient to bring complete balance between the broken creation and it's creator
(see Hebrews 7:27; 9:12; 10:10, and Jude 3).

One implication of this truth is that the legal transaction of reconciliation between broken creation – including man – and God is completed. What is not completed is restoration from brokenness to shalom (completeness). Restoration is a process that began at the
cross and will continue until Christ returns as King and makes all things "new." As Jesus'
disciples, there is nothing we can do in the biblical sense of reconciliation. That was done
by God in the shedding of Christ's blood on the cross – a once for all transaction.

What we do is not reconciliation in the biblical sense. However, Jesus' disciples are to be
ambassadors of the good news of God's reconciliation. We are to be laborers in the work
of restoration – working from the brokenness (the vandalism caused by sin) of creation
toward that ultimate shalom of God's compassionate loving intentions.

How do we "do" the task of restoration? We meet the criteria God has established in His
design for our living. That "how" is articulated in God's instructions for how we are to
live. Two of the primary locations of these instructions are found in the Ten Commandments (Exodus 20) and in their summary, the Great Commandment. The relationship between living according to God's instructions and restoration is explained in 2 Chronicles
7: 14. This tells us that the healing (restoration) we anticipate and desire is brought about
by a partnership between God and the people who are called by His name.

—Bob Moffitt

Prayer Starter: *Lord, thank You for reconciling me and give me strength and direction for
restoration.*

GOD WILL GUIDE

The secret things belong to the Lord our God, but the things that are revealed belong to us and to our children forever, that we may do all the words of this law. (Deuteronomy 29:29)

God does not hold us responsible for what He has not revealed to us. Hence, there is great freedom in decision making!

God is like a coach in professional football. In college football the quarterback is continuously waiting for the coach to tell him what play to execute next. While in professional football, the coach trusts that the quarterback knows the playbook, so He can choose whichever play He feels best to execute.

Similarly, God has given us the Bible as a playbook to help us make decisions. When we make decisions according to the Bible, we know that we are within God's will. When the Word is silent about a particular decision, God has given us freedom. Of course, the only way to enjoy this freedom is to trust that God will guide us when we wander in the wrong direction.

—Joe Gordon

Prayer Starter: *Lord, help me make decisions that are according to Your Word. When Your Word is silent, help me walk by faith.*

PASSING THE BATON

Only be careful, and watch yourselves closely so that you do not forget the things your eyes have seen or let them slip from your heart as long as you live. Teach them to your children and to their children after them.
(Deuteronomy 4:9)

My father's family was an example of the spiritual baton (much like passing of the baton in a relay race), being carried by some of his siblings while others dropped it and didn't pick it up again until many years later. Dad was one of four raucous, fun-loving boys. My grandparents were wonderful, odly parents that raised all four sons with the same godly instruction and admonition.

All four brothers chose to receive the spiritual baton, but two brothers chose to fumble the baton in their early adult years. During their segment of the race, these two brothers did nothing to prepare their children to receive the spiritual baton. Unfortunately, their children were raised in a spiritual desert and they did not receive the spiritual teaching and admonition that their fathers could have provided. Consequently, their lives were never grounded in the Word; they had no personal relationship with Jesus. Thus they had nothing to pass on to their own children - the next generation - and they too are left wandering in that same spiritual desert.

The hurt and pain that comes from residing in a spiritual desert brought suicide into one family; others experienced divorce, alcoholism and other forms of instability in their lives. As a result, today we see three generations from the sons that received the spiritual baton walking with Jesus, and three generations of the two brothers that fumbled the baton not walking with the Lord. These two brothers picked up the baton later in life, but it was too late for them to train their children to carry the baton to the finish line.

As evidenced in my grandparent's family, the responsibility is placed on the parents to train their children in the ways of the Lord. But the children also have a responsibility to believe and accept Jesus Christ as their Lord and Savior and receive the spiritual baton.

—Ron Goble

Prayer Starter: *Lord, may my children have a receptive heart for Jesus.*

MIRROR, MIRROR ON THE WALL…

…You are precious in my sight… (Isaiah 43:4)

Mirrors can often reflect a distorted view of who we really are. We look in a full-length mirror and see our imperfections from head to toe. We look in a magnifying mirror and see our flaws enlarged. We look in a three-way mirror and see views that affect our self-image.

Take a good look at how Jesus sees you, not how you see yourself. Imagine that Jesus is standing by your side looking in the mirror with you. He is smiling, for you are precious in His sight! (Isaiah 43:4). He loves you more than life itself (1 John 3:16). He sees you with eyes of acceptance (Romans 15:7). He values you with all His heart (Matthew 10:31). Through Him you are forgiven (Nehemiah 9:17).

You see blemishes, ugliness, and imperfections. He sees you with love, forgiveness, and acceptance. Take time to see yourself through the eyes of Jesus!

—Susan Miller

Prayer Starter: *Lord, so often I base my image on a negative or false perception of who I really am. Help me to see myself as You see me. Remind me that my true identity is found in You, not in a mirror.*

HOW TO PRAY FOR THE LOST

"Thy kingdom come, thy will be done, on earth as it is in Heaven."
(Matthew 6:10)

In teaching us to pray, the Lord says we should specifically pray that His kingdom (meaning His rule, His reign) should come—should be advanced—on this earth. One critical way in which this occurs is through the conversion of lost souls. To pray "Thy kingdom come" means to pray, at least in part, for lost relatives and friends to come to a true knowledge of Jesus Christ as their Lord and savior.

For every lost soul we pray for, we should ask God for at least three things: 1) to orchestrate circumstances so the person will come into contact again and again with the Word of God, for "faith comes by hearing a word about Christ" (Romans 10:17); 2) to grant that person an awareness of his/her sin and the repentance that leads to salvation (2 Corinthians 7:9-10); and 3) to cause that person to submit his/her will to the will of God in acknowledging Christ as Lord and Savior (John 6:44; Mark 3:35). This is Scripture-based, evangelistic prayer.

—John Politan

Prayer Starter: *I pray that those who are on my heart this hour, Lord, would hear the word of Your Gospel, have a godly sorrow for their sin, and turn to You for salvation.*

MIND READER

We are destroying speculations and every lofty thing raised up against the knowledge of God, and we are taking every thought captive to the obedience of Christ. (2 Corinthians 10:5)

"Sometimes I wish God didn't know what I was thinking," a teenager confessed to his youth pastor. "I try to keep my mind clean, but a lot of junk keeps cluttering my brain cells – stuff I don't want God to know about. What do I do?"

"I understand your struggle," his pastor responded gently. "And when I'm trying to clear my head of the junk, I remember Luther's saying: 'I can't stop birds from landing on my head, but I can prevent them from building a nest in my hair.'"

The teen laughed and then vowed that when the next bad thoughts crept into his mind, he'd "drive them out" and not let them build a nest.

That's something those of us who are older should do as well! In a fallen world, there are so many pictures and thoughts that can spring (or are sprung) into our mind. But that's where the choice comes in to deal with those images by "taking them captive" and asking the Lord to make a way of escape. Any "nest building" in your mind? Ask the Lord to forgive you and give you his strength to drive those negative or ungodly thoughts away!

—John and Cindy Trent

Prayer Starter: *Lord, whether it's an angry thought or a lustful thought, or any thought that is "junk" in our minds, help us drive it away. Thank You for Martin Luther's reminder on how to deal with them. It takes more then one "trip" for a bird to build a nest. Lord, help us not allow any "nests" that dishonor You to build up in our head or thinking.*

WORDS OF HOPE AND HEALING

A gentle answer turns away wrath, but a harsh word stirs up anger. (Proverbs 15:1)

I was at a spa with a few friends celebrating a birthday. I was there to focus on our friendship and relax. In the quiet room alone with the masseuse, I decided to break the silence and ask her about her background. I prayed and asked the Lord for help in directing our conversation. As I asked her about her view of God, the mood shifted from peace to hostility quickly. "I have a sister who is a Bible thumper," she seethed, "And I don't care what any of you have to say!" I was taken aback! I knew this anger wasn't directed at me, but I also knew I had a responsibility to try and calm her and get to the real answer.

I could have been demanding and told her I was paying her for a service and she better get her attitude right or I would tell her supervisor! I could have given her a quick reply and changed the subject. But the Lord was leading my words as I had asked Him to do. It was time for a gentle answer to turn her wrath away.

"Who has hurt you? Who has misrepresented God to you? All He wants is for you to understand how much He loves you, but you are so angry with Him. What has happened?"

She instantly softened and we ended our conversation on a better note. I was to plant a seed of healing for her that day. As an ambassador for Jesus, my job was to love her and give her grace when she needed it most. What will your job be today?

—Tracy Goble

Prayer Starter: *Lord, help me to bring words of hope and healing today to those I meet.*

LIVE IN THE MOMENT

Come now, you who say, "Today or tomorrow we will go to such and such a city, and spend a year there and engage in business and make a profit." Yet you do not know what your life will be like tomorrow. You are just a vapor that appears for a little while and then vanishes away. Instead, you ought to say, "If the Lord wills, we will live and also do this or that." But as it is, you boast in your arrogance; all such boasting is evil. Therefore, to one who knows the right thing to do and does not do it, to him it is sin.
(James 4:13-17)

How much of our lives and the time we could spend in relationship with God do we waste in trying to control that which is not ours to control? "The mind of man plans his way, but the Lord directs his steps" (Proverbs 16:9). We are certainly called to consider the future and to lean on the wisdom God provides us in planning our way in this life, but when we go beyond that and try to control that way, we move into the arrogance about which James warned us. Even worse, since we have been "called according to His purpose" (Romans 8:28b), it is a sin when we rely on ourselves for the control of the future. Like all sin, our attempt to control the future is ultimately fruitless. Like all sin, it is a vain attempt to usurp the sovereignty of God.

So where does God want us to live? He wants us to live in the moment - not in the past which we cannot change, or the future which we cannot know. Rather, He calls us to live simply in the moment, relying on His unfailing provision. Jesus said it best: "But seek first His kingdom and His righteousness, and all these things will be added to you. So do not worry about tomorrow; for tomorrow will care for itself" (Matthew 6:33). We have enough trouble just handling today. Embrace the freedom that comes from relying solely on God for the control of the future. Rely solely on God for His grace to cover your past. Rely solely on God as you live each moment in the joy of an unfettered relationship with the Lord of the universe. Rely solely.

—Jim York

Prayer Starter: *Lord, I want to rely solely on You.*

GOD SEES INSIDE

Judge not, that you be not judged. (Matthew 7:1)

The people who looked like they were the most righteous people in Jesus' day were the scribes and Pharisees. They fasted at least once a week, they gave tithe to the Temple, they commonly were praying on the street corners, and they followed the strict letter of the Law.

But Jesus says in Matthew 5:20 that unless your righteousness surpasses that of the scribes and Pharisees, you will not enter the kingdom of Heaven. What Jesus was getting at was that the scribes and Pharisees looked good on the outside, but inside they were still corrupt. In Matthew 23:27, He called them whitewashed tombs because they look good on the outside but inside they are dead. Their sins had not been forgiven. In fact, they thought they were so good they did not need to be forgiven.

We look on the outside, but God looks at the heart. We only see what people want us to see; God sees it all. I think I see now why God wants us to be very careful not to judge others because we do a very poor job of it. Let's leave the judging to the professional (God) - He is really the only one who does it perfectly.

—Paul Wegner

Prayer Starter: *God, in my heart let me not judge others but leave that up to You.*

FEAR-BASED

Be strong and courageous. Do not tremble or be dismayed for the Lord your God is with you wherever you go. (Joshua 1:9)

Lie: My fearful feeling is truer than God's Word.

There have been times in my life when I let my fears rule my perspective, and even restrict my activity. I'll never forget the challenging panic-attack months. During a panic-attack, I truly felt like I was dying. My heart raced. I couldn't catch my breath, and I felt like I had to get out of there…wherever I was. I remember a meeting at church, when suddenly, a wave of nausea and panic swept over me. Then the evil one tried to convince me never to return to that room…that meeting. My panic warped my perspective on reality.

My thinking was the problem, not the location. Recently I watched a friend's dog's fearful reaction to a stuffed horse. Cooper barked and the hair on his back stood on end. He was so frightened. But it was a faux horse! It was deception – it looked true but was not. It looked like something to be feared, but he was wrong – his senses deceived him. He didn't read it right. My panic warped my perspective on reality. My thinking was the problem, not the location.

—Nonie Maupin

Prayer Starter: *Dear Lord, I need You to transform my fear into strength and courage. Help me realize You are always with me.*

REFLECT

Remember your leaders, who spoke the Word of God to you. Consider the outcome of their way of life and imitate their faith. (Hebrews 13:7)

You and I have so much to be grateful for. Reflect on those whom God has placed in your life to be a blessing and encouragement.

God has put many special people in my life's path for nearly 70 years. I was raised in a Christian home and had the influences of Christian parents.

Growing up I had the privilege of participating in a vibrant home church where a youth director was personally encouraging and trained me for Christian leadership. I have made many meaningful relationships along the way. Many of them have significantly impacted my life as they have modeled the Christian life for me.

As a missionary for over 45 years, many colleagues and mission leaders have encouraged and used the Scriptures to strengthen my faith and ministry. There was a Brazilian co-worker who challenged me weekly to memorize Scripture, share Christ with those I met daily, and to stay accountable in a discipleship relationship. This was a mutual experience. How helpful a friendship can be!

We are to remember those whom God has placed in our lives who have taught, guided and encouraged us. Thank God for those whom He has put into your path.

Maybe you are in need of someone to help you on the path of life. Ask the Lord for that someone special.

—Bill Keyes

Prayer Starter: *Lord, You know my every need. You created me and want me to grow. Help me remember those people whom You have already used in my life for my spiritual and emotional encouragement. Thank You for _____ in my life and please bring someone I can encourage today.*

CONTENTMENT

I know how to get along with humble means, and I also know how to live in prosperity; in any and every circumstance I have learned the secret of being filled and going hungry, both of having abundance and suffering need. (Philippians 4:12)

Paul calls on us to set our minds "on the things above, not on the things that are on earth" (Colossians 3:2). Ultimately therefore, genuine contentment results from our communion with God the Father and with His Son.

The most familiar passage from Paul on the subject is Philippians 4:10-14, where Paul describes his contentment in want or plenty. Paul knew how to be content whether he had plenty or whether he was in need. The secret was drawing on Christ's power for strength.

Paul was content because he could see life from God's point of view. He focused on what he was supposed to do, not what he felt he should have. Paul had his priorities straight, and he was grateful for everything God had given him. Paul had detached himself from the nonessentials so that he could concentrate on the eternal. Where is your focus today?

—Patrick Sullivan

Prayer Starter: *Heavenly Father, please help me to see Your perspective on contentment as I look to Your Word.*

THE KEY IS SERVING OTHERS

...And whoever wants to be first must be slave of all. (Mark 10:44)

Marion Mill was born in a fairy tale royal palace in Hungary. Her first spoon was solid gold. They sent her to school in Vienna where she became an actress and there she met and fell in love with a young medical student named Otto.

Otto and Marion married and went to live in Hollywood, California. There, as they "set up house," he began to dabble in movies. He became so interested in movies and in directing movies that he gave up his medical practice and went on to become the internationally famed movie director Otto Preminger. Marion's beauty, wit, and irresistible charm brought her everything a woman desires. In Europe, New York and Hollywood, she became a famous international hostess. But Otto's princess could not handle the fast life of Hollywood. She dove into alcohol, drugs and numerous affairs. Her life and life-style became so sordid, even for Hollywood, that Otto Preminger divorced Marion. She tried to take her own life three times, unsuccessfully, and finally moved back to Vienna.

There at a party, she met another doctor – Albert Schweitzer, the well-known medical doctor, musician, philosopher, theologian and missionary. Schweitzer was home on leave from his hospital in Lambarene, Africa. She was so fascinated by Schweitzer that she asked him if she could talk to him alone. For almost six months she met with Dr. Albert Schweitzer every week. At the end of that time he was going to go back to Africa and she begged him to let her go with him. Schweitzer surprised everyone by agreeing. Marion, the young princess, who was born in a palace, went to a little village in Lambarene, Africa, and spent the rest of her life emptying bed pans and tearing up sheets to make bandages for putrid sores on the poverty stricken nationals.

She wrote her autobiography. I love the title of it – *All I Want is Everything*. When she died, Time Magazine quoted from her autobiography these words: "Albert Schweitzer says there are two kinds of people. There are the helpers and the non-helpers. I thank God He allowed me to become a helper, and in helping, I found everything."

—Jim Borror

Prayer Starter: *A helper Lord. Please let me be a helper to You and all I meet.*

EYES PEELED

For the eyes of the Lord range throughout the earth to strengthen those whose hearts are fully committed to Him. (2 Chronicles 16:9)

"Keep your eyes peeled, Tim." It was advice I often heard while growing up. Sometimes it was one of my parents reminding me to stay alert to needs of a younger sibling or it was a friend wanting me to locate someone or something they needed. The point was to keep my eyes open and lids "Peeled" back so that I wouldn't miss something important.

God has His eyes peeled for you. And he's not just hanging out in one place hoping He might catch you bringing your spiritual "A Game" to Him. He's moving from Main Street to the least traveled back roads of civilization searching for those people who claim His name and live for Him with their whole heart—regardless of whether or not there's anything in it for them.

He's got His eyes peeled for those who are living devoted lives, even when all hell is breaking out around them. And just when you think the pressure is too much, you get this sudden sense of His presence and power. That's because He not only has His eyes peeled for the fully committed, He wants to empower them to be strong and courageous—faithful followers of the God of grace.

—Tim Kimmel

Prayer Starter: *O Lord, thank You that obedience to You never goes unnoticed. Help me when I'm inclined to stray and strengthen me for the challenges ahead.*

A BETTER OUTCOME

But a man must examine himself, and in so doing he is to eat of the bread and drink of the cup. (1 Corinthians 11:28)

Here are some things to focus on for the rest of this year to ensure a better outcome:

1. Self-examination – are you doing your best? Make a careful exploration of who you are and the work you have been given, and then sink yourself into that. Don't be impressed with yourself. Don't compare yourself with others. Each of you must take responsibility for doing the creative best you can with your own life. (Galatians 6:4-5)

2. Use of time – where and how do you spend your time? Some folks save it, others make it, most waste it, several kill it, and a few are actually on it. Many try to manage it and end up losing it. Time is a taker. Once past, it never returns. How it's spent determines the satisfaction of life. (Ephesians 5:15-16)

3. Victory over defeat – are you winning or losing the battle? Victory is gained only in Christ. He goes before you. Put on the full armor of God and keep it on! (Ephesians 6:11)

4. Free in Christ – are you free from bondage? (John 8:31-32). Living in freedom from bondage requires faith in Christ. "For freedom Christ has set us free: stand firm therefore, and do not submit again to a yoke of slavery." (Galatians 5:1)

5. Spiritual gifts – are you serving with your spiritual gifts? Every Christian has at least one. "To each is given the manifestation of the Spirit for the common good." (1 Corinthians 12:4-11) Don't leave home without them!

—Darien Bennett

Prayer Starter: *Lord, search my heart. Help me to live my life for You, using the gifts You have given me and standing firm in Your love.*

PROMISE OF PEACE

Be anxious for nothing, but in everything, by prayer and supplication, with thanksgiving, let your requests be made known to God: and the peace of God, which surpasses all understanding, will guard your hearts and your minds in Christ Jesus. (Philippians 4:6-7)

This is a great promise from God. He tells us to let Him know our concerns and requests through prayer. He promises to give us His peace and to protect our hearts and minds in Christ Jesus.

When I first read these verses as a new Christian at age 31, I was moved to tears knowing that I could experience the peace of God, and that He would guard my heart and mind in Christ Jesus. These words of truth have brought wonderful peace and comfort to me over the years.

This was especially real to me when I battled staph infection and had five surgeries in eight months. Many days I would read Philippians 4:6-7, pray, and then experience the peace of God as He would calm and guard my heart and mind in Christ Jesus.

When speaking with men that are experiencing anxiousness and fear, I have seen God's peace come over them and guard them after reading these verses and praying.

What a great promise from our Lord!

—Larry Roberts

Prayer Starter: *Dear Father, help me to be anxious for nothing today. Help me, in everything, to pray and present my requests to You with thanksgiving. Thank You for giving me Your peace.*

CHEWING GUM

Likewise, husbands, live with your wives in an understanding way, showing honor to the woman as the weaker vessel, since they are heirs with you of the grace of life, so that your prayers may not be hindered. (1 Peter 3:7)

Somewhere in my childhood it was impressed on me that it was ungentlemanly and unladylike for an adult to chew gum. It was okay while you were playing sports or in a casual setting but if a person was dressed up, it was considered out of character for him or her to chew gum. It has always been a "thing" with me.

After many years of marriage, I noticed that my wife was chewing gum a lot. This was happening not just while she was in a casual setting, but when she was dressed up. Not only that, but she had a very annoying ability to make the gum "pop" as she chewed it. Since I knew that she was aware of my obsession about the subject, I convinced myself that she was doing it to irritate me – sort of a "passive-aggressive" maneuver. I became irritated that she would do something purposely to annoy me.

After I gave my life to Christ and the Holy Spirit started teaching me the ways a husband is to love his wife in an understanding way, my attitude began to change. I began to pray that God would take this "thing" about gum away from me. I began to thank Him for such a beautiful wife, and for one who had this amazing dexterity to make the gum pop, which I could not do.

Soon things began to change. Does my wife still chew gum? I honestly do not know. Either she quit or I do not notice it anymore. Either way, I thank God for removing the critical spirit that I had harbored for so long.

—Bob Cain

Prayer Starter: *God, I sometimes struggle with selfishness and fail to understand the other person's point of view. Help me to surrender my will in favor of serving them.*

THE "COST" OF A SOLID FOUNDATION

He is the same yesterday, today and forever. (Hebrews 13:8)

One man had a dream of purchasing property and building a retirement home on a beautiful lakefront lot. He finally realized his dream and built his dream house, as close to the lake as the county would allow. He put in for his permit, and after months of waiting, received permission to build a dock and dock-house for his boat.

But then came a choice. The builder he hired gave him an option to anchor his dock and dock-house and save a lot of money. After all, he'd spent so much money already on his dream home, he didn't want to splurge on the dock. But within three months of his dock and dock-house being completed, a "once-every-twenty-year" flood ripped out the cheap fasteners and he lost all that had been built.

This true story only affected the man's dock, but it's another reminder that cutting the "cost" and ignoring putting in a solid foundation that goes all the way to bedrock isn't worth what we "save" in the long run. That's true in a house, a dock-house, or in our marriage. We need to build our life on the Rock – on the One who doesn't change, doesn't vary, doesn't wear out, and is the "same, yesterday, today and forever."

—John and Cindy Trent

Prayer Starter: *Lord, in Matthew 7:27, we read that, "The rain fell, and the floods came, and the winds blew and slammed against the house – and great was the fall." Lord help us to build our lives on the rock, starting today and everyday.*

IN THE WORLD

Religion that is pure and undefiled before God, the Father, is this: to visit orphans and widows in their affliction, and to keep oneself unstained from the world. (James 1:27)

Certainly you've heard the cliché, or maybe you've even said it…some variation of the idea that a Christian needs to be "in the world but not 'of' the world."

This idea is articulated in James that exhorts true followers of Jesus to serve society's disenfranchised and marginalized, all while remaining uncompromised by worldly trappings.

The challenge comes when putting this ideal into practice. Too often, despite best efforts, we see failed results including:

• "Three Monkey" Christians – these are the Christians who isolate themselves under the umbrella of "see no evil, hear no evil, speak no evil." While they are not "of the world," nor are they "in the world."

• The "Carnal Christians" – these are the Christians who think they need to indulge in every worldly vice to be relevant. They may be "in the world," but they are marked by being "of the world" as well.

God offers us no shortage of opportunities to be "in the world," to reach out to others and to speak out the saving name of Jesus while doing so. Missions, ministry, and service-based outreach are the means and method by which Jesus has afforded us the chance to share His love and truth with others.

Here, "religion" is not a matter of man-made ceremonial observance. It is an expression of worship and devotion. It involves a determination to remain morally uncompromised, so that as God affords you the chance to serve others and tell others about Him, your own life's circumstances would not get in the way of God's message. In this way you may be "in" while not "of" the world.

—Jamie Rasmussen

Prayer Starter: *Jesus, while I am in the world, give me the strength and endurance to not be of the world , but of You alone.*

LOVE COMES ALIVE WHEN YOU GIVE IT AWAY

Beloved, let us love one another, for love is from God; and everyone who loves is born of God and knows God. (I John 4:7)

A children's song says: "Love is something if you give it away, give it away, give it away. It's just like a magic penny—if you give it away you end up having more!"

I love the story of the little boy who moved into a new neighborhood. He was shy and quiet, and his name was Chad. One day he came home and said, "You know what, Mom? Valentine's day is coming and I want to make a Valentine for everyone in my class." His mother's heart sank and she thought, "Oh, how I wish he would not do that." Every afternoon she would watch all of the children coming home from school, and they would be laughing and hanging onto each other, books under their arms—all except Chad. He always walked behind them. But she thought she would go along with Chad. So glue, paper and crayons were purchased. For three weeks Chad painstakingly made thirty-five Valentines.

When the day came to deliver the Valentines, he was so excited! This was his day. He stacked those Valentines under his arm and ran out the door. His mother thought, "You know, this is going to be a tough day for Chad. I'm going to bake some warm cookies and give him some milk when he comes home from school, and maybe that will ease the pain. He probably won't be getting very many Valentines."

That afternoon she had the warm cookies and the milk out on the table. When she looked out the window, sure enough, here came the big gang of children, laughing, and Valentines under their arms. They had really done well. And there was Chad, coming up behind. He was walking faster than usual and she thought, "Bless his heart, he is ready to burst into tears. His arms are empty." He came in the house, and she said, "Darling, Mommy has some warm cookies and milk for you." But his face was all aglow. He just marched right by her and all he could say was, "I didn't forget a one—not a single one!"

Life's greatest joy is to give your love away. It isn't a song until it's sung. It isn't a bell until it's rung. It isn't love until it's given away.

—Dale Galloway

Prayer Starter: *Thank You Jesus for giving us all the Father's love to put into practice.*

WHAT NEEDS TO BE DONE

Benaiah . . . Went down into a pit on a snowy day and killed a lion.
(2 Samuel 23:20)

The pit is a cistern; a large hole dug in the ground to hold the water supply for the city. All the falling water from rain or snow is captured and channeled from all over the city into the cistern. This is done so the city can have water.

Over the long dry summer, the cistern has become dry. But now, the first snow of the season will soon flow into it to provide the water the city needs for the months ahead.

But a lion has gotten into the cistern and is trapped there. Unless he is killed and taken out, he will contaminate the water and it will be unfit to drink. Someone has to go into the pit and kill the lion. Who will do that?

The lion is frantic; pacing in a small space, unable to jump out, and ready to attack anyone who comes near. And snow is falling. Anyone who goes into the small, closed-in space of the cistern will have slippery footing on the rocks. Who will volunteer?

For the sake of God's people, Benaiah takes on a job that no one else wants. Despite the risk or inconvenience, he does what needs to be done so that God's people will have what they need.

—Don Sunukjian

Prayer Starter: *Lord, give me a heart that cares for Your people, and a willingness to put myself out to serve them.*

BESIDE OURSELVES

For if we are beside ourselves it is for God, or if we are of sound mind, it is for you. For the love of Christ compels us... (2 Corinthians 5:13-14)

Have you read a passage 500 times and, at the 501st reading, wondered, "What in the world does that mean?" Recently, while reading 2 Corinthians 5:13, I glued myself to the phrase, "beside ourselves." I have verbalized in the past that I've been "beside myself." Since studying Paul's usage of that phrase, I am convinced I did not know what I was saying! However, I now am able to say, with understanding, that I desire to be "beside myself"–for God!

The phrase, in Greek, speaks of being "amazed, thrown into wonderment." It also means to be "out of one's mind!" Paul was accused of being "beside himself" in his defense of the Gospel (Acts 26:24). Paul was impassioned for Christ. He was burdened for mankind lost without Jesus. In Romans 9:1, we find Paul mourning over his lost Jewish brethren. Paul's love for his fellow Jews and his deep grief over their unbelief carried him – beyond himself. Paul's love was not sensible and calculating. His love brought him to the point of abandonment of himself. There was no self-realization in Paul's commitment to declaring the Gospel. He was not concerned about what people thought of him. Nor was He riveted on his physical well-being.

Do we have a desire to be "beside ourselves?" How can we boldly step out for God? 2 Corinthians 5:14 proclaims, "the love of Christ compels us." "Compels" means "pressure that causes action." What action will you take today for the cause of the Gospel?

—Cathy Wilson

Prayer Starter: *Lord, cause us to be bold for You as we share Jesus with a lost and dying world.*

RULES TO LIVE BY

You shall love the Lord your God with all your heart and with all your soul and with all your might. (Deuteronomy 6:5)

Maybe you are a fan of the TV show *NCIS* like I am, and you have heard Leroy Jethro Gibbs refer to his rules, an extensive series of guidelines (50+) which make up a code that he lives by and teaches people he works closely with.

The last couple of days I have been busy gathering a few of my personal rules and, if you don't mind, I would love to share them with you:

Rule #1: Whatever you do, do it with all your heart.

Rule #2: Wherever you are, be all there.

Rule #3: Don't just take up space – make your life count.

Rule #4: Pay attention when God speaks.

Rule #5: If you can bless a worthy person, do it.

Rule #6: Respect authority and submit to it.

Rule #7: Hang around good people and they will rub off on you.

Rule #8: Chase every detail down when people are involved.

Rule #9: Stick together – it's safer!

Rule #10: If you can pray with someone in the moment, do it.

Rule #11: When faced with a choice to encourage or discourage, always encourage.

Rule #12: Value compassion – it brings people together.

Rule #13: Embrace informal authority as far more valuable than formal authority.

Rule #14: Use the hug – slug – hug approach if forced to correct someone.

Rule #15: Understand that being the boss leads to even more restraints – not less.

Rule #16: To be successful you must build a strong support system and maintain it.

Rule #17: Cherish laughter – it is an instant vacation.

Rule #18: If you are in charge of a meeting, end at the posted time.

Rule #19: When you lead, do so excellently by being diligent and careful.

Rule #20: Life brings strange twists – adapt!

—Holly DelHousaye

Prayer Starter: *Lord, help my life rules to all come from loving You first.*

NOT A SUGGESTION

"All authority has been given to me... Go, therefore, and make disciples"
(Matthew 28:18-19)

If you, in Arizona, got a letter from someone you didn't know personally, inviting you to come to dinner at his home on the east coast, at your expense, would you seriously consider it? Probably not. But if the letterhead said "The White House," would you think about that invitation differently?

Matthew 28:18-20 is commonly referred to as "The Great Commission" but is, in fact, usually a "Great Omission" in the lives of most Christians. Attending church, contributing an offering, doing good deeds, going on mission trips, and other worthwhile activities are all commendable, but are not fulfilling the Great Commission.

Jesus formally made disciples (and we get to read about it in the Gospels) and then told His disciples to make disciples. This is His strategy to reach the world. He did not command us to build church buildings, but He commanded us to build godly men and women who would multiply their faith to others. He focused on 3 who would pass on their training to the rest of the 12, who would train 72, who would keep multiplying what they had received to others.

Would you be willing to share what you have received spiritually with three others, making sure they were training others? What if the letterhead with this directive said it comes from "The Supreme Commander of the Universe"? That's what Matthew 28:18 tells us. Did you get your letter?

—Dave Cottrell

Prayer Starter: *Lord, I will obey Your command to make disciples. Fill me with Your Spirit and show me how to obey.*

REDEEMED

…As Christ loved the church and gave Himself up for her…(Ephesians 5:25)

When Paul wrote this he was referring to all the people Christ died to redeem. He didn't just mean those who were alive after Christ had died, but also those who looked to God for their salvation before Christ even came to earth.

Jesus said that He would build His church (Matthew 16:18) by calling people to Himself. This pattern of church building is a continuation of the process of building the church before Christ came to earth, for in Old Testament times God was continually calling His people to Himself to be a worshiping assembly before Him.

Because we cannot see the spiritual condition of people's hearts, the true church in its spiritual reality as the fellowship of all genuine believers is invisible. Only God can see the condition of people's hearts. But the church is also visible. The visible church will contain genuine believers as well as others who do not truly believe or follow the claims of Jesus. We should, with benevolent judgment, consider all to be members of the universal church who appear to be believers from their confession of faith and their pattern of life.*

—Wayne Grudem

Prayer Starter: *God, thank You for Your church.*

EVALUATION

But… (Revelation 2: 4, 9, 14, 20; 3:1)

An essential, yet stress-filled part of the business professional's work experience is the annual performance evaluation. Sometimes the employee is pleased to hear that their hard work has been recognized and the person is commended. Sometimes though, the review includes the hard news that the employee's effort was disappointing or substandard. The most difficult evaluations seem to be when the employee is completely unprepared for a critical review, because they have a completely inaccurate view of themselves and the work they have done.

In Revelation 2 and 3, Jesus delivers seven assessments to seven churches. With each of these Jesus makes it clear that each church has an incomplete or incorrect view of itself. With each, Jesus takes the time to correct their wrong thinking:

- Ephesus: they had abandoned their first love.
- Smyrna: they lived in poverty; He reminded them of their spiritual wealth.
- Pergamum: some of them held to the heretical teachings.
- Thyatira: they tolerated evil leadership and practiced sexual immorality.
- Sardis: they thought they were alive, but were spiritually dead.
- Philadelphia: acknowledging they had little power, He encouraged them to persevere.
- Laodicea: they thought they were rich; He assessed them as lukewarm, nauseating, poor, blind, naked, and wretched!

It is a simple reality that most churches are ill-equipped to accurately assess themselves. We typically underestimate our weaknesses and limitations and overvalue our accomplishments. All the while we minimize our total dependence upon God's Holy Spirit and wrongly appraise the worth of our human efforts.

Some of the most loving actions of a concerned Savior include assessing our works, evaluating our efforts, and correcting our wrong self-perceptions. It is an act of grace for Jesus to intervene, to set us straight, and to encourage us to move forward confidently in our new, enlightened understanding.

With every "but" (or "yet," depending upon translation), Jesus is saying, "I love you." He loves you so much that He wants you to know the truth about who you are, how you are, and what you are doing. Only by knowing the ultimate truth about ourselves can we become what God intends us to be. His love is truth. His truth sets us free.

—Bryan McAnally

Prayer Starter: *Lord, help us to know our true strengths and weaknesses.*

SPIRITUAL WALK

Therefore, confess your sins to one another, and pray for one another so that you may be healed. The effective prayer of a righteous man can accomplish much. (James 5:16)

God affords the one who is faithful to Him many and varied resources with which to engage in the spiritual walk, the test, and the battle. Chief among these resources is prayer. In the context of these verses, confession, coupled with prayers of petition to God are commanded.

Prayer is necessary not only to make our requests known to God, but also to align our will and desires with His sovereign will and loving desires for His creatures.

When one is ill and the church elders, the body, and the individual are praying for healthful restoration, an opportunity arises to search oneself and confess any known sins. To ask the Holy Spirit to search his or her heart and reveal any unknown sins is an excellent practice. Many, but by no means all, manifestations of sickness may be linked to sinful thought patterns and behaviors. By confessing sin and asking for healing, God may in His will allow physical healing. Ultimately He will heal the Christ follower spiritually and in every way.

—David Walther

Prayer Starter: *Lord, search my heart. Those areas of my life where I fall short make known that I may repent and confess and be healed in You.*

FREEDOM

Now the Lord is the Spirit, and where the Spirit of the Lord is, there is liberty.
(2 Corinthians 3:17)

"We are endowed by our Creator with certain inalienable rights," says the 1776 Declaration of Independence. It does not say endowed by government or politics, or wealth or education. No, it's just the simple but profound idea that every individual possesses God-given rights. Throughout history, most men and women have been born in chains. Under this declaration, they are born to be free.

Ronald Reagan said in his 1967 gubernatorial inaugural address, "Perhaps you and I have lived with this miracle of freedom too long to be properly appreciative. Freedom is a fragile thing and is never more than one generation away from extinction. It is not ours by inheritance; it must be fought for and defended constantly by each generation for it comes only once to a people."

—Barry Asmus

Prayer Starter: *Dear Lord, it matters not that other people love America as much as I do. But it does matter whether they love You. Biblical freedom teaches that we can be set free from the curse and destructiveness of human sinfulness. Thank You for sending Jesus.*

GOD'S LINE OF WORK

…Being diligent to preserve the unity of the Spirit in the bond of peace. (Ephesians 4:3)

Peacemakers, Jesus said, "Shall be called sons of God." Peacemakers, those who work to resolve conflicts, will be recognized as doing God's work. The man or woman who is a maker of peace is in the same line of work as God.

The book of Romans closes with, "Now the God of peace be with you all" (15:33). 2 Corinthians ends, "The God of love and peace shall be with you" (13:11). 1 Thessalonians closes, "May the God of peace Himself sanctify you entirely" (5:23). And Hebrews concludes, "May the God of peace…equip you in every good thing to do His will" (13: 20-21). God is the God of peace, and those who know Him know what He's about: peacemaking.

Reconciliation is peacemaking and is the work God has given us: "God…reconciled us to Himself through Christ, and gave us the ministry of reconciliation…He has committed to us the word of reconciliation. Therefore, we are ambassadors for Christ" (2 Corinthians 5:18–20). The first peace is peace with God - salvation. Yet, the ministry of reconciliation doesn't stop there. For Christ's sake, our peace is also with one another. Jesus prayed for our unity in order "That the world may believe that Thou didst send me" (John 17:21).

—Darryl DelHousaye

Prayer Starter: *Lord, show me my relationships needing Your peace and reconciliation. Help me be a peacemaker for Your sake.*

OUR FOUNDATION

And the rain fell, and the floods came, and the winds blew and slammed against that house; and yet it did not fall, for it had been founded on the rock. (Matthew 7:25)

Have you ever felt life seemed to contradict and battle against God's Word?

- Discouraged in quiet disappointment from shattered dreams?
- Silently wondering why God hasn't released you from some of the circumstances you seem unable to escape?

You are not alone. All people experience sorrow and disappointment in life to some extent. But for the Christian, it is not the trials and sorrows that should be the focus. The difference of how the Christian comes through their journey of circumstances is what should set every Christian apart from the world.

In Matthew 7:25 and 27, the exact same circumstances came against each house. The only difference was the foundation which had already been laid. When He is our focus and joy, our foundation will hold, regardless of circumstances.

It is through life's journey, including the battlefield of trials, circumstances, questions and even doubt about God that the Christian should emerge as a mature and victorious image of God's character and love. This is a current day victory walk even in the midst of life's challenges, sorrows, and disappointments. That's what the victorious Christian life is all about!

—MaryAnn Morton

Prayer Starter: *Dear Father, my desire is to live these present days pleasing in your sight and care, regardless of the winds of adversity.*

REJOICE; HE COMFORTS

Praise be to the God and Father of our Lord Jesus Christ, the Father of compassion and the God of all comfort, who comforts us in all our troubles, so that we can comfort those in any trouble with the comfort we ourselves receive from God. (2 Corinthians 1:3-4)

When my husband and I were sent to the mission field ten years ago, I was filled with inexplicable joy. Looking forward to a joyful and pleasant journey serving my Lord overseas, I soon discovered that obeying my calling would be more of a grieving journey. This was not because of the obvious losses that came with the "package" (although difficult indeed): living far away from family and friends, adjusting to a new culture, living with a low budget in an expensive country, and not being there for family milestones (weddings, pregnancies, births, graduations, etc.) All these we had been prepared for.

After dealing with almost each of these, the unexpected and most difficult one hit our door: infertility. Tears and questions to God took place. Loss, not joy, described my mission work.

But in the depth of my pain and tears poured during my quiet times, my loving Father was there bringing His comfort. It wasn't easy. It required that I unlearn old patterns and change some of my faith paradigms. It was through my suffering and His comfort that I learned to know, love and experience God in ways I hadn't before. Henri Nouwen said in The Wounded Healer, "It is in our own woundedness we can become a source of healing for others." Those words became true to me. God not only comforted me in my troubles but in His timing. He allowed me to become a mother, gifting me with twins!

He also equipped me to become a source of healing to other infertile women because I had been there and I was comforted by God. He even opened doors for me to minister to other moms now! Our God is amazing. He is able "to accomplish infinitely more than we might ask or think" (Ephesians 3:20). He turned my mourning into dancing and I will thank Him forever (Psalm 30:11,12).

—Fanny Pineda

Prayer Starter: *Dear God, You are the God of all comfort. I am aware that my journey in life might not always be pleasant. When grief occurs, may I be able to experience Your comfort, so that I can later comfort others in the same way.*

SWORD OF THE SPIRIT

Take…the sword of the Spirit, which is the Word of God. (Ephesians 6:17)

Here in Ephesians 6 Paul calls us to take the sword of the Spirit, which is the Word of God. In the original language, the word here for "Word" is used of the Gospel; that is the good news of salvation.

The Spirit gives it power and penetration like the thrust of a sword. So by preaching the Gospel in the power of the Spirit, we will free unbelievers from the dominion of the devil by opening their eyes to the glory of Jesus Christ. In other words, we wield the sword of the Spirit when we preach the Gospel to an unbeliever.

I can't help but think of a noble swashbuckler who jumps on board a ship to free captives from pirates. That's the Christian! He's jumping into the darkness to free unbelievers from the oppressors of sin and Satan. Isn't that an exciting picture!

—Joe Gordon

Prayer Starter: *Lord, give me the courage to preach the Gospel today.*

THE BLESSING BOOK

O Lord hear my prayer, listen to my cry for mercy: in Your faithfulness and righteousness come to my relief. Remember the days of old; I meditate on all Your works and consider what Your hands have done. (Psalm 143:1-5)

Have you ever had a time in your life when you could not see God working in your life, even though you were spending a lot of time in God's Word and additional time in prayer? A number of years ago, I experienced that in my life and it created many questions. I asked, "God, where are you? Lord, are you listening to my prayers? Do you even care? Have you completely forgotten about me?" I did not ask my questions in a normal tone of voice. Some were shouted at God with a lot of emotion, as I wanted to be certain He heard me and that I got His attention.

Several days after a prayer session like that, I awakened and began to thank God for the many blessings He had given to my family and me. I can clearly remember that He impressed on my mind that I should start making a list of each of those blessings. I bought a small notebook and divided it into several sections: family blessings, spiritual blessings, financial blessings, the blessing of wonderful friends, business blessings, and personal blessings. I reflected on the days of old.

After I finished, I went back and read each one. I was impressed with the number of blessings I had received and how many of them had developed over several weeks and months. Some took several years to come to fruition. There were many times I had no clue about what God was doing in my life, but He was preparing gracious blessings for me.

I learned, "Be patient and wait on the Lord." He will, when the time is right, provide the answers to my prayers. By focusing on my blessings, I could start to see how God had been working all along.

—Ron Goble

Prayer Starter: *Lord, help me to count my many blessings and wait for You.*

FOLLOW THE LEADER

Therefore be imitators of God, as beloved children; and walk in love, just as Christ also loved you… **(Ephesians 5:1-2)**

We all come from different places and different backgrounds and that certainly affects the direction we take in life. One thing I know for sure, you're moving in the right direction if you're following the leader – Jesus Christ. To know Him is to love Him, and to follow Him is life-changing.

Remember playing "follow the leader" as a child? To play this game you did exactly what the leader did. Similarly, as Christians, we are to "be imitators of God" (Ephesians 5:1a). Our leader Jesus beckons for us to follow Him. Jesus said, "come, follow Me" (Matthew 19:21). The more you read, study, observe, and understand the life of Christ, and then imitate Him, the more your life will be an overflow of Him. By imitating Christ and following Him, you are not only taking a step in the right direction, you will be changing the course of your life!

—Susan Miller

Prayer Starter: *Lord, I want to follow You, know You, and be more like You. I want to change the direction of my life. Take my hand and lead me gently into a deeper knowledge of You.*

SPIRIT VERSUS FLESH

Peter said to Him, "Even if I have to die with you, I will not deny you." All the disciples said the same thing too. (Matthew 26:35)

Thank God for His grace and loving kindness to us who, although passionate in our faith and commitment, still are weak and fail in our service to Him. In today's reading Peter and the other disciples spoke boldly of their commitment to serve Jesus, even if that meant death.

A conflict exists between the spirit and the flesh. Jesus says to His disciples, "Watch and pray that you do not enter into temptation" (Matthew 26:41). Paul says in Romans 7:25, "With my mind I serve the law of God, but with my flesh the law of sin." Matthew Henry in his commentary says, "Our impotency in the service of God is the great iniquity and infidelity of our nature, and it arises from these sad reminders of corruption, which are the constant grief and burden of God's people. Yet it is our comfort, that our Master graciously considers this, and accepts the willingness of the spirit and pities and pardons the weakness and infirmity of the flesh; for we are under grace, and not under the law."

Today, take comfort in knowing that God knows our heart, and even in our failures there is hope for a new day. Even with Peter's weakness and failure, the Lord in His grace used Peter to build His church. Is there an area in your life where you perhaps have failed and you now need to accept God's grace and forgiveness so that you can be a useful instrument in service to Him?

—Mark Upton

Prayer Starter: *Lord, thank You for Your loving kindness and grace as demonstrated in Your forgiveness of me for my failure to ...*

THE RIGHT WAY TO USE OUR WORDS

Let my tongue sing of your Word. (Psalm 119:172)

Church history tells us that Charles Wesley was hesitant to talk about his new found faith when he first became a Christian. He asked a friend if he should "treasure in his heart" his conversion and keep it to himself or if he should tell others about what had happened to him?

The advice he received? His friend told him, "If you had a thousand tongues, you should use every one of them to tell others about Jesus."

Good advice! In fact, Charles Wesley not only became one of the most famous preachers of all time, but he wrote over 6,000 hymns! That's a pretty impressive use of one's "tongue" to sing praise to God!

We're not going to tell you that you've got to try and sing at your church. (Unless of course God has given you that gift!) But all of us—good "singers" or not—can lift up our voices to praise the Lord. You don't have to be in the choir, but lift up your voice and make a joyful noise – even if it's more noise than you'd like!

—John and Cindy Trent

Prayer Starter: *Lord, one thing we know that lifts up our heart is to sing praises to You. Help us lose our self-consciousness about singing (or any self-assurance we have if we can sing) and just focus on praising You with our tongue. You're worthy of our praise, and thank You for how much it draws us together.*

THE CRITICAL MISSING PIECE

But I will sing of Your strength; I will sing aloud of Your steadfast love in the morning. For You have been to me a fortress and a refuge in the day of my distress. O my strength, I will sing praises to You, for You, O God, are my fortress, the God who shows me steadfast love. (Psalm 59:16-17)

I recently prayed with someone about a huge burden in their life. They started their prayer like this: "Lord, please go with me as I confront this problem."

It was a normal prayer. But it made me realize once again that we have a critical missing piece in our prayer lives. On the whole, we are lacking praise.

We have been taught that praise should be part of our prayer lives, but so many of us jump right into our requests. Could it be that praise is the secret to unlocking our prayer lives so we can line up with God's will for us?

I finally started to understand this when I joined a group of praying mothers. The format is very disciplined. The first thing we do is open Scripture to read about an attribute of God. As we go to prayer, we begin with praise, speaking back the attribute we just read about and praising God for this quality. For example, in the above Scripture we would pray back, "Father, I praise You, because You are my strength. You give me steadfast love because You are love. I praise You because You are my fortress, I can hide in You, and I know in my distress I can run to You."

When I start my prayers with concentrated praise for who God is, all of a sudden my heart changes. I realize that the burden which felt so large and heavy feels smaller because I see God for who He is…able to conquer everything that I face! He is God and I can trust Him! God doesn't need me to advise Him. When I praise Him with Scripture, the Lord gives me wisdom about what He wants me to do.

—Tracy Goble

Prayer Starter: *Father, I praise You because You are my strength and my fortress. Teach me to praise You.*

HOLD SHORT

For as the Heavens are higher than the earth, so are my ways higher than Your ways and my thoughts than Your thoughts. (Isaiah 55:9)

As a private pilot, I have frequently heard the tower instruct me to "hold short" when I have requested clearance to take off. This is the tower's way of saying, "I know you think you're ready to go, but I can see things from up here that are invisible to you at ground level. I need you to wait patiently until the circumstances are right for you to proceed. Only when I know it's safe will I give you the clearance to take off." As a pilot, I willingly accept the air traffic controller's command. But as a child of the King I have often tried to ignore God when He tells me to "hold short."

We pay lip service to the knowledge that God knows what's best for us, but then we rebel against Him. As Rich Mullins said, "I'd rather fight You for something I don't even want than take what You give that I need." If we step back and look at this from God's perspective as much as we are able, we will quickly realize that it is not about God denying us something good but rather it is His will that we have something better. While we may yearn to take off and soar on our own adventure, we need to constantly listen to our Heavenly Father's provision for our safety and well-being. You see, His ways are higher than our ways!

— Jim York

Prayer Starter: *Lord, help me to gratefully acknowledge Your desire for my best. Help me to "Hold short" when You wish me to wait on Your timing.*

PROPHET OF GOD

I am not a prophet, nor the son of a prophet. (Amos 7:14)

Amos was a farmer, but God called him to do a job for God that was very difficult, but fit him perfectly. Amos farmed in Judah and God sent him to the northern tribes of Israel with a message of judgment. However, when he got there the message was not well received. In fact Amaziah, the priest in Bethel, told Amos to go back home and make his money at home. See, Amaziah thought that Amos was a false prophet (which were prevalent in the northern kingdom), and that he pronounced judgment to make a living. Commonly the king would pay them off, then they would announce nice things for the king and everyone was happy. Amaziah thought that Amos was encroaching on his territory so he told him to go home and do his prophesying.

However Amos was a farmer and God called him with a message of judgment on Israel. Thus, Israel had better listen because Amos was not doing it for the money. Basically what Amos was saying was, "I am not like you, Amaziah, and I am not doing this for the money. I am a farmer, but God called me with a message of judgment and you had better listen to God." Is God urging you to speak truth to someone, even if it makes you uncomfortable? Obey God today.

—Paul Wegner

Prayer Starter: *Dear God, help me to hear Your Word and act on it.*

GOD COULDN'T LOVE ME

For God so loved the world that He gave His only Son, so that everyone who believes in Him will not perish but have eternal life. (John 3:16)

Lie: God couldn't love me.

The Gospel message can't be that simple. Some have suggested that if we tell ourselves positive affirmations often enough we'll begin to believe them. Several years ago, Stuart Smalley was a fictional character on Saturday Night Live. Played by Al Franken, Stuart Smalley was a self-help expert. His daily affirmation went like this: "I'm good enough, I'm smart enough, and doggone it people like me." He decreed that if he said that to himself often enough he would feel better. In addition to the irony, this and other self-help messages are simply that - helping yourself.

When God says "I love you," He means "you." And it's so much more than any positive affirmation the world may bring.

He intends for the smallest child or the oldest adult to understand the Gospel message. It's simple and profound. An old, favorite children's song says: "Jesus loves me this I know, for the Bible tells me so." It's that simple. Believe it.

—Nonie Maupin

Prayer Starter: *Heavenly Father, when You say the world, that means me, and I choose to stand on Your truth.*

HELP FROM THE LORD

I will lift up my eyes to the hills- where does my help come from? My help comes from the Lord, the maker of Heaven and earth. (Psalm 121:1-2)

A few years ago our HIV/AIDS medical team drove to an isolated village to visit some of the volunteers we had trained to work in the community. It was a muddy drive in the hills. I was driving our big Toyota SUV. I can drive, but my mechanical skills are close to zero. We had a wonderful visit and one of our Tanzanian team led two people to Christ that day. We came out to our car rejoicing.

But the car would not start. I was the only driver and the person with the most knowledge of cars! I tried starting it several times with no response and we were in a village with no gas stations or mechanics. I said to the group, "Let's pray and ask God to help us."

As soon as we finished praying, a man came up to us and asked us if we needed any help. Apparently, he was a driver of the same type of SUV as ours and was on leave in the village. He was easily able to fix the problem with our car.

We drove back filled with thanksgiving to God who had sent us help when we called to Him.

—Lyndall Rothery

Prayer Starter: *Lord Jesus, we thank You that our help comes from You. Help us to remember to look to You for help today. Help us to always turn to You for our help.*

SUFFERING HARDSHIP

To you it has been granted for Christ's sake, not only to believe in Him, but also to suffer for His sake. (Philippians 1:29)

When sin entered the world, suffering came along with it, yet God uses affliction to instruct and discipline His people.

To the Philippians, Paul wrote, "To you it has been granted for Christ's sake, not only to believe in Him, but also to suffer for His sake" (Philippians 1:29). He not only suffered for Christ, but also for the sake of the church (2 Timothy 2:10). Those who wish to represent Christ and serve His church must be willing to suffer for His name. In verse 9 of 2 Timothy 2, Paul says that he "suffers hardship" as if a criminal.

I think the reason that Paul had such a good perspective on suffering was because he had such a burden to serve Christ. When he was in prison, he viewed himself as a prisoner of Christ, not of the Roman government. The early church considered it a privilege to suffer for the name of Christ. In Acts 5:41, the apostles "went on their way from the presence of the council, rejoicing that they had been considered worthy to suffer shame for His name." When we see our suffering as a way of serving Christ, as Paul did, it will help us endure and find the truth God is trying to teach us.

—Patrick Sullivan

Prayer Starter: *Heavenly Father, we thank You for Your constant love for us. Give us Your perspective on the trials that we encounter.*

Other passages where Paul speaks of suffering:

Romans 8:17; 2 Corinthians 1:7; Galatians 3:4; Philippians 3:10; 1 Thessalonians 2:2; 2 Thessalonians 1:5; 2 Timothy 2:12; and 2 Timothy 3:12.

IN THE SPIRIT

But the hour is coming, and now is here, when the true worshippers will worship the Father in spirit and in truth, for the Father is seeking such people to worship him. (John 4:23-24)

I John, your brother and partner in the tribulation and the kingdom and the patient endurance that are in Jesus, was on the island of Patmos on account of the Word of God and the testimony of Jesus. I was in the Spirit on the Lord's Day... (Revelation 1:9;10a)

Just as there are two rails on a track, which a large train can run on with amazing stability, our worship has two rails...spirit and truth. It's clear throughout the Scriptures that God is the source of truth and that Jesus is in fact that Truth, so our worship is in and through Jesus.

That second rail is slightly more elusive, in that our worship is also in spirit. When Jesus talked with this Samaritan woman in John 4, He clearly articulated that a time was coming when worship would not be confined to a specific time, space or human mediator, but that worship would be in the spirit realm. John, while exiled on the Island of Patmos, understood that nothing could stop him from worshiping. There was no physical separation, lack of resources or limitations that could keep him from being "in the spirit".

When you know how to worship, you can do it anywhere, anytime, anyway. I love the way one pastor put it when he wrote, "if you can't seem to find God, then stop what you are doing and start worshiping. He'll find you, for the Father seeks those who will worship Him."

—Troy Peterson

Prayer Starter: *Holy Spirit, lead me to a place of worship that is grounded in the truth of Christ and free to experience You at all times.*

YELLOW OR GOLD

So the Word of the Lord has brought me insult and reproach all day long. But if I say, "I will not mention Him or speak any more in His name," His Word is in my heart like a fire, a fire shut up in my bones. I am weary of holding it in; indeed, I cannot. (Jeremiah 20:9)

Silence is indeed golden. To embody that inner nobility that holds its tongue when criticized, insulted or maligned…well, it's a personal wealth of character that beats anything you can store in a bank.

But there's another type of silence that isn't golden – it's yellow. You're inclined to embrace it when the criticism, insults and maligning aren't actually aimed at you, but at the Lord you represent. There's nothing new about this dilemma. Jeremiah faced it every day. Back then, people wanted to hear edited truth and comfortable advice. They didn't want to know their lives weren't aligning with God's heart and they wanted to intimidate anyone who tried to tell them otherwise.

Sound familiar? The people closest to us aren't always crazy about us verbalizing our faith. They especially get antsy when we speak God's truth into their life. But when God's Spirit has set you free from the tyranny of your shame, His transforming power and presence in your life cannot be contained. And for the sake of those who still walk in darkness, it must not.

—Tim Kimmel

Prayer Starter: *Dear Lord, help my life to be a living example of Your love and then give me the passion for others that helps me speak clearly and boldly of Your gracious truth.*

GETTING TO KNOW GOD

You shall love the Lord your God with all your heart and with all your soul and with all your mind. This is the great and first commandment. And a second is like it: you shall love your neighbor as yourself. (Matthew 22:38-39)

This passage makes it crystal clear that God desires an interpersonal relationship with us, His children. He has adopted us into the family of God and given us eternal life. Perhaps of equal significance to the believer, though, is that we are able and called to respond to Christ daily. Beyond our coming to believe in Him, God wants us to really get to know Him. He wants us to love Him, honor Him, and to reflect Him in who we are as much as in what we do.

David Ferguson, in his book Relational Discipleship, shows us how the love within the Trinity works. As Jesus always yields to the Father, the Father always reveals His will to the Son:

Ask and it will be given to you; seek, and you will find; knock, and it will be opened to you. For everyone who asks receives, and he who seeks finds, and to him who knocks it will be opened. (Matthew 7:7-8)

As we yield to Him in obedience, and ask, He will reveal those things He wants us to know about Him and ourselves.

Take some time today to hide away with God and ask Him to reveal the areas of resistance in your life.

—Donald Farr

Prayer Starter: *Father, I ask boldly for insight and wisdom and for the desire to triumph over the disobedience in my life – revealing any other areas You want to bring into Your light.*

REFUSE TO PICK AT ANOTHER

Above all, keep fervent in your love for one another, because love covers a multitude of sins. (I Peter 4:8)

In reading an article about turkeys, I learned from an expert that when a turkey is wounded and has a spot of blood on its feathers, the other turkeys will peck at that spot until they literally peck the wounded turkey to death. When I read that, my first reaction was, "How cruel!" My second thought was, "How dumb turkeys must be to keep pecking at the wound of a fellow turkey." Man has the ability to be smart or dumb. You can be smart and refuse to pick at another's wound, or you can be dumb like the pecking turkeys.

Since picking is such a dumb thing for us to do, why then do we sometimes do it? We mistakenly think that by making the other guy look bad, it makes us look good. We are trying to build up our own sinking egos. The truth is that it makes us look even worse than the guy we're trying to make look inferior. Picking always hurts the picker more than it hurts the picked. God has a better way for you and me to live. It's called the way of love. "Love overlooks a multitude of faults."

Yes, smarter than a dumb turkey—that's you! God's happy lover!

Recognize the fact that no one is perfect. If you loved only perfect people, who would you love? Not me, nor anyone at church, not your mate, not sinners and certainly not yourself.

—Dale Galloway

Prayer Starter: *Jesus, teach me to love others Your perfect way and not my imperfect way. This day help me to expect more of myself than I do of others.*

YES, SIR!

And Jesus said to them, "Follow me, and I will make you become fishers of men." And immediately they left their nets and followed Him. (Mark 1:17-18)

One of the basics of early introduction to army discipline at West Point is that of "instant and unquestioned obedience" to an order. When given a command, the only acceptable response is, "Yes, sir!" When that is so well ingrained, it stays with you for a long time.

Several years ago our church hosted an outreach event. My wife, Georgann, and I invited another couple with whom we had shared the Gospel on several occasions. At the event I was seated between Georgann and the other lady. The speaker asked a rhetorical question of what would you say if you knew God was telling you to do something? Without hesitation, I whispered under my breath, "Yes, sir!" I had no intention that anyone should hear me say it; it was a simple, spontaneous response, just like I would say to my commanding officer in the Army.

Soon thereafter, the lady who was our guest committed her life to Christ. As she did so, she told me that the instant she heard my muttered answer to the question at the outreach event was when the scales were removed from her eyes and she understood, for the first time, the concept of being committed to obeying God. In the ensuing years she has become a fully devoted follower of Christ and has led others to Christ and taught Bible studies to women. You never know when a subtle word or action will have an eternal impact.

Are you hesitating to do what you sense God is asking you to do?

—Bob Cain

Prayer Starter: *Father, help us all to respond to you the first time You ask us to do something. You are commander, and we want to respond with "Yes, sir!"*

A SPIRITUAL FAMILY

Do not rebuke an older man, but exhort him as a father, younger men as brothers, older women as mothers, younger women as sisters, with all purity. (1 Timothy 5:1-2)

Anne's father divorced her mother, walked out on the family and never looked back. She tried over the years to build a relationship with him, but he never cared to try. The day after she got engaged to an outstanding Christian man, her father passed away and she never got to say goodbye. However, she didn't have to walk down the aisle alone. Anne and her fiancé had gone through a pre-marital preparation course at their church, where each couple was given a "mentor" couple to coach and encourage them. And it was Alan, an older man and their mentor from the class, who she asked to walk her down the aisle.

When Paul wrote to Timothy in today's verse, he wasn't telling him that everyone in the church was related to him physically. Rather, he was telling him that those who have the same spiritual Father, share a bond so close that they can "be there" for each other in this life, and they'll share all eternity together too!

Remember, "the wolf loves lone sheep." One of the greatest assets we can have in our lives are committed Christian friends. We may not have had the best family growing up, but God gives us the family of God when we become believers.

—John and Cindy Trent

Prayer Starter: *Lord, thank You that You provide a spiritual family to help us grow. Lord, plug me into a class of like-minded friends and help me build friendships with other people that honor You. Allow me be the kind of friend that helps others stay strong and grow in their love for You.*

ACTS OF PRAISE

Therefore I will praise you among the Gentiles, and sing to your name.
(Psalm 18:49)

There is a lot of conversation taking place amongst the western churches and among Christians in these days about the matter of praise. Some people feel it is best to be reserved in praise, not expressing their adoration with any outwardly demonstrations. Others feel as though their praise is incomplete if they aren't raising both their hands, swaying in the pew, and speaking out words of devotion.

The Scriptures seem to affirm both extremes of these preferences, validating that worship should be intensely personal and freely external. However, there is another expression of worship that is likewise valid and appropriate, but often not expressed with the same passion or fervor. This "other" expression of praise is acts of meaningful service.

Not many people think of sharing the Gospel as an expression of praise. Rather it's often considered a daunting labor requiring specialized knowledge, accompanied by overwhelming risks and a high likelihood of failure. However, the Bible consistently presents "proclamation" of God's love and goodness as an act of praise. The Psalmist declared that it was right to praise God to the Gentiles. In the New Testament, Romans calls "beautiful" the feet of those who bring the good news of God's salvation in Jesus.

God has blessed you with a story to tell. It is a story of love, of pursuit, of redemption, and of relationship. He wants you to tell your story to others. He expects you to tell your story to others. I encourage you to tell your story to anyone who will listen. Do it as an expression of praise. It's a story worth telling, and it is beautiful in the ears of your loving Lord and Savior.

—Jamie Rasmussen

Prayer Starter: *Lord, help me to praise You in all ways. Open my eyes to opportunities to praise You all around. Help me to follow Your leading.*

MY PURPOSE IN LIFE

I will give thanks to You, O Lord my God, with all my heart, and will glorify Your name forever. (Psalm 86:12)

I had been taught that we are supposed to glorify God, but nobody ever told me what that meant. What is "glory" and how do we "glorify" God?

1 Corinthians 15:41 begins, "There is one glory of the sun, and another glory of the moon..." Each of these gives a different light because of their different attributes. The sun is a giant nuclear reactor, its elements producing light and heat that give life to our planet millions of miles away. The moon is a big dead rock that cannot produce even 1 watt of its own light, but may reflect the sun's light.

God is like the sun, full of light and power for life. I am like the moon, unable to produce any light of my own, but able to reflect God's light to others as I walk in the power of His Spirit. Those who do not know God walk in darkness, just as at night people cannot see the sun, but they can see the moon brightly reflecting sunlight. Jesus said we are the light of the world. Our job is to shine noticeably with God's love so that when people want to know how we have so much light, we can introduce them to our Lord and bring them to the Father.

—Dave Cottrell

Prayer Starter: *Remind me daily, Lord, as I look up to the sun or to the moon, that You have given me a special job to do.*

YOU GOTTA HAVE HEART

For this reason I bow my knees before the Father, from whom every family in Heaven and on earth derives its name, that He would grant you, according to the riches of His glory, to be strengthened with power through His Spirit in the inner man, so that Christ may dwell in your hearts through faith; and that you, being rooted and grounded in love, may be able to comprehend with all the saints what is the breadth and length and height and depth, and to know the love of Christ which surpasses knowledge, that you may be filled up to all the fullness of God. (Ephesians 3:14-19)

I have a new love for the book of Ephesians. The prayer that Paul prays for them in Ephesians 3:14-21 is unbelievable. It's my prayer for my family, church family and everyone else. He prays with such eloquence…but more important, he prays with such heart.

Many people don't want to pray because they can't make it sound wonderful. I used to feel like this, but now I know that when I pray my simple words, Jesus takes them and makes them sound beautiful to the Father – as long as they come through my heart. He is our advocate to the Father. I have heard some prayers with fancy words that sound flowery but hollow. The song says it – you gotta have heart! – A heart for Jesus.

—Sue Phipps

Prayer Starter: *Lord, thank You for hearing our prayers. Thank You for being our God. We pray You fill us up with Your Spirit and love.*

WORK

*The Lord bless you and keep you; the Lord make His face to shine upon you
and be gracious to you; the Lord lift up His countenance upon you.
(Numbers 6:24)*

In the eighth book of the Bible, Ruth's story unfolds during Israel's reign of Judges. Even though the Jews deserted God's land because of famine, God remained faithful. When Naomi returns to Judah, her daughter-in-law Ruth returns with her and marries Boaz to carry on the family name (and becomes an ancestor of David and Jesus). Imagine the happiness of the people when Boaz returned from Bethlehem and greeted the harvesters with, "The Lord be with you." And the harvesters shouted back to Boaz, "The Lord bless you" (Ruth 2:1–4). Don't you wish your workplace would be that friendly?

As Christians we often say, "The Lord be with you." What does that mean? If the Lord is with you—and He is—God is in it. The garbage man is every bit as important to the health and well-being of a society as the doctor. Every job and every task can be done with gratitude and for the glory of God.

God calls what He does work, and that it is good. Ecclesiastes 3:13 says, "That everyone may eat and drink and find satisfaction in all his toil—this is the gift of God." It is God-like to work.

—Barry Asmus

Prayer Starter: *Dear Father, help me to see that work is worship. It is good because it is from You.*

PRESSED

Thy hand has pressed down on me. (Psalm 38:2)

My mother taught me how to properly iron a shirt or blouse. (For those of you who are not familiar with an iron – it is a hand held implement with a heated flat steel base used to smooth clothes and linen!)

First, you iron both sides of the collar, then you iron and crease the sleeves and then you iron the rest of the garment. Impressed? Well, don't be – because even though I do know how to iron – ironing has fallen on hard times in my home. I must confess that I buy things that need the smallest amount of maintenance possible – and even pass on things I like because of the amount of time I would need to invest to keep them looking nice.

When I cannot escape ironing, I do several things. I look for hanging threads and cut them off; I square up the seams and make sure everything is matched; and sometimes, I even poke small snags back into the reverse side of the material.

Recently when I was ironing, I was thinking how important it is to iron items once in a while because when I do, I bring them back to their most perfect state. This thought led me to think about how God sometimes has to press me to get me back to alignment with Him and His perfect plan for my life.

I do know that sometimes when I am pressed, it is because of my own foolish choices. And then, sometimes when I am pressed, it is because of the sins of others over which I have absolutely no control.

The truth is that when I am pressed back to my foundation, I eventually must turn my focus back to God alone and let Him trim my hanging threads, square up my seams and poke my snags back where they belong. This is ultimately exactly where my Heavenly Father wants me to be – looking up and walking in humility!*

—Holly DelHousaye

Prayer Starter: *Lord, keep my eyes on You as I walk through this day.*

PROMISES FOR FAITHFUL

To the one who conquers… (Revelation 2: 1, 11, 17, 26; 3: 5, 21)

Living by faith and not by sight requires contending for it. Ask a woman who has prayed for years to be blessed with a child in her womb. Ask the dad who has begged God nightly for His wayward child to return to family and faith. Ask the church who intercedes for unbelievers, serves the marginalized, and gives grace liberally.

Jesus is compassionate in the fight for faith, knowing well that there are many times when the Christian doesn't feel like a warrior, much less a conqueror. Jesus understands that the opposition is relentless and that temptations are significant. He knows that pitfalls are abundant and that your flesh strives to betray you at every turn. He knows that on your own, you will fail.

Yet, in each of His seven letters to the seven churches, Jesus offers a promise to "the one who overcomes." Here is some of what He promises to the one who overcomes:

- To eat from the tree of life
- To not be hurt by the second death
- To be given hidden manna
- To be given a white stone with a new name on it, known only by Jesus
- To be given authority over nations
- To be clothed in white garments
- To never be blotted from the book of life
- To be made a pillar in the temple of God
- To have God's name written upon him
- To sit with Jesus on His throne

You may not feel like a conqueror right now. You may be waiting for your prayers to be answered. You may be in the middle of your faith being tested. As you fight for your faith, see this cavalcade of promises as more than just a bounty of victory. Instead, first see it as a promise that victory awaits you personally. In a series of messages to churches, Jesus makes a point to offer promises to individual overcomers. Victory is possible. It is available. It is inevitable through Jesus. Also see His promises as expressions of love and relationship from a caring, compassionate, and generous God who is eager to reward you for your faithful, faith-filled walk through this life.

—Bryan McAnally

Prayer Starter: *Help me Jesus to have the strength to come through to the end as Your faithful follower.*

SAVED BY GRACE – FOR WHAT?

For we are His workmanship, created in Christ Jesus for good works, which God prepared beforehand, that we should walk in them. (Ephesians 2:10)

One of the first Bible references I memorized (after John 3:16), was Ephesians 2:8-9 ("For by grace you have been saved . . ."). As a young adult, it was very reassuring to know that my salvation was a result of God's grace – there was nothing I could have done to earn it, and there is nothing I can do to lose it. Unfortunately, through much of my early Christian life, that was exactly what I did – nothing. Sure I went to church (most Sundays), read my Bible (if I had time), even served (occasionally). But by and large, I was the consummate "pew-sitter." I was content to rest in the knowledge and promise that I had God's gift of eternal life.

I don't have the space to tell you the details of how God changed my life. (Let's just say that being humbled, broken and repentant were involved.) I now know that although my salvation was indeed a gift, it was also a gift with expectations. God has a purpose for my life, and His desire is for me to do the good works He prepared for me. He does not want a relationship that is relegated to sitting together in a pew. His desire is a relationship of walking (or working) together to further His kingdom.

—Don Baltzer

Prayer Starter: *Lord, what good works have You prepared for me?*

MONEY

The silver is mine, and the gold is mine, declares the Lord of hosts.
(Haggai 2:8)

It all belongs to Him and He entrusts it to us so that through it we would glorify Him. Money provides many opportunities to glorify God: through investing and expanding our stewardship and thus imitating God's sovereignty and wisdom; through meeting our own needs and thus imitating God's independence; through giving to others and thus imitating God's mercy and love; or through giving to the church and to evangelism and thus bringing others into the kingdom.

Yet because money carries so much power and so much value, it is a heavy responsibility and it presents constant temptations to sin. We can become ensnared in the love of money (1 Timothy 6:10), and it can turn our hearts from God as Jesus warned in Matthew 6:24. He also warned against accumulating too much that we hoard and do not use it for good: "For where your treasure is, there your heart will be also." (Matthew 6:21)

But the distortions of something good must not cause us to think that the thing itself is evil. Money is good in itself and provides us many opportunities for glorifying God.*

—Wayne Grudem

Prayer Starter: *God, help me use Your money for Your glory.*

RESTORATION

Now it came to pass, in the days when the Judges ruled, that there was a famine in the land. And a certain man of Bethlehem, Judah, went to dwell in the country of Moab, he and his wife and his two sons. (Ruth 1:1)

The setting of the book of Ruth is gloom! And, it gets "better." In their attempt to flee from famine in Israel, Elimelech takes his family and travels approximately 50 miles to enemy territory where they "sojourn." In Hebrew, "sojourn" means "to turn aside from the road." Elimelech dies and his two sons follow in death. We see three funerals at the outset of the book of Ruth. What was this family thinking as they fled from the Promised Land?

What are we thinking at times? Have we turned aside from the road – from the abundant life that God has given us in Christ? Have we turned aside—this year, this month, this week—today?

God's grace pursued those who were left in the family of Elimelech. In the midst of a destitute situation, God pursued and delivered Naomi and her daughter-in-law, Ruth. At the end of the four chapters in the book of Ruth, we are invited to a wedding! God's grace pursues us even in the midst of struggles and brings about restoration. God is always about restoration.

Following the wedding of Ruth and Boaz, the Lord gave Ruth conception and she bore a son who became a "…restorer of life…" to Naomi.

—Cathy Wilson

Prayer Starter: *Lord, even in the midst of difficult circumstances in my life, please cause me to respond to Your grace, knowing that You are a God who restores.*

GOD'S LOVE

We love, because He first loved us. (1 John 4:19)

At times I am consumed with God's love for me. I may be thinking that I am minding my own business, ("busy-ness") when I am struck. Other times, during my waking moments, I have a real sense of His presence. The reminder He gave me this morning was simple but clear. It didn't come in an audible voice, but an enveloping, calming understanding. I would like to share it with you and have you insert your own name and apply it to yourself today:

I have created you, _____. I loved you before you knew Me and poured My love into you. I am your God. I made everything and My desire for you is to love Me. Fall deeply in love with Me as I draw you near. I have all of your best interests at heart. My instructions written in love are for you, _____. As you know Me more and love Me more, so love those around that I have placed in proximity to you. Love those you do not know and love your enemies also. Let all know of My perfect love in your inner most being and allow this to flow onto others.

— David Walther

Prayer Starter: *Lord, allow this to not only inform me, but allow me to live this.*

PRAYER

I will guard my ways, that I may not sin with my tongue; I will guard my mouth as with a muzzle. (Psalm 39:1)

I have often regretted my speech, but never my silence. Having participated in more than a thousand meetings these past 30 years, I have heard many things I wanted to criticize. A disciple of H.G. Wells once pontificated, "Man is a splendid creature who goes from strength to strength in an ever-widening circle of achievement. He is finally taking control of his life, believing in himself and saving himself." How hard it is to hold your tongue when people make boastful statements like that!

You want to exclaim, "You shall have no other gods before Me!" Or ask, "Why do you make man himself more central to significance and purpose than God?"

But our best resort is to pray. In alignment with God's purposes, prayer defeats darkness and changes lives. Fighting for souls in prayer is a fight that brings glory to God. Matthew Henry once said, "Since my lips are the door to my words, let grace keep that door, that no word may go out which in any way dishonors God or hurts others." Prayer is the key.

—Barry Asmus

Prayer Starter: *Dear Lord, no matter how hard I try to justify my existence through knowledge, wealth, fame or power, it will not be enough. Only an identity built on You will go the distance. Only You can bear the burden of Godhood. Only by prayer can we see what is seeable of an invisible God.*

BEAT THE SYSTEM

For whatever is born of God overcomes the world: and this is the victory that has overcome the world...our faith. (I John 5:4)

The verb here translated as "overcome" is *nikao* for which the noun is *nike*—meaning "conqueror." We find the name on some of our aerial missiles as well as our running shoes. John spells out for us just how we can be conquerors in this world, how we can overcome the pressures of this age and beat the world's system: we overcome by love, (1 John 5:1) knowing people are the great worth. We overcome by obedience, (1 John 5:2–3) knowing God's commands are the great concern. We do what is right, no matter what others say or how we're feeling about something: our thinking is clear and we obey God rather than man. And we overcome by faith (1 John 5:4)—which is the key to the whole thing. The key to loving others and obeying God is our faith! A child of God who loves his God will continually overcome the moving and molding pressures of this age. We aren't overcomers because we're smarter or sharper; we're overcomers because we have placed our confidence, not in the opinions of a hundred different people, but in the truth of one—Jesus the Christ. We have trusted Him for our salvation; we honor Him as our Lord.

Overcoming this age is a central issue for eternity: "To him who overcomes," Jesus says in Revelation, "I will grant to eat of the tree of life...I will give him some of the hidden manna...I will give him the morning star...I will grant to him to sit down with me on my throne, as I also overcame and sat down with my Father on His throne" (Revelation 2:3).

—Darryl DelHousaye

Prayer Starter: *Lord, help me to have faith in You and know I am an overcomer.*

BEING RENEWED

…Be transformed by the renewing of your mind… (Romans 12:2)

Did you notice the Scripture above does not say to be renewed by different circumstances or relationships, but to be transformed by the renewing of our mind? This teaching goes beyond just masking a situation with positive mental thinking.

Have you ever been consumed with letting your mind run rampant with images of things you either did or didn't do in the past? Through biblical principles and guidance, the intent of God's desire and purpose for our lives emerges in brilliant display. We come to the understanding that God doesn't hold past regrets and mistakes against us. Through His sacrifice, He has made it possible for us to move beyond our mistakes. He gives us strength, peace, and comfort, enabling us to move forward – with our souls restored.

Even though we sometimes have to live with the consequences of past decision making, we should not be living with the heavy bricks of regret dragging around our ankles. Christ came to set us free, and one of the main issues of freedom is with what we fill our minds.

Without deliberate intent and consistent discipline to daily renew our mind in Christ, a Christian will often be frustrated with an up and down emotional relationship with the Lord. You see, what obsesses us possesses us. God knew that when He created us. And so this is His very clear and direct teaching: "Be transformed by the renewing of your mind."

—MaryAnn Morton

Prayer Starter: *Dear Father, I come to You, accepting Your desire for my mind to be renewed in and through You. I desire to be made complete and whole in You. I focus my mind and desires on Your Word.*

PROMISE OF LIFE

Simon Peter replied, "Lord, to whom would we go? You have the words that give eternal life. We believe, and we know you are the holy one of God."
(John 6:68-69)

We first came as missionaries to Asia, sent by Scottsdale Bible and her sister church in Argentina, Iglesia de la Puerta Abierta, ten years ago. We knew we were leaving behind many people we loved and that the road ahead would be hard. Yet we knew it was God's plan and we were glad to follow it.

There were many hard times, but by far the most difficult was the death of our baby girl. We had four beautiful months together before the Lord took her home. The pain of losing her was terrible and also led to my confusion. Somehow along the road I had mistakenly believed that since I had left everything to serve God, He somehow "had to" bless me. When my baby died, I was left very confused and did not understand how it was possible that after so many prayers and miracles, Alondra was not with us anymore. During those dark times after her death I was faced with many questions. Does God care? Why did this happen to us? Is there a God at all? As I contemplated alternatives to what I've always believed to be true, Peter's words in the Gospel of John kept ringing in my ears. "To whom should I go? You have the words that give life!"

As I look around me here in Asia, I see other alternatives to trust. Buddhists are burning incense sticks in their temples and Muslim prayers wake me up early in the morning. I could also choose disbelief. But among all these choices, only Jesus promises life. His words tell us about Heaven and how He defeated death with His own life. He promises eternal life with Him and abundant life here on earth.

I still don't have answers for all of my questions. God is still teaching me so much about Himself. But in the grief, I'm glad to know that death is not the end. There is more life coming than what I am living here on earth.

—Marilina Vega

Prayer Starter: *Lord, thank You that You give us life here, and even more*
– the promise of life in Heaven with You.

TRUTH AND LIES

God, who never lies... (Titus 1:2). You are of your father the devil...and has nothing to do with the truth, because there is no truth in him. When he lies, he speaks out of his own character, for he is a liar and the father of lies. (John 8:44)

Lying contradicts the character of God, which is unwavering.

If you think that the Bible is over the top here by equating all lies with the devil, then think of lies as an action that exacerbates sins we're hiding with our lies.

If you lie because you believe the truth will embarrass you, then you're exacerbating your pride. If you lie because you're too lazy to explain the entire truth, then you're exacerbating your slothfulness. If you lie because you believe the truth will hurt others, you're exacerbating your people-pleasing. All lies are of the devil because they make our hidden sins worse!

It is never right to lie because all lying is sin.

— Joe Gordon

Prayer Starter: *Lord, help me speak truthfully today.*

BLESSINGS

O Lord hear my prayer, listen to my cry for mercy: in your faithfulness and righteousness come to my relief. Remember the days of old; I meditate on all your works and consider what your hands have done. (Psalm 143:1,5)

Our God is the Father of all blessings. One example of a blessing we received was in the mid-1970s when we lived in El Centro, California. We attended a small, country church in Imperial with about 70 people. We became good friends with a single mom who had five young children. Two of the kids were twin boys about eight years of age. The mid-70s was a time for long hair for boys, but the father of these twin boys did not like long hair. So their mother would bring them over for me to cut their hair short, prior to their going to visit their dad. Little did I know what that would lead to, but God knew.

In 2006, when my wife was diagnosed with pancreatic cancer, we had a conference call with Dr. Bryan Clary the head of surgical residency at Duke University and a world-renowned pancreas and liver specialist. Yes, Dr. Clary was one of the twins whose hair I had cut 34 years before. Dr. Clary guided us through the initial stages of the battle we faced, and recommended Dr. Daniel Von Hoff, the leading doctor involved in pancreatic cancer research, who treated Kathy for three and a half years. As I told him about Dr. Clary, Dr. Von Hoff pulled out his latest book on pancreatic cancer and pointed out to me that Dr. Clary had written a chapter in the book. God began 34 years earlier preparing this blessing for my wife to have this incredible medical team to treat her pancreatic cancer. The oncologist she was seeing told us that she was four years ahead of the general public with the treatment she was then receiving.

The old hymn says, "Count your blessings, name them one by one. Count your many blessings, see what God has done."

—Ron Goble

Prayer Starter: *So many blessings from You Lord....Thank You for...*

BLOOM WHEREVER GOD PLANTS YOU!

May your roots go down deep into the soil of God's marvelous love. (Ephesians 3:17)

Sometimes we can't see the big picture, or instant results when we move to a new community. We choose not to put roots down because it's so hard to start over again. It's not always clear to see what God is doing, or why He is doing it, so we distance ourselves from a relationship with Him and with others.

Many times God will transplant us through a move to grow deeper roots in our relationship with Him. It is in the confusion and chaos of change that God teaches us about His faithfulness. It is through being uprooted and transplanted that we come to know Him and trust Him like never before. Once our roots grow deep in the soil of God's love, we begin to grow from within, seeds of hope begin to emerge, and then peace and contentment begin to break through the surface of our hearts. It is knowing God's faithfulness, trusting in Him, having hope, peace, and contentment, that we can begin to "bloom" again!

—Susan Miller

Prayer Starter: *Oh Lord, I will make the choice to grow deep roots in you and to "bloom" where You have transplanted me.*

TRUTHS OF GOD

But Thou art a God of forgiveness, gracious and compassionate; slow to anger and abounding in loving kindness... (Nehemiah 9:17)

Do you think much about Gods loving kindness, His forgiveness and compassion? You get angry, don't you, when someone you love does not listen to you and does what they please? Do you think much about how hard it must be for God to hold back His anger on generations who do not believe in Him?

Let me suggest that today you don't stop at reading just verse 17. Take out a pen and read through the entire 9th chapter of Nehemiah and make note of all the things God does. If you do you will be rewarded as you discover that God is not idle waiting about – God is active.

Here are some of the truths you will discover: God pursues us. God makes Himself known to us. God speaks to us. God provides for us. God listens to us. God fulfills all His promises. God does all this even when we are arrogant and turn from Him, when we are stubborn and do not listen, when we disobey, and when we do acts of contempt.

After making a list of all the things God does for us, make a list of the areas in your life where you right now need to ask God for forgiveness. Now give this list to the Lord and praise Him for His loving kindness.

—Mark Upton

Prayer Starter: *Lord, I am so thankful that You are active in my life and that You pursue me and care so deeply about me. Lord, forgive my …*

A LIGHT FOR MY PATH

Your Word is a lamp to my feet and a light to my path. (Psalm 119:105)

Two young climbers set off to climb the "Dom," the highest mountain inside Switzerland, higher than the more famous Matterhorn. The "Dom" reaches 14,900 feet and their goal was just to go half-way to the "high hut," a cabin where they could rest before making the summit the next day. However, hours into their climb, the weather began to change.

While they were still far from the "high hut" and safety, it began to mist. Then it began to rain. As daylight began to fade, the rain turned to snow. They were freezing (not having worn enough cold weather gear) and in danger of hypothermia or worse. That's when a light went on. Actually, it was a lantern – hung up by the "high hut" keeper just in case some travelers needed it's light!

That's a true story that pictures something very important to each of us as well. Namely, in the world we live in, with so much sin and sickness, it's easy to lose our way. But in the same way that "light" guided those two hikers to safety, God's Word can "light our path" and lead us to a place of safety and warmth.

—John and Cindy Trent

Prayer Starter: *Almighty God, we are so grateful to You for lighting our path. And most of all, thank You for "The light of the Word," who is Your Son, and our Lord, Jesus. Lord, is does get dark, cold and scary at times in this world. Thank You for guiding us, leading us and showing us Your ways.*

A PROMISE AND A TEST

If anyone is in Christ, he is a new creature; the old things passed away; behold, new things have come. (2 Corinthians 5:17)

Whenever I have heard this verse quoted, it is presented as a glorious promise of the power of God working in the life of a believer—usually a new believer. What a joy to know that the old things that plagued our lives when we were sinners are now a relic of the past. We are now new people entirely, remade by God with new things to look forward to. Praise God!

But this verse is more than just a promise; it is also a test designed to help us. It asks the question, "Are you truly in Christ?" If a person says he is in Christ, but the old things remain and new things have not come, then the test says, "No, this person is not in Christ." This is important to know!

Paul told the Corinthians to test themselves to see if they were truly in the faith (2 Corinthians 13:5). Peter lists a set of qualities that should become present in the life of a believer, saying that if these qualities are not present, a person needs to make certain that he is truly Christ's (2 Peter 1:3-11).

Many get upset at the suggestion that someone who says he is a Christian might not be, but if someone has believed something other than the genuine Gospel, then he still needs to receive Christ. Millions have believed in religion that does not include the cross or that fails to truly give Jesus authority as Lord. Many will come to Him on that day saying "Lord, Lord!" But will be cast out (Matthew 7:21-23). Better to test now and make sure that we are truly His.

—Dave Cottrell

Prayer Starter: *Dear God, don't let me be deceived. Let me examine and test my life by Your Word, and do whatever is needed…*

GOD'S PRESENCE

For those whom He foreknew, He also predestined to become conformed to the image of His Son, so that He would be the firstborn among many brethren; and these whom He predestined, He also called; and these whom He called, He also justified; and these whom He justified, He also glorified. (Romans 8:29-30)

As I have dealt with the sorrow of losing my wife to cancer at a young age, I found myself getting into the habit of hiking in the Phoenix Mountain Preserve for an hour or two just about every day. This has become a wonderful time of prayer and reflection. I found myself engaging in long talks with God about the "why" and "what." Why had He allowed this to happen? And what is His plan for my life going forward?

While the answers were sometimes slow in coming, I did find a frequent sense of God's personal presence in my heart. One day I found myself marveling at the fact that I was in a conversation with the Creator of the universe. As quickly as that thought came to me, I found myself asking why He would waste His time talking with me? I almost expected to see a burning bush as I realized that God made me the way He did for His pleasure! We can boldly come before His throne to receive the inestimable gift of His guidance.

At the beginning of time as we know it, God foreknew that I would be walking on this trail today and that He would be moving in my heart and soul to comfort me with His matchless presence. How can I feel anything but profound gratitude in His presence?

—Jim York

Prayer Starter: *Lord, open my heart to sense Your personal presence in my life.*

CAN AN OLD PROPHET LEARN?

O Lord, how long shall I cry for help, and you will not hear? (Habakkuk 1:2)

Habakkuk, the seventh century prophet, started off by complaining against God. He wondered how long God was going to sit idly by while Habakkuk's calls go unheeded? Then he wondered why God let sin abound in this world (Habakkuk 1:3-4)? If Habakkuk ran the show, things would be different.

God responds by saying that He is doing something so great that Habakkuk could never imagine it. God is going to raise up the mean Babylonians to punish the sin that is rampant in Israel. Habakkuk is stunned—how could God use the wicked Babylonians to punish a less wicked nation? That did not sound fair. But rather than answer Habakkuk's question, God allowed His plan to work out, and sure enough, by the end of the book Habakkuk is a changed prophet. He realizes that God does not have to answer to him and that all Habakkuk can do is trust in an amazing God who can do things Habakkuk never dreamed of.

I wonder what it is going to take for me to quit complaining against God's plan and instead to just rest in His providence, knowing that God knows best? I love Habakkuk's final response even though he can see no reason to rejoice, "Yet will I exalt in the Lord."

—Paul Wegner

Prayer Starter: *Lord, help me to always trust You.*

OUT-OF-CONTROL THOUGHTS

And the peace of God, which surpasses all comprehension, shall guard your hearts and your minds in Christ Jesus. (Philippians 4:7)

Lie: Even God can't help me with my out-of-control thoughts.

When our thoughts spin like a carnival Ferris wheel, it's easy to think that we have no control over them; yet, we do. It's a novel idea to realize that we do not have to entertain every thought that comes into our mind. That's all they are...just thoughts. Out-of-control thoughts are generally negative, worrisome, and degrading. However, God can give us control over our thoughts. He is capable of guarding my mind and soothing my thoughts.

Italian violinist Niccolo Paganini (1782-1840) was playing a beautiful piece of music before a large audience. Suddenly one string on his violin snapped, yet he continued to play, improvising beautifully. Then two more strings broke, and he completed the composition playing with only one string. When the applause eventually stopped, he nodded at the conductor to begin the encore. The violinist smiled at the audience and shouted, "Paganini...and one string!" Placing his instrument under his chin, he played again with only that one string.

Just as Paganini chose through perseverance to play with one string, we can choose our thoughts. Life is full of difficulties that are out of our control, but our thoughts? God can guard my mind and yours. Just ask!

—Nonie Maupin

Prayer Starter: *Lord, I humbly ask that You guard my heart and my mind in Christ Jesus.*

SURRENDER TO GOD

Brothers, join in imitating me, and keep your eyes on those who walk according to the example you have in us. (Philippians 3:17)

Today, take an extended time to consider how passionate you are for your relationship with Christ. If you are ready to take the plunge, ask God to deepen that passion, to make your heart desire more than anything else – an ever deepening intimacy with your Savior. Then, as a matter of choice – yield and surrender to Him the things that have been in the way of that desire. Watch Him change you and grow you into the man or woman He designed you to be.

If you are not ready for the plunge, that's ok, keep in your heart that "there is no condemnation to those who are in Christ." The gnawing in your heart for God, though small it may be, can and will grow if you'll acknowledge it to Him and ask Him to help you want what you don't want now.*

—Donald Farr

Prayer Starter: *Lord Jesus, help me take the plunge.*

REMEMBER

I thank Christ Jesus our Lord, who has given me strength, that He considered me faithful, appointing me to His service. (I Timothy 1:12)

This is the verse that the Lord gave us in November 1972 when we were appointed members of Wycliffe Bible translators and left for Mexico the following fall to attend jungle camp. We arrived in Mitla, Mexico, in February 1974 to serve as children's home parents, caring for children of other missionaries while they went out to remote villages to work with the indigenous groups to do translation and literacy work.

The children lived with us and attended the mission school. It was in May of 1974 that we met with the missions committee of Scottsdale Bible Church and became a part of the outreach team. We served eight years in Mexico and then were required by the government to leave along with others in the mission.

Next, after serving 16 years in Lomalinda, Colombia, we were evacuated because of the rebels fighting the government and those who grow the coca plant. Our next assignment took us to Nairobi, Kenya, for the next six years, and God blessed us greatly as we served the missionary children there. Again, the government required us to leave the country and we began serving at the international linguistic center in Dallas, Texas, in 2003. It was difficult to pick up and move, especially to a different language and culture. We faced all sorts of trials during our service, but God equipped us each time to not only endure, but to have joy in serving.

One who is called does not quit in the face of adversity, but gains strength from the one who is faithful. Today, will you quit or will you look to God for strength?

—Gary and Charlotte Shingledecker

Prayer Starter: *Lord, help me to be Your faithful follower each day no matter where You lead.*

"I AM"

God said to Moses, "I AM who I AM. This is what you are to say to the Israelites. 'I AM' has sent you." (Exodus 3:14)

"I AM." Three simple letters, two small words. Yet these three letters revealed the name of God to the world. They knocked over a legion of Roman soldiers. They comforted a Samaritan woman. They enraged the Pharisees. And they indwelled the Apostles. They are full of truth and power and glory.

The name God gave us for Himself is Yahweh or "I AM." In modern language, we use this phrase along with descriptive adjectives such as, "I am tall," "I am sad," or "I am hungry." By definition, these statements are limiting. You are tall or short. Or you are happy or sad. You cannot be both. "I am in Arizona" or "I am in California." You can't be in both places.

There is no such limitation in "I AM." Instead, it encompasses all. It describes God's timelessness and His unchanging nature. It speaks to His self-existence and need of nothing. "I AM" reminds us that He was and He is and He will be. The Greek translation is *ego eime* and includes the concept of "He is being," which reminds us of His active nearness in our lives.

How lucky we are that even in giving us His name, He reminds us of our proper relationship with Him. We have limits. We are constantly changing. We are dependent. We have needs. With the simple name "I AM" we are reminded that He is Creator and we are His creation.

—David Scholl

Prayer Starter: *Father, I thank You for Your limitless nature and constant reminder of…*

THE UNCOMPLICATED CHRISTIAN LIFE

Make it your ambition to lead a quiet life, to mind your own business and to work with your hands, just as we told you, so that your daily life may win the respect of outsiders and so that you will not be dependent on anybody.
(1 Thessalonians 4:11)

The Christian life isn't complicated. The disobedient Christian life is extremely complicated. When we put one dumb choice next to a foolish statement and then lean them both against a lazy life, we shouldn't be surprised when we end up in bondage and dependence on others. When we pick and choose the parts of the Bible we like and ignore the rest, we shouldn't be shocked that we're on the outside looking in when it comes to being respected for our beliefs.

God wants us to long for Him and to make choices about how we live our lives in ways that align with His heart. He says, "Lead a quiet life." In other words, don't make the kind of noise that brings negative attention to His reputation. Whether it's political opinions that degrade our detractors, gossip, or even God's truth delivered in a shrill voice, we're called to rise above these. It's the logical first step of a life that doesn't nose its way into other people's private affairs, but rather focuses that energy toward a hard day's work.

Today is a great day to practice turning all of this into a habit.

—Tim Kimmel

Prayer Starter: *Dear Lord, help me live in quiet peace with You today, to mind my own business and to pull my weight.*

FORSAKE SIN

Thy kingdom come, Thy will be done, on earth as it is in Heaven.
(Matthew 6:10)

In addition to the conversion of lost souls, a second way God advances His kingdom on earth is when His children continue to develop a greater awareness of sin in their own life, a greater desire to forsake that sin, and a greater longing to persevere in holiness. To daily pray "Thy kingdom come" is to daily pray, in part, that God would give us an awareness of the areas where we fall short in obeying His Word (Psalm 51:6-7), the grace to confess (1 John 1:9), recognition that He is *Jehovah-rapha* – "The God who heals and restores" (Psalm 103:1-5), and the perseverance to obey.

What does your soul need healing from today? What do you need to confess and forsake in your life today? To the extent we forsake our sin, and ask God to enable us to walk in holiness, to that extent we further advance His kingdom rule on earth, demonstrate our love for Christ, and have greater assurance of our salvation (1 John 2:3).

—John Politan

Prayer Starter: *Lord, I pray that You will make me more aware of areas in my life where I disobey Your Word and fail to manifest Christ. I humbly ask for Your grace and power to work in my heart and mind to forsake my sin and to strive to persevere in holiness today for Your glory.*

WHAT WILL I CHOOSE?

Not that I am speaking of being in need, for I have learned in whatever situation I am to be content. (Philippians 4:11)

When our daughter was in high school several years ago she attended the Junior-Senior Prom in the spring of her senior year. She had a great time and the next day a huge group of her classmates was planning a desert picnic northeast of Scottsdale. She was more excited about the picnic than she had been about the prom. It was going to be a great day interacting with classmates who would soon be scattering "to the winds" of colleges all over the state and the country.

Saturday morning my wife, Georgann, and I awoke early and ventured into the kitchen. To our dismay, the sky was gray and rain was falling. It was the type of rain that those of us who have lived in the desert know is not a rain shower, but an all day drizzle. Our first thoughts were of our daughter and the disappointment she would suffer from a cancelled event that she had not only looked forward to for so long, but had actually been one of the key planners for the event.

We were drinking coffee and reading the soaked paper when Melissa groggily walked out to the breakfast area. We said nothing, but held our breaths anticipating the tears of disappointment of our wonderful daughter. Our hearts were broken for her.

She walked to the window and stood there looking out for what seemed like an eternity. We were expecting a cascade of tears. Finally, she said, "I guess I have a decision to make." I was stunned, but managed to ask what that decision might be – an alternate venue for the picnic? Another day?

"No", she said, "I have to decide whether I will be content or not."

That morning I learned—from my child—what the apostle Paul meant when he said, "…I have learned in whatever situation I am to be content." How is your contentment level today?

—Bob Cain

Prayer Starter: *Lord, the plans I have are not working out like I wanted, but You are in control, so I pray for contentment in this circumstance….*

WHO HOLDS THE HEART OF THIS HOME?

...For God sees not as man sees, for man looks at the outward appearance,
but the Lord looks at the heart. (I Samuel 16:7b)

There is a wonderful place
A space so secure and warm,
That all who are privileged to live there
Call it home.
Who holds the heart of this home?
The walls are colored with laughter
And the floors with wall-to-wall memories.
Each space testifies to the
Bustling energy and joy of blended lives.
Who holds the heart of this home?
It's more than an address
Or a statement of achievement and style.
It's a tender oasis from the storms of daily life,
A place of peace and rest.
Who holds the heart of this home?
Cheerleaders for life dwell here
As do living testimonies for faith.
Imperfect saints work out the walk of wisdom
In the halls of this home.
Who holds the heart of this home?
For every damaged day and sharp defeat,
Home is the balm for the wound.
For every cutting word and ungracious event,
Home is the kindness we crave.
Who holds the heart of this home?
And every bad memory of family and childhood
Is swallowed in the embrace of a now happy home.
The time for forgiveness and healing is here
In the sanctuary of home.
Who holds the heart of this home?
So, those who build a home instead of a house,
A deliberate and prayer-laced place
Rather than a sterile designer's delight,
Do well.
Who holds the heart of this home?
You hold the heart of this home!

—David and Donna Otto

EARS TO HEAR

I love the Lord, because He has heard my voice and my supplications.
(Psalm 116:1)

We have a good friend who has five children and is fond of telling this favorite story:

It seems that it was supper time, and his entire family was seated around the dinner table. Everyone was talking at once, except the youngest son who was five years old at the time. Like watching a tennis match, he kept looking from one family member to another, waiting for some kind of opening or break in the conversation so he could get a word in edgewise.

Finally, frustrated beyond endurance, he stood up on his chair and screamed at the top of his lungs.

Everyone instantly stopped talking, their eyes riveted on this child.

"What's the matter around here?" The boy shouted, "Doesn't anybody have any ears?"

That's a funny story, but it's true in too many homes! In other words, there are times when it's easy to feel like we can't get a word of meaningful conversation spoken or when we don't feel listened to. One of the greatest gifts we can give our spouse and children is the gift of our "ears." We need to listen to others just as God hears us and listens for our voice.

—John and Cindy Trent

Prayer Starter: *Lord Jesus, thank You that You don't just "talk" but You listen to us. We pray we can have "ears" for each other, ears that hear each other's heart, and needs, and goals, and dreams. And help us to listen for Your voice for our lives as well.*

NEW BELIEVERS ADDED

And the Lord added to them day by day those that were saved. (Acts 2:47)

In a church of our size it's easy to get lost in the crowd. For some people that's exactly why they come. They want to be anonymous. But that isn't what attracts most people to Scottsdale Bible. In fact, I suggest that "getting lost in the crowd" isn't in the best interest of anyone at church, and it is one thing that our church must aggressively work against as we move forward.

When I read the book of Acts, I see God unfolding a perfectly strategic plan to accomplish a perfect purpose. As His Holy Spirit moved and filled the 120 people present in the upper room, the resulting outpouring was a massive initial addition of 3,000…and more added daily to them who were being saved. As easy as we can see that it is for people to get "swallowed up" in the crowd here, imagine that it was even easier in an environment like that where God was doing so much, so fast, among so many.

One reason the early church grew so dynamically in its onset is because they understood that when new believers were added to the church, they were added to "them," not "it." They understood that the church was people, and when new believers were added it was a testimony to the growth of the community.

God is adding to His church. He is not adding them to class rosters or to a worship service attendance count or to a list of donors. He is adding them to His community of faith, which we are a part, too. He is building relationships. We are the church. You are the church. God in His goodness is adding to us, for His name's sake, to accomplish His perfect purpose.

—Jamie Rasmussen

Prayer Starter: *God, open Your church wide and fill us with Your Holy Spirit that new ones will be added to us daily.*

THE PUNCH LINE OF THE GOSPEL

For God did not send His Son into the world to condemn the world, but to save the world through Him. (John 3:17)

It was lunch time—McDonalds—crowded. Standing in that group was a young mom with three small kids. Two construction workers slipped in behind them. Somehow they missed the memo that you turn down the "construction site language" when you are standing around young ears.

I'm sure the mother thought she was doing the right thing for her kids. Lots of well-intended people do misguided things. Regardless, she turned around and lit into those two men with a righteous rage. She gave them the "How dare you…" intros to her tirade, unloading a biblical lecture on their lack of class. Then she finished her vent by quoting John 3:16 and suggesting they turn their hearts and their vile tongues over to God.

I felt embarrassed for these men, sad for this woman and her kids, and disappointed on behalf of Christ's work on the cross. These were lost men talking the way lost people do. Sure, they lacked tact, but that tends to be a problem of lost people. Then I thought of Jesus sharing those words to Nicodemus for the first time. What many don't realize is that John 3:16 is the set up, but John 3:17 is the punch line. "God didn't come to condemn the lost world, He came to save it." And that is still true today.

—Tim Kimmel

Prayer Starter: *Dear Lord, give me eyes of grace as I look at people who don't know You. Help me live in response to the need of their heart rather than in reaction to the misdeeds of their life.*

QUESTIONS OF GOD

Come, let us reason together. (Isaiah 1:18)

There are 288 question marks in the book of Job. Seventy-eight of the questions are from God Himself – questions like: "Job, where were you when I laid the earth's foundation?"

Life is full of questions: how do I justify my existence? What is my purpose for living? Should I impose my beliefs about God on others? But many questions come from others: why does God allow suffering, evil and death? You don't think there is just one true religion, do you? Doesn't evolution disprove the Bible? Why should I believe what you are saying?

Perhaps our best responses are empathetic, Spirit-filled answers. It is a God-thing when our answers are bathed in the Word and the Spirit is guiding our lips. We know that no other religion outside the Bible has declared that God created the world out of love and delight. We know the source of the idea that God is love is the Bible itself. God is not afraid of our questions, because an honest pursuit for answers brings us back to His Word, and back to the truth that God created us in order to have a relationship with us.

—Barry Asmus

Prayer Starter: *Dear Father, Your Word promises that You are merciful and gracious. For we know that as high as the Heavens are above the earth, so great is Your steadfast love towards those who fear You. I have so few answers, but I'm thankful that You have them all. I do know that when I'm weak, that's when You are strong.*

UNITY IN CHRIST

…With all humility and gentleness, with patience, showing tolerance for one another in love, being diligent to preserve the unity of the Spirit in the bond of peace. There is one body and one spirit, just as also you were called in one hope of your calling; one Lord, one faith, one baptism, one God and Father of all who is over all and through all and in all. (Ephesians 4:2-6)

These verses are powerful. We must be gentle, humble, patient, bearing with one another – making every effort to keep the unity of the Spirit through peace. Christ is our peace – Christ is our unity. As Jamie has pointed out, we are a very divergent church with many different factions under Christ, but listen to this next statement by Paul: "It was Jesus who gave some to be apostles, some to be prophets, some to be evangelists and some to be pastors and teachers, to prepare God's people for works of service, so that the body of Christ may be built up until we reach unity in the faith and in the knowledge of the Son of God and become mature, attaining the full measure of perfection found in Christ."

To me this full perfection will be when I die, but the important part here is that we are all headed in the same direction…coming from many directions but headed to the same place. Imagine a spot out in front of you. Open your fingers wide and point to that spot – that's where we are. Now close your fingers and point to the same spot – that's how we're heading. Do we all have to agree on everything? Absolutely not, but we all have to envision ourselves huddled around Christ going to the same place.

—Sue Phipps

Prayer Starter: *Jesus, become my everything. Lead me and all those around me toward You.*

THE GRATIFIED LIFE

Cast your bread upon the waters, for you will find it after many days.
(Ecclesiastes 11:1)

I woke up this morning thinking about a satisfied life, but before I could get out of bed that concept had already moved to a "gratified life." Let me explain. A satisfied life equals a contented life but a gratified life equals a life that brings pleasure, keen enjoyment, and delight – often in surprising ways!

Many years ago I made the choice to intentionally invest myself into each person that God brought across my path. I promised Him I would be faithful to step up, be alert and match the openness of others and the depth to which they were willing to go! Over the years, this commitment to go deep in relationships has developed into a concept I call life-to-life exchange.

By life-to-life exchange, I mean I give of myself, sometimes extravagantly, and when it is a profitable relationship – I receive something rich, fulfilling and extravagant in return. It is much like what Solomon said in his journal in the book of Ecclesiastes, chapter 11, verse 1.

This return cannot be expected or manipulated, but when I find it, it adds fantastic mystery and adventure to my life! Life-to-life exchange is the most profitable investment I can make and the foundation of a gratified life.

—Holly DelHousaye

Prayer Starter: *Dear Lord, help me to give of myself to others sacrificially with no expectation of return.*

LISTEN

He who has an ear, let him hear...(Revelation 2:7, 29; 3:6, 13, 22)

I grew up with an older brother who taught me several "indirect lessons." He accomplished this through the age-old technique of messing up and getting disciplined. Because of his occasional poor decisions and the lectures that always followed, I learned important lessons about truth-telling, curfew-breaking, and other things that we've agreed will never show up in print.

While I had plenty of failures in my own right, I truly benefitted from hearing and overhearing the discipline and correction he received. Now as a parent myself, there are times when I make sure that all my children hear the lessons I'm teaching to one specific child, so they all may benefit.

In Jesus' seven letters to the seven churches, He concludes five of those messages with a statement, "He who has an ear, let him hear..." Jesus wants us to be clear that there is a personal application for each person, as well as for the specific churches being addressed.

Perhaps it is because we can each identify with each of the churches. There are times when you will forget your first love. There are times when you will feel poor, but are spiritually rich. There are times when you will be lured by false teaching, or tempted by immorality. There will be times when you are behaving badly, or lukewarmly. There will be times where you need encouragement to persevere. None of these experiences are unusual to the human experience. And Jesus wants you to know through His message to these churches, that He is able to speak truth into your life and your common circumstance as well.

Likewise, the warning and promises that Jesus offers the churches are available to you as well. Remember, you are part of the church. Jesus faithfully offers you individually life, authority, a new identity, eternal relationship in God's presence, and everlasting residence in Heaven.

"He who has an ear, listen..." is an idiom for you to pay attention. Jesus speaks to you, now. He who is faithful and true has a message that is real and relevant and life-changing. Listen up, and believe!

—Bryan McAnally

Prayer Starter: *Lord, open my heart and mind to Your words to me each day.*

THINKING OF YOU

May the God of hope fill you with all joy and peace in believing, so that by the power of the Holy Spirit you may abound in hope. (Romans 15:13)

I had just finished telling a friend of mine, a self-proclaimed atheist, that I was facing major surgery the following Monday morning. His response was heartfelt: "I'm so sorry to hear that. I'll definitely be thinking of you." As he walked away it struck me that that's the only thing he could offer - to hold me in his thoughts. No promise in the power of prayer, no peace that God was in control, and no hope, other than the skill of the surgeon's hands.

What a difference. As believers, we serve the God of hope—He is a sovereign God—one who loves us, who cares for us, who answers prayers, who gives us joy and peace in believing – and most importantly, He is a God who desires that we live our lives in abundant hope. I am reminded of the chorus to an old hymn written by Ira Stamphill: "Many things about tomorrow, I don't seem to understand; but I know who holds tomorrow, and I know who holds my hand." And knowing "who holds our hands" forms the foundation for our hope!

—Don Baltzer

Prayer Starter: *Lord, teach me how to rely only on You—and not on myself—so that I may experience a life filled with abundant hope.*

WISE CONTROL

*Be fruitful and multiply and fill the earth and subdue it, and have domin-
ion over the fish of the sea and over the birds of the Heavens and over every
living thing that moves on the earth. (Genesis 1:28)*

The entire earth belongs to God for He created it. To "subdue" the earth meant to exercise wise control over it in such a way that it will produce useful goods for the people who
"subdued" it.

This command therefore implied an expectation that Adam and Eve and their descendants,
as God's image-bearers, would investigate, understand, develop, and enjoy the resources of
the earth with thanksgiving to God who had entrusted such a responsibility to them. This
implied not merely harvesting food from the vines and trees in the Garden of Eden but
also domesticating animals, developing the mineral resources of the earth, and eventually
developing dwelling places and means of transportation, learning artistry and craftsmanship,
and so forth.

The ability to develop and enjoy the resources of the earth in this way is an ability unique to
human beings, one that is shared neither by animals nor angels.

—Wayne Grudem

Prayer Starter: *God, help me to be a wise steward of all Your resources with gratitude to You.*

HOLD ON TO GOD

...And a certain man of Bethlehem, Judah, went to dwell in the country of Moab, he and his wife and his two sons. The name of the man was Elimelech, the name of his wife was Naomi, and the names of his two sons were Mahlon and Chilion — Ephrathites of Bethlehem, Judah. And they went to the country of Moab and remained there. (Ruth 1:1-2)

This Jewish family known as Ephrathites (which means "fruitful"), lived in Bethlehem (which means "house of bread"), located in the area known as Judah (which means "praise"). They traveled 50-60 miles to reside/dwell/remain in Moab. Why? God had given them the Promised Land. He had given them a virtual paradise! I know there was a famine in the land... but God had given it! There was a famine in the land in Isaac's day and God instructed Isaac not to escape to Egypt (Genesis 26:1-3). God told Isaac to dwell in the land He had given the children of Israel, and that He would be with him and bless him.

Hadn't Elimelech remembered the accounts of God's provision for His people? And why, Elimelech, did you go to Moab, of all places? The Moabites were the people who refused to give the children of Israel bread and water when God delivered them from Egypt (Deuteronomy 23:4). And, the Moabites worshipped pagan gods! God excluded the Moabites from entering the assembly of the Lord. Why, Elimelech, did you take matters into your own hands and run away from God?

How are we faring in difficult circumstances? Are we heeding God or disrespecting Him? That's a rather blunt statement. However, if we are running away from God and what we know to be His truth, we are not respecting Him.

In the face of struggles and hardship, think "GTAA": Grab the truth of God's Word. Thank Him for the situation in which you find yourself. Ask Him how you should respond. Ask Him what you are to learn.

—Cathy Wilson

Prayer Starter: *Lord, please reveal to me Your truth. Please grant me your understanding. Please give me a thankful heart. Please cause me to stand firm and wait upon You!*

TURN BACK TO TRUTH

My brethren, if any among you strays from the truth and one turns him back, let him know that he who turns a sinner from the error of his way will save his soul from death and will cover a multitude of sins. (James 5:19-20)

Brothers and sisters, James implores his hearers: should anyone among you be on the wrong path, wandering around having lost their direction, moving away from God's truth—you must turn your brother or sister back to the truth.

As you are reading this, perhaps the names and faces of individuals whom you know are in need of your intervention to turn them back to the truth have come to your mind. Perhaps others are reading this today and your name and face have come to their mind. Prepare your heart accordingly.

—David Walther

Prayer Starter: *Lord give me clarity and boldness in speaking the truth in love to those whom I know who are wandering from Your truth. Lord, search my heart, is there anyway in which I am wandering from Your truth? Give boldness to those who know me to help me see those things I cannot see. Please convict me now, prompt me to confess, repent and to be right with You, Jesus.*

REJOICE

Rejoice in the Lord always, again I will say rejoice. (Philippians 4:4)

The apostle Paul was at the end of his life and he said, "Rejoice." He was imprisoned many times, endured countless beatings- oftentimes very near death, five times received 39 lashes with a whip, three times beaten with rods, one time stoned almost to death, three times shipwrecked and lost in the raging sea for a night and a day. His life was filled with danger from rivers, threats to his life, toil and hardship, sleepless nights, hunger and thirst, often without food and frozen from exposure to the cold.

How could so many lousy, bad luck things happen to one man? Ask Paul. "When I am weak, then He is strong. I will boast of my weakness. I will cling to Jesus. My grace is sufficient for you, for my power is made perfect in weakness. Do not be anxious about anything but in everything by prayer and supplication with thanksgiving, let your requests be made known to God. For I have learned to be content in all things. I can do all things through Him who strengthens me. For me to live is Christ and to die is gain." Will you respond today to the Lord and rejoice in your circumstances?

—Barry Asmus

Prayer Starter: *Lord, thank You for Paul. He has truly put the significance of my trials in perspective and gives me hope. Faith and suffering are equal gifts of God's grace.*

JESUS IS FOR REAL

For there are three that bear witness, the Spirit and the water and the blood; and the three are in agreement. (1 John 5:8)

Scholars have called 1 John 5:6-12 the most perplexing passage in that epistle. Yet John didn't write it to be perplexing. A recurring word in the passage 1 John 5:6–12 is "witness" –*marturia* in Greek, a testimony of evidence, a witness to fact. What fact? "That God has given us eternal life, and this life is in His Son" (1 John 5:10).

John gives three witnesses from God for this fact, for "on the evidence of two or three witnesses a matter shall be confirmed" (Deuteronomy 19:15).

First, John says Jesus "came by water" (1 John 5:6). This was Jesus' baptism, when God's voice from Heaven said, "This is My beloved Son, in whom I am well-pleased" (Matthew 3:17). Second, John says Jesus also came by "blood" (1 John 5:6). "Blood spoke of death, for the life of the flesh is in the blood…it is the blood by reason of the life that makes atonement" (Leviticus 17:11). False teachers in John's day were saying Christ did not have a human body because bodies were evil, and good would never take on evil. But if Jesus Christ did not have a body that would bleed. He could never die as "the Lamb who takes away the sin of the world." His blood, His death on the cross, proved that He was the promised Messiah and the Son of God. The third witness from God, John says, "is the Spirit," (1 John 5:7) who bore witness to Jesus in His miracles, and continues to bear witness in the Bible.

The credibility of your faith rests in the credibility of the one you say you believe in. God's own witness confirms it: Jesus is for real.

—Darryl DelHousaye

Prayer Starter: *God, my faith rests in Jesus who You confirm with Your witnesses that He is real.*

GOD'S VOICE

Let us lay aside every weight, and the sin which so easily ensnares us.
(Hebrews 12:1)

Have you ever become aware of a pattern of sin (or "weight" that could easily lead into sin) in some area of your life? The "weight" may not be sin in itself, however when God speaks to one of His children and says they need to eliminate this "weight" and they do not, that is where the disobedience comes in. It is not so much an issue of the literal act in itself being sin, as it is an issue of obedience.

The act of ignoring an area in life that God has given light and brought to our attention is dangerous. To cover or justify it through time and ongoing repetition can enable a person to continue with a false justification and attitude, thinking God will just "wink" at this area. Many times this "weight" is not noticeable by others.

How easy to become complacent and no longer sense the voice of God because of the repetition of our sin. The longer we continue in this sin, the less strength we have to overcome. God brings to our minds those "weights" that slow us down in his work. These seemingly small issues to us, at the moment, may not seem important or worth disturbing our habits and lifestyle. However, when God says to lay something aside, obedience to that light is as important as the outward, more noticeable sins and weights.

—MaryAnn Morton

Prayer Starter: *Father, uncover the secrets of my heart and open my eyes to Your holiness. I commit to be sensitive to Your inner tug concerning weights that hold me from Your desired blessings and ministry to others. I long to be released from the chain of my quiet sinful ways!*

SHARING JESUS

Jesus answered her, "If you knew the gift of God, and who it is that is saying to you, 'give me a drink,' you would have asked Him, and He would have given you living water." (John 4:10)

Imagine if Jesus had approached sharing the Gospel the way we do. If He witnessed "our way," He would have hoped the woman at the well noticed there was something different about Him by the way He drank His water, and maybe asked Him about it.

Maybe she would have noticed His "my-dad-created-the-world- in-6-days, what-did-your-dad-do?" T-shirt and asked Him to explain it. Maybe she would have overheard Hillsong blaring through His iPod earbuds and asked what the lyrics meant.

I better stop before this gets preposterous.

I'm sure glad that Jesus didn't do it the way we do.

No…He did it His way. He spotted her and recognized that God put her in His life. So He took the initiative. He broke the silence with her and used something as non-threatening as a drink of water to lead into a spiritual conversation. He immediately steered the conversation to Himself (since He is the Gospel, after all).

As they talked, He kept the conversation on Himself, refusing to be distracted by the less important matter of religious squabbles or derailed by the diversion of the woman's scandalous history. As a result, many in the entire village came to believe in Him.

Through His own experience with the woman at the well, Jesus showed us that we should be willing to talk about Him to anyone, anytime, no matter the differences. Recognize every person as someone God has put into your path for this reason. Never be shy about starting a spiritual conversation, but be creative and determined to steer the conversation to Jesus. Be disciplined to avoid distractions and derailers. Above all, point people to Him, so He can do His miraculous, life-changing work in them and others in their community.

Share Jesus with others the way Jesus shared Himself with others. To do anything else will leave a parched person thirsting.

—Bryan McAnally

Prayer Starter: *Jesus, help me to share You boldly and clearly with others, allowing Your Holy Spirit to touch their lives.*

FAITH

So faith comes from hearing, and hearing through the Word of Christ.
(Romans 10:17)

It is certainly true that this passage is claiming that initial faith in Christ comes from hearing the inspired Word about Christ, but it is also true that much of the faith we need for day-to-day living comes from hearing the Bible's message.

So, are you plagued with doubts, fear, or anxiety? God's Word enables our faith to be strong when we struggle with doubts.

Read, memorize, meditate, study, and pray through the Word of God for a faith that is strengthened by God Himself!

—Joe Gordon

Prayer Starter: *Lord, please use the divinely inspired Word of God to strengthen my faith when I feel weak today.*

TRUST FOR THE FUTURE

Trust in the Lord with all your heart and do not lean on your own under-standing. In all your ways acknowledge Him, and He will make your paths straight. (Proverbs 3:5-6)

These two verses have been life verses of mine since college. Why then? Well, I needed to select a Scripture to accompany my senior picture for the yearbook and this one seemed as good as the many other options that people typically choose.

Maybe it seemed especially relevant because I didn't know yet what I was going to do post-graduation. Wendy and I had already set our wedding date, just a few weeks after I would walk the line, but the future was definitely uncertain. My family lived in Oregon, she lived in Pennsylvania, and I was currently going to school in misery...excuse me, Missouri. It's one thing to get married, it's another thing to support yourself and your new wife. I was searching for a pastoral position to begin using the training I had received in school, but unsure of the next steps.

Have you ever been there? I tend to be a self-sufficient individual with plans in-hand, so dependence on others doesn't come naturally. Maybe you can see where this is going. Too often we are guilty of trying to "make" things happen in our strength and knowledge.

I have since had many opportunities to put my trust in God's ways and plans rather than my own. He knows better. His way is straighter. Try it.

—Troy Peterson

Prayer Starter: *Lord, teach me to trust You more...*

THE IMPACT OF ONE LITTLE WORD

For I, the Lord, do not change… (Malachi 3:6)

Moving is change. The loss of friends, community, home, job, and even your church family can often be emotionally devastating.

The impact of change, whether through a move or some other kind of loss, can also bring fear and anxious thoughts to your mind – fear of what lies ahead, and anxiety over all the unknowns that come with change. Be reassured through God's Word in Scripture:

Cast your cares on the Lord and He will sustain you. (Psalm 55:22)

When I am afraid, I will trust in you. (Psalm 56:3)

There is comfort in knowing that God never changes! He will give you peace and hope for each day. Be assured that God can handle whatever changes come your way and He will enable you to get through the changes in your life. You may not know what the future holds, but you know who holds the future.

—Susan Miller

Prayer Starter: *Lord, walk with me through the changes in my life this year. Equip me to face change in a way that will glorify You and draw me closer to You each day. Comfort me with Your peace and hope.*

DETERMINATION

It's hopeless! For we are going to follow our own plans, and each of us will act accordingly to the stubbornness of his evil heart. (Jeremiah 18:12)

"The price of success is hard work, dedication to the job at hand, and the determination that whether we win or lose, we have applied the best of ourselves to the task at hand" said Vince Lombardi. "Determination is the wake-up call to the human will," said Anthony (Tony) Robbins. "A leader, once convinced that a particular course of action is the right one, must….be undaunted when the going gets tough," said Ronald Reagan.

Determination is a motivator for success; however, the challenge is what the focus of that determined energy is. In Jeremiah 18, the Lord spoke of Himself as a potter of clay who takes our very lives and shapes them to accomplish His will. He also speaks of those who choose not to allow the Lord to fashion them into great instruments of success for His glory. These are determined people who choose to follow their own course. Their hearts are fixed on their own desires and not moldable by the Lord.

Determination is a powerful thing. Examine your heart. Are you determined to let the Lord mold you into a mighty man or woman of God for His glory or is your heart stubborn and set on a different course?

—Mark Upton

Prayer Starter: *Lord I have allowed You to shape me in all areas of my life except …*

I CAN READ YOUR MIND

He who gives an answer before he hears, it is folly and shame to him.
(Proverbs 18:13)

"I know what you're thinking!" A little girl told her mother. When her mom said, "So what am I thinking?" She said, "You were thinking how happy I'd be if you took me to get an ice cream!"

When a precious young child says something like that, it's very cute! However, there's a much more negative side to "mind reading" with our family and friends. Here in the book of Proverbs, it's clear that answering before we really listen doesn't put us in the "wise" camp. But if we're honest, it's so easy at times to already "know" what someone is going to say when they begin a sentence or thought – and just complete it for them.

Ask the Lord for the wisdom, love and patience to really listen to our loved ones and others in our life as well – and only then share our answer.

—John and Cindy Trent

Prayer Starter: *I'm so impatient at times, Lord. You know that. And You know, too, that I often "just know" what my family or friends are thinking – even without waiting for them to share their thoughts. Help me to be wise and not foolish and to really work at listening, and rarely answer before I hear.*

RECEIVE

Give and it shall be given to you… (Luke 6:38)

"Give" is one of those words from God that is inclusive in every circumstance… a clear demand. What are we to give? Everything! We give all that we are and have now or in the future. If you are to be part of this benevolent cycle of the universe, you must give or the cycle is broken by you.

"Give" is also a practical word. Where are you experiencing your greatest present need? Jesus promises the giver will receive more. Are you experiencing not having enough time? Give more of your time away. Not experiencing love? Love someone more. Have a lack of energy? Try more exercise. It's a universal promise from our Savior.

—William Anthony

Prayer Starter: *Lord, help me to give more of myself away.*

DON'T FORGET

Remember this, keep it in mind... (Isaiah 46:8a)

When the Scripture says, "Remember..." it's prudent to do so! As a student is expected to master key concepts in a a class, God sometimes spells out key things to remember. When it also says to "fix in mind, take to heart," God is clearly giving a foundational thought meant to anchor the essence of who we are. Such an imperative comes in Isaiah 46:8-9. "Remember, this, keep it in mind, take it to heart, you rebels. Remember the former things, those of long ago: I am God, and there is no other; I am God, and there is none like Me."

So we're to remember, fix it in our minds and take it to heart...the former things of long ago. These are the miraculous interventions God did, such as delivering Israel from bondage in Egypt parting the red sea, providing manna and water in the wilderness and delivering their enemies into their hand as they entered the Promised Land. God doesn't seem to do the same miracle twice. In other words, we're not to learn a "formula" of how God works; rather, we're to learn to depend directly on Him as we learn to walk with Him. We're also to remember the times we've seen God work directly in our lives, answering prayer, leading or speaking to us, sustaining us, and transforming us. Finally and above all, we're to remember there is no other God than Him or like Him...daily. Remember!

—John Milligan

Prayer Starter: *Lord, help me to remember daily all the times You have been faithful.*

LONGING FOR HOME

But according to His promise we are waiting for new Heavens and a new earth in which righteousness dwells. (2 Peter 3:13-15a)

A friend of mine died yesterday and it got me thinking about Heaven. Wouldn't it be nice to live in a world where righteousness reigns and where justice is upheld? We look at this world and it just seems like there are so many things that are wrong and unfair. I know that this world will never be a place where justice and righteousness rule and I will just have to live with that. But I wonder if the injustice in this world causes us to long even more fervently for Heaven.

C.S. Lewis made an interesting statement: "If I find in myself a desire which no experience in this world can satisfy, the most probable explanation is that I was made for another world." I guess this is what is happening. I am longing for another world, one in which righteousness and justice are the standard. No wonder it is called "new Heavens and a new earth" – it will be so much different than the present one.

—Paul Wegner

Prayer Starter: *Lord, Your creation is so glorious. But I also long to be with You in Heaven.*

PERFECTIONISM

Not that we are adequate in ourselves to consider anything as coming from ourselves, but our adequacy is from God... (2 Corinthians 3:5)

Lie: God expects me to be perfect.

Perfectionism is like an octopus with tentacles that reach into a few or many areas of life. Some people are "closet perfectionists," that is, much of life may not look orderly or organized, but their sock drawer is neat and color coordinated. I know someone who neatly organizes the artificial sweetener packers, but I wouldn't call her a perfectionist.

These are mini perfectionisms. The problem deepens though when perfectionism consumes my life. I know because I'm a rehabilitated perfectionist. It consumed my thoughts and guided my behavior. It was so important to appear perfect to others. I nit-picked every detail in order to condemn myself for past mistakes or exalt myself for being perfect. In my thoughts, past conversations were never good enough and future ones could be perfect (In a perfect world only!).

You see, perfectionism demands a right or wrong, a black or white, or an absolute outcome. But it is a frustrating, elusive, and exhausting endeavor. At the very least, perfectionism will cripple one's heart. Instead realize any adequacy we now or will ever have comes from God alone.

—Nonie Maupin

Prayer Starter: *Dear Lord, I don't know what I was thinking striving for perfection. You are the only perfect and Holy One. You are God and I am not!*

UNRESERVED COMMITMENT

...But I followed the Lord my God fully. (Joshua 14:8b)

Leading approximately 100 Scottsdale Bible teens on a weekend venture to see the Havasupai Falls has always been etched in my mind and heart. We left the day after school recess began and drove to the Grand Canyon area. We began our journey in what was, for most of us, a wilderness experience of the first order. As challenging as it truly was to keep body and mind together, it was well worth the spiritual victories that were won in all of our lives. And we learned, as with many men of faith such as Abraham, Moses, Joshua, David, John the Baptist, Paul and our Savior Jesus Christ, that the wilderness environment is a well-established classroom of effectiveness. Caleb is also a biblical character who demonstrated in his wilderness journeys that his unreserved commitment did indeed carry him through to the end of his long and arduous trail of adventure with God.

Three times in Joshua 14 it declares that Caleb wholly followed God. It is one thing to follow God. But it is another thing to wholly follow God. We may say, "I have followed God for several years, now I have earned credits to do as I please." For Caleb, it was a 24/7 commitment to the Lord for a lifetime. The important thing to remember is that God wants all of us all of the time in order that He can bless our lives in ways we could not possibly otherwise experience. And this will be accomplished to the praise and glory of His name. Will you be like Caleb and wholly follow the Lord?

—W. Sherrill Babb

Prayer Starter: *Lord, take more of my life until I am wholly devoted to You.*

UNDERSTANDING THE BIBLE

Be diligent to present yourself approved to God as a workman who does not need to be ashamed, accurately handling the Word of Truth.
(2 Timothy 2:15)

Most Christians know the importance of studying the Bible. This book is our authority for all spiritual matters. It gives us wisdom for life. The Word of God is a biography and history of the Father, Son, and Holy Spirit as they interact with man, revealing His character and His perfect love for us and His desire to have an eternal relationship with us. There is no other book like it.

Many people find it difficult to understand the Bible, however. Fortunately, there are plenty of great resources available to help you understand the Bible. You can read books or attend classes that teach you how to observe, interpret, and apply Scripture. But most people neglect the best resource of all.

A good dictionary is the first tool for understanding the Bible, or any book for that matter. There are so many words we hear and use that we think we understand, but might be surprised to discover their true definitions: prodigal, glory, disciple, pastor, etc.

My first two rules of biblical interpretation are as follows (recite aloud and memorize):

- Rule #1: when reading the Bible, you come to a word with 6 or more letters—stop! Make sure you understand what that word means!

- Rule #2: when reading the Bible, you come to a word with 5 or fewer letters—stop! Make sure you understand what that word means!

A man who learned these rules brought a case of dictionaries to our class. He wanted everyone to experience the joy he now had as a result of better understanding the Bible. Try it.

—Dave Cottrell

Prayer Starter: *Lord, help me to understand Your Word, and then to obey Your Word every day.*

REJOICE

I praise You because I am fearfully and wonderfully made; Your works are wonderful, I know that full well. (Psalm 139:14)

While living in Nairobi, Kenya, Char was teaching first grade. Our science class was learning about the human body and how it works. We concentrated on our hands and how God made them so wonderfully. We do not have to adjust screws or apply oil or grease to our hands. As we opened and closed our hands one of the boys became very excited and said spontaneously, "Let's give God a clap!" And all the children clapped loudly for God.

Our Bible class followed and since all the children were so excited about the things God was doing, I gave them an opportunity after our devotional to accept Jesus Christ into their hearts. After a time of prayer, I asked if anyone had accepted Jesus today and if they wanted to share that with the class. The same boy raised his hand and said, "I accepted Jesus in my heart and it sure feels good!"

—Gary and Charlotte Shingledecker

Prayer Starter: *Thank you Lord, for the opportunities you give us each day to serve You. Let us marvel and rejoice in Your goodness to us today!*

GOD'S BETTER IDEA

*Fathers, do not exasperate your children, instead, bring them up in the training and instruction of the Lord. (**Ephesians 6:4**)*

Our children are pros at pushing all the wrong buttons on us. But that's a two-way street. They may know how to bring the worst out of us, but no one on earth wields as much power to do the same thing to them as we parents do. Like it or not, we are the gatekeepers of our children's self-perception. How we view them plays a huge role in how they ultimately view themselves.

It's easy to slip over the thin line that separates them from being people God has entrusted to our care, to being objects with certain labels…like students, or athletes, or the kids that live in our house. Once we start viewing them as objects, we're inclined to evaluate their performance in that role. They can end up the student who is operating way below his/her potential, the lazy athlete or the ungrateful kid living in our home, when value is tied to performance.

Exasperation happens when we do things that cause our kids to resent us--like consistently focusing on what's wrong with them. God has a better idea. He's dealing with us through the power of His grace. His advice is "Why don't you treat your kids the way I treat you?…with grace."

—Tim Kimmel

Prayer Starter: *O Lord, please help me view the people I love most through the lens of Your grace and encourage them through the power of Your love.*

THE BOOK OF LIFE

…The book of life of the Lamb who was slain. (Revelation 13:8b)

Recently, my son showed me one of his favorite phrases in the Bible. It is contained in Revelation 13:8. This is a dark part of Revelation dealing with the beast. However, the end of verse 8 contains a beautiful reference to Jesus and the book of life. Verse 8 ends with, "…the book of life of the Lamb who was slain." This references the book of life where the names of the elect have been written before the foundation of the world. My son suggested this phrase would make a great title for the book we call the Bible. It is true.

The greatest story ever told is the story of the Lamb who was slain. The beginning and the end have been written. It is perfect. It is His great play and we are blessed to be players in it. As Christians, our names are written into the story. We need to pause more often and be thankful that through God's grace alone we have been cast in His play! He is in full control and the drama is unfolding just as He wrote it.

Rejoice in this truth! Celebrate the glory of the story! Ask God to reveal the role He has cast for you. Most of all, live abundantly, walk worthy and glorify Him in your role in the book of life of the Lamb who was slain.

—David Scholl

Prayer Starter: *Lord, thank You for Your grace to include me in Your perfect story. Help me to know …*

GREATER TRUST

Thy kingdom come, Thy will be done, on earth as it is in Heaven.
(Matthew 6:10)

One way in which God's kingdom is enlarged in this world is by believers exercising greater faith by trusting Him more in everything.

A traveler could not continue his journey without crossing a frozen lake. Fearful that the ice might break, he crawled for hours attempting to reach the other side. Nearing the middle of the lake, he heard a noise behind him. Glancing over his shoulder he was shocked to see a farmer crossing the lake driving a team of horses and a fully loaded wagon. Explaining that the ice was several feet thick and could easily support the weight, the farmer finally encouraged the traveler to get into his wagon and ride to the other side. Just like that traveler, we so often behave the same way. We refuse to trust in God's providential care in every circumstance, thinking it too dangerous to surrender to His will.

Will you trust Jesus Christ with everything in your life? Your marriage? Your singleness? Your children? Your lack of children? Your occupation? Your lack of an occupation? Your health? Your lack of health? Meditate today on 2 Chronicles 16:9 and Proverbs 3:5-6. Trust God in everything and you will find that "the ice is thick."

—John Politan

Prayer Starter: *Lord Jesus, give me the grace to trust You in every area of my life.*

LISTING APPOINTMENT

...Do not be anxious about anything, but in everything by prayer and supplication with thanksgiving let your requests be made known to God. And the peace of God, which surpasses all understanding, will guard your hearts and your minds in Christ Jesus. (Philippians 4:6-7)

Many years ago, before I surrendered my life to Christ, I was the general manager of one of the largest residential real estate companies in Maricopa County. One of our strategies was to market homes on behalf of custom homebuilders who did not have their own marketing departments. It was a major source of revenue for our company, and therefore, very important to secure the accounts.

On most occasions, the negotiation for the account was done over lunch. Sometimes I would meet with a builder alone and sometimes the president/owner of my company would meet with us. Over time, I found that when I was meeting the builder alone, I would not enjoy the meal very much. I was too tense about whether or not I would obtain the account. When the president was there, I completely relaxed and enjoyed the meal. That was because I knew if we did not obtain the account, it was out of my hands. My thought was if the president could not get the job done, then certainly I could not have gotten it done!

Many times I have found myself fretting about an issue before I realized that I needed to give it over to God. To paraphrase what I said above, "If He could not get the job done, then certainly I could not get it done!" Not only do I enjoy meals more now, but I enjoy life more since learning to trust God, and allowing myself to enjoy His peace!

—Bob Cain

Prayer Starter: *God, I am really stressed out. Would You please guide me through this situation concerning...?*

LIKE PURIFIED OIL

May he kiss me with the kisses of his mouth… for your name is like purified oil. (Song of Solomon 1:2-3)

Do you know how they used to purify oil in Jesus' day? One method was to take a series of trays and stack them, one on top of another. In the top tray would be a large stone. In the tray directly beneath it were smaller stones, and on down in size until the final tray was filled with fine gravel.

The unrefined olive oil was then poured through each layer of rock and gravel so that all the impurities would be filtered out and the pure oil collected at the bottom.

In the book the Song of Solomon, we get a picture of a God-honoring marriage. There's certainly a desire for closeness and intimacy! ("May he kiss me with the kisses of his mouth.") There's a reason why Solomon's bride is so desirous of kissing him. "For your name is like purified oil." Like oil poured through trays of rocks to remove the impurities, Solomon has taken seriously the need to live an upright life.

No one is perfect. That's part of why we need a Savior. But when we choose to read our Bible, watch our tone of voice, pray with our spouse, treat our children with honor, be hospitable, and follow through with our friends, we build a track record of trust that makes a difference.

—John and Cindy Trent

Prayer Starter: *Lord, thank You for the reality of Your Word. It calls us to a high calling – like doing what's right and having a life of purity. But our relationship with You isn't based on "good works" or being "perfect" in Your eyes. You forgive us when we fall short and You keep us moving toward a righteous life. Help me, Lord, live the kind of life that shows those around that I'm committed to You!*

THE SHAPE OF THINGS

Do not be conformed to this world, but be transformed by the renewal of your mind, that by testing you may discern what is the will of God, what is good and acceptable and perfect. (Romans 12:2)

We care about the shape of things. I don't mean whether they are in round tubes or square boxes. I mean "the shape" of people's lives, situations, attitudes, or opportunities. Don't believe me? How often have your heard phrases like these?

- You're in great shape!
- Shape up!
- Things are taking shape.
- Don't get bent out of shape.
- Any way, shape, or form.
- Ship shape!

We humans have the unique ability to be shaped by our circumstances, by our relationships, and by our opportunities. Unfortunately that "shaping" happens naturally, particularly if we take a passive approach to life and let it "just happen" to us.

God has a better plan. Rather than being shaped (or "conformed") to the world, He wants you to be changed, or transformed. He wants to make you different from your natural mental, emotional, and spiritual "shape." The key is to take a step of action to move away from being passively conformed, to being changed by the active renewal of your mind.

Renewing your mind is the ongoing activity of thinking deliberately about the matters of your life, considering all things in the light of biblical truth. Inevitably, confronting the conventional "shape of things" with the transformational perspective of God will change you.

It's really quite a claim when you consider it. God has promised that if you let Him renew your mind, you will be able to test everything you encounter and be able to discern the Father's good, acceptable, and perfect perspective.

Let God's Word renew your thinking and discover the shape of your increasing faith in Jesus!

—Jamie Rasmussen

Prayer Starter: *God, renew my mind and transform me into Your disciple. Increase my faith.*

GOD'S REBUILDING

We…are being transformed into His likeness with ever-increasing glory, which comes from the Lord, who is the Savior. (2 Corinthians 3:18)

Our house needs a make-over. We returned from vacation and the house sighed, "I'm dingy."

I have to agree.

The interior paint is old. We've lived here 16 years and haven't painted yet. Well, we just painted the bedrooms where handprints showed up.

The new carpet we installed when we moved in was pretty much ruined by the time the movers left. The kitchen cabinets feel mysteriously "sticky", and our daughter Sarah says, "The cabinets are too dark. Paint them white, Mom."

I don't look forward to the process of making improvements in our house. Why can't everything just stay new and clean? It makes me look forward to my Heavenly home where everything is fresh.

In the meantime, I realize that God is doing a radical rebuild on me. He is not just repainting the walls; He is rebuilding me in the image of His Son. He is pulling out the habit of snapping at people and replacing it with a spirit of kindness. He is replacing self-focus with God-focus. He is prying my hands off of my belongings and reminding me that all I have is His. He is painting out self-indulgence and replacing it with an appetite for His Word. He is tearing down self-protection and replacing it with vulnerability.

—Nell Sunukjian

Prayer Starter: *Dear Lord, thank You that You are not interested in merely improving me, but in a radical change from the inside out into the image of your dear Son. I choose this day to co-operate with You, Lord.*

FRUIT INSPECTORS

*But the fruit of the spirit is love, joy, peace, patience, kindness, goodness,
faithfulness, gentleness, and self-control. Against such things there is no law.
(Galatians 5:22-23)*

Several years ago, before our children were born, some friends from the church invited Kristina and me to spend a weekend at their cabin up in Oak Creek Canyon. In addition to hiking, fishing, and working on a big puzzle, one of the memorable things we got to do was pick buckets full of blackberries. There were eight adults and two kids on that trip, if I remember right, and after awhile the berry-picking got a little competitive. Someone even fell in the bushes and refused to let any of her "competitors" help her up. She finally managed on her own, but came out covered with scratches all over her arms and legs. When it was over, there was some good-natured boasting about who picked the most berries and who had the most scratches.

It made me think about how often—in the Christian life—our boasting is not so good-natured. We can get pretty serious and sophisticated in our efforts to let others know how much fruit we've borne or what sacrifices we've made to get what we've gotten – after all, we've got the scars to prove it!

The Bible doesn't call us to be fruit inspectors or orchard managers, but simply to abide in a loving relationship with our Heavenly Father through Jesus Christ. This is the soil and climate in which the Holy Spirit can produce His fruit in us.

Rather than boasting about our fruit, let us be thankful! If my friend from church would invite me to stay at his cabin and send me home with a bucket of blackberries, how much more is God willing and able to supply all my needs?

—Joe Bubar

Prayer Starter: *Lord, thank You for Your gift of abundant, eternal life and for the 'fresh fruit' that Your Holy Spirit is producing in me.*

I WANTED THE LOBBY

Be still and know that I am God. (Psalm 46:10)

I have lost track of the number of times I have stayed in hotels.

500? More? I really don't know. But most hotels I stay in have elevators, and for every hotel visit, I must ride the elevator four times a day. If I have stayed in 500 hotels for three days each stay…well, you do the math. That number does not include buildings, department stores or hospital elevators. I tell you this because I want to assure you that I am a veteran elevator rider.

Think about how many elevator rides you have taken.

More than once, ok, often, ok ok, frequently, when the door of the elevator opens, I just go through it. It goes something like this: the door opens, I exit, I turn right, then left, and then I turn red. I have done it again…I am on the wrong floor.

I hear someone say, "This is the seventh floor." (But I am headed for the lobby.)

If I catch the mistake quickly enough, I can take my red face and hop back on the elevator. But usually the doors are too far closed. You are nodding—you have had the same experience. Actually, I surveyed some fellow elevator riders recently, and everyone agreed to having done the same thing repeatedly. Why? Here are my conclusions: I'm not thinking, I'll follow anyone, or I'll walk through any open door.

Suddenly the elevator doors are a symbol; they are like the doors in my life. A door opens and I feel the need to walk through. A friend initiates, a job is offered, or an idea pops into my head, and I exit what I am doing, and go through the doorway. Just because a door opens does not mean I need to move. I am not designed to enter every hallway or room.

"Be still and know that I am God. Be steadfast, immovable. Wait and see." These are the patterns of the Scriptures. It is true that God does open doors for us to walk through, but not every doorway is made for me to walk through. Some doorways are for me to catch a view and keep riding to my destination. My goal is the lobby, not another tour of the seventh floor. His destination is best!

—Donna Otto

Prayer Starter: *Lord, help me to "wait" for Your leading instead of taking every door that opens.*

BODY CARE

Blessed be the God and Father of our Lord Jesus Christ, the Father of mercies and God of all comfort, who comforts us in all our affliction, so that we may be able to comfort those who are in any affliction, with the comfort with which we ourselves are comforted by God. For as we share abundantly in Christ's sufferings, so through Christ we share abundantly in comfort, too. **(2 Corinthians 1:3-5)**

"Mom, I feel dizzy. . . ." These four little words are what I said to my mom before:

- My heart stopped beating and my mom administered CPR on me for 6 minutes.
- My husband, Tom, in Arizona, received a dire phone call from my mom, in Ohio, as she accompanied me in the ambulance.
- I was placed in a hypothermic coma to try to save my brain cells.
- I had had a cardiac arrest – at 47.

What we experienced after these events was truly the body of Christ in action:

- Prayer, and more prayer–from the minute Tom called Pastor Jamie, people began praying for me.
- Phone calls, emails, Facebook messages to get the word out happened immediately.
- Cards sharing beautiful and encouraging words and Scriptures were kindly sent.
- House cleaning – inside and out (after the historic haboob dust storm!) was lovingly done.
- Meals were faithfully prepared for weeks.
- Childcare for our four girls joyfully took place.
- Driving me and our girls to and from school and all our activities was patiently volunteered.
- Gift cards for our girls to enjoy a fun day of shopping were thoughtfully given.

In the midst of our afflictions, the body of Christ comforted us abundantly. In doing this, they were also able to rejoice with us in the miracle that God performed in our lives!

—Jennie Sharda

Prayer Starter: *Heavenly Father, thank You for the way in which You provide comfort to us through Your body of believers. Help us always to remember the ways in which we have been comforted, so that we may in turn comfort others to Your glory. Amen.*

HIS SPIRIT SPEAKING

Hear what the Spirit says to the churches. (Revelation 2:7, 29; 3:6, 13, 22)

A quick look through the Bible's pages shows that there are epistles written to fourteen churches. People are most familiar with the letters written by Paul to the churches in Ephesus, Collosae, Thessalonica, Philippi, Galatia, Corinth, and Rome. Even though these epistles were written to these specific churches, they were distributed among all the churches of that day, and over time have become part of canon. Today you can find these letters easily in your Bible's table of contents. These epistles have blessed you personally, and they have been the inspired source used by your pastors to preach messages of unity, hope, encouragement, direction, perseverance, joy, and faithfulness to your church.

The Bible includes seven additional church epistles that are often overlooked because they aren't set apart as individual "books" of the Bible. These are the seven letters dictated by Jesus to the apostle John, recorded in the book of Revelation. In five of the letters, the message concludes with the command, "Hear what the Spirit says to the churches."

In this simple instruction, Jesus clarifies that His message is unique in that through it, He speaks to the individual listener, to every listener, to the specific church being addressed, to every church exposed to the message, and to the church universal and historic.

It's common for a local congregation to try to identify with one of the seven Revelation churches. Most churches easily see the Smyrna or Philadelphia comparison and avoid being compared to Sardis or Laodicea. Yet Jesus wants every church today to understand that it has some of each of the seven churches in its personality. There is a bit of Ephasus, Smyrna, Pergamos, Thyatira, Sardis, Philadelphia, and Laodicea in every congregation. Accordingly, there is a congregational message to be heard, listened to, and followed.

Each church is exhorted to "Hear what the Spirit says." This reveals that the spirit of God is speaking now to our church in an ongoing way. He continues to speak through a timeless message given long ago. His Spirit is speaking even now to our church, guiding our future and directing our path.

—Bryan McAnally

Prayer Starter: *Lord, help all in our church to hear Your words directed to each of us.*

OBEDIENCE

For by grace you have been saved through faith. And this is not your own doing; it is the gift of God, not a result of works. (Ephesians 2:8-9)

The New Testament clearly teaches that justification (forgiveness and being counted righteous before God) comes to people only through faith in Christ. Jesus is offered to sinful humanity as Savior by God's grace alone.

But then Paul immediately says that God wants Christians to live in obedience to Him: "For we are His workmanship, created in Christ Jesus for good works, which God prepared beforehand, that we should walk in them." It is impossible to listen to the teachings of Jesus in the Gospels without hearing dozens upon dozens of moral commands, standards, warnings, and promises telling Christians how they should live in order to please God in their daily conduct. Therefore it must be seen as a matter of great importance to God that His people, who have been justified by faith alone, live every day of their lives walking in obedience to God's moral standards.

Empowered by the Holy Spirit, daily obedience expressing faith, loyalty, and love toward Christ will have a transforming effect.

—Wayne Grudem

Prayer Starter: *Help me be obedient to You today. I love You, Jesus.*

NO FEAR

I sought the Lord, and He answered me; He delivered me from all of my fears. (Psalm 34:4)

Psalm 34 speaks of God's protection and care for those who trust in Him. "No fear" was a slogan that was commonly seen on T-shirts – I wish I still had mine. Each of us has a "No fear" T-shirt given to us by the Holy Spirit, and we can confidently wear it every day; but it does take a disciplined desire of the heart to remind ourselves of it.

There are three simple phrases in today's verse. "I sought the Lord" – God longs that we seek regular fellowship with Him just as we would with our spouse, parents, or children. They long to simply hear our voice. When we seek Him we know He listens. The second phrase says "He answered me" – He is always there for me. Anytime I call He answers. But it gets better. The third phrase says, "He delivered me from all of my fears." What a promise!

Although we don't know what surprises or challenges lay ahead for us today, we do know that we can approach today without fear.

—Tom Sharda

Prayer Starter: *Lord, help me to remember these three simple phrases and your promise as I start my day. Whatever today holds let me approach it without fear.*

HOW TO PRAY

Elijah was a man with a nature like ours, and he prayed earnestly that it would not rain, and it did not rain on the earth for three years and six months. Then he prayed again, and the sky poured rain and the earth produced its fruit. (James 5:17–18)

Pray like Elijah! The name Elijah for James' original audience would have immediately inspired awe and respect. The name Elijah literally means, "YHWH (Yahweh) is my God." Elijah was known as one of the great, unwavering, bold prophets who God used in powerful ways. In 1 Kings 17 and 18, we learn that, by the Word of the Lord, Elijah confronted evil King Ahab, told him that there would be not rain - and there was no rain. He then told Ahab years later when there would be rain and there was rain. Elijah also multiplied flour and oil for a starving widow and her child, restored life to that same child, and called down consuming fire of the Lord before the prophets of Baal.

Such mighty acts can only be achieved through God's special empowerment. Although Elijah did these amazing things, James is quick to tell us that Elijah was a human being—just like you and me. James uses Elijah here as a model of how we are to pray!

—David Walther

Prayer Starter*: Lord, give me the confidence to pray like Elijah.*

TRUTH

Sanctify them in the truth; Your Word is truth. (John 17:17)

During the summer of 2009, my family and I traveled to Beijing, China, and walked on the Great Wall. A long gondola ride up the mountain and then another ride on a steep incline followed by another 500 steps dug into the rock, and there we were: standing on one of the highest points of the great wall and able to see for miles in every direction. This great wall, built over thousands of years, is a wall connected deeply to the earth, rising high to prevent enemies of China from entering.

But it didn't work then and is even more irrelevant today. Why? The reason is because modern telecommunications make boundaries porous. Information can now go over, around and through any physical barrier erected by man.

More important, there is no wall that can keep out the truth. Truth is stronger than any weapon. Tyrants fear mere individuals because they wield the enormous power of liberty rooted in truth. And both liberty and truth answer to a higher authority. "You shall know the truth and the truth shall set you free . . . If the Son has set you free, you shall be free indeed." (John 8:32, 36). "For no one can lay any foundation other than the one already laid, which is Jesus Christ" (2 Corinthians 3:11).

—Barry Asmus

Prayer Starter: *Dear Jesus, You are truly the way, the truth and the life. Only Your truth can bear the weight of a sinful world.*

THE DIVINE DESIGN

The Lord is…not wishing for any to perish but for all to come to repentance. (2 Peter 2:9)

God so loved the world…if it's true, how does He let all those people know?

You and I are created and redeemed to love, that we might glorify God by doing it.

"Beloved, let us love one another, for love is from God" (1 John 4:7). Love is from God. The source of all worth, for anything of worth, is in God. It is God who created everything, and it is God who sets the value on what He has created. When you take away God from anything…you take away its inherent worth.

"Everyone who loves is born of God, and knows God" (1 John 4:7). Those who know God know the worth of what God has created. "The one who does not love does not know God" (1 John 4:8). Those who do not know God do not know the worth of His creation.

"For God is love" (1 John 4:8). This is not something God does; it's something He is. Love is an attribute of God; as God is holy, so God is love. There is something in God which moves Him to give worth to what He makes. God values what He creates, no matter how it turns out—as compared to us, who value what we make only if it turns out the way we want.

What pain and misery is there around you? What have you done lately with the influence or power you have to relieve it? We are a people who care! This is part of God's plan. His divine design: to use us in carrying out His love, so others will know.

—Darryl DelHousaye

Prayer Starter: *God help me to carry out Your love.*

GOD'S GRACE

Now they took wives of the women of Moab: the name of the one was Orpah, and the name of the other Ruth. And they dwelt there about ten years. (Ruth 1:3)

Hold on! Here we are in the book of Ruth reading about a Jewish family living in a virtual paradise (Bethlehem, Judah). They leave the land and travel to enemy territory. And then Elimelech and Naomi's two sons (Jewish boys), marry Gentile women. What's wrong with this picture? The law that God gave to the children of Israel did not allow the descendants of Abraham, Isaac, and Jacob to marry Gentiles. Psalm 19:7 tells us that the law is good, it reflects who God is. The law is perfect, restoring the soul. The problem is that we, as sinful mankind, cannot keep the law. God, in His grace, reveals to us our sin and our need of Jesus.

God's grace pursues the family of Elimelech and God brings about restoration. While the theme of the book of Ruth is, "The glory of God," the subtheme is, "What the law didn't allow, God's grace allows."

In the book of Ruth, Boaz, a good Jewish boy with Gentile blood in his background (Matthew 1:5), marries Ruth, a Gentile. Boaz and Ruth are the great-grandparents of King David of Israel. And these people are all in the genealogy of Jesus (Matthew 1).

—Cathy Wilson

Prayer Starter: *Thank You, Lord, that Your grace reaches out to all mankind. I am so thankful that Your grace has pursued and captured me!*

REQUESTS OF GOD

…(1) Search me, O God, and (2) know my heart. (3)Try me and (4) know my anxious thoughts; and (5) see if there be any hurtful way in me… (numbers and italics added) **(Psalm 139:23-24)**

Have you ever lost something of value and hunted and hunted, searching and looking every place you can think of – even retracing your steps to places you have recently been? It is a deliberate effort and intent. To request God do this in your life becomes life-changing, as He gently but clearly shows areas that need to be made new.

Here the Psalmist has made five requests; requests that imply a desire to be exposed in all areas of life and accept changes as God deems necessary. To ask God to search, then try and know one's heart and thoughts leaves room for nothing hidden. For the request to reveal the hurtful, negative or sinful ways leaves no question this is a deeply serious request. It goes beyond a casual glance. This is a request of a person wanting to move beyond where they currently are.

Although God is the only one who already knows our hearts, to humbly open and present oneself to the searching care of our loving Father, are deeply intimate moments spent in His presence. The trusting Christian who makes these requests to God is requesting changes in their lifestyle of thoughts, attitudes, actions and results in changed lives. These changes will affect one's relationships and entire life. To pray this Psalm is a journey to having one's soul freshly restored and made whole. Will you pray it today?

—MaryAnn Morton

Prayer Starter: *Dear Father, I bow before You, desiring Your cleansing and restoring search through every area of my life. I ask for Your strength in stopping undesirable old habits, thoughts, and actions, and pray for Your strength in making new ones.*

PRAYING ALOUD

My Father, if it be possible, let this cup pass from me, nevertheless, not as I will, but as You will. (Matthew 26:39)

Our Heavenly Father is a personal God. So, He desires us to pray aloud, since praying silently can often result in prayers that are short and jumbled.

Can you imagine if we spoke to each other with just our minds? It would be nuts! "Did you like that movie? Oh! I smell popcorn! Boy, I really need to look into buying a new mattress. What did you like about that movie?"

But, when we pray aloud, we use our minds as if we're speaking to a person; hence, making our relationship with God more personable.

When Jesus prayed in the Garden of Gethsemane, He went ahead of His followers some distance and "fell on His face and prayed, 'My Father, if it be possible, let this cup pass from me; nevertheless, not as I will, but as You will.'"

Now, how was this prayer recorded unless Jesus prayed aloud? So go someplace where you won't be overheard and pray aloud.

—Joe Gordon

Prayer Starter: *Lord, enable me to speak to You as my personal God.*

IDENTIFIED IN CHRIST

For the Son of Man came to seek and to save the lost. (Luke 19:10)

Garbage Collector	Divorce Attorney	Tax Accountant
President of the USA	Housewife	TeleMarketer
Porn Star	Pastor	Surgeon
Pest Exterminator	Imam	Pimp
Career Criminal	New York Times Editor	Graphic Designer

By habit or tradition, we assign value to a person based on their title in relation to "what they do." Read through this list above, and see how these different titles bring out different feelings in you.

Once, Jesus had an important conversation with a man named Zacchaeus. Luke identifies this guy as a short, rich, chief tax collector. Even if Luke wasn't "ranking" him, it's evident that the people did. They called him a "sinner" and they thought less of Jesus because He chose to spend some time with this man of low value.

Jesus had a different label for Zacchaeus, though. He called him, "A son of Abraham." In Jesus' estimation, he was a child of promise and an heir of blessing. Jesus was able to make this distinction and assign proper value to Zacchaeus, because Jesus Himself was not merely the sum of others' estimation of Him as a prophet, a priest, a rabbi, or the son of a carpenter. He was all these things and much more. He was (and is) Messiah.

As Messiah (or Christ, if you prefer the Greek version of the same title), Jesus seeks out and saves people who are lost. People like Zacchaeus. Like me. Like you.

In seeking you out, Jesus identifies you not by the rank-and-value titles assigned to you by this world, but by the title of relationship given by God alone. He is seeking God's children, regardless of the title attached to them by choice or by circumstance.

In saving you, He is restoring your relationship with God into its proper context. This relationship isn't based on whether you're rich or poor, tall or short, Jewish or Gentile, or any other factor. It's based on the true you…who you are as God's adopted child.

Refuse to be defined by anything less than the full expression of your relationship with God through Jesus. Moreover, refuse to identify anyone else by a lesser title unworthy of their identity. Share Jesus with the lost, with hopes that they, too, may be identified in Christ as an heir of God's blessing.

—Bryan McAnally

Prayer Starter: *Lord Jesus, help me to regard myself and others as being Your child and heir.*

THE FOUR R'S

Let the Word of Christ richly dwell within you… (Colossians 3:16)

Relying on the Word of God is essential with a busy lifestyle. God's Word will rest your body, renew your mind, restore your soul, and refresh your spirit!

…And Thy words became for me a joy and the delight of my heart… (Jeremiah 15:16).

Begin to rest…are you worn-out and weary from a busy schedule? Come to me, all who are weary and heavy-laden, and I will give you rest (Matthew 11:28).

Begin to renew…do you need a new start in life? And do not be conformed to this world, but be transformed by the renewing of your mind… (Romans 12:2).

Begin to restore…have you been running on empty? He restores my soul; He guides me in the paths of righteousness for His name's sake (Psalm 23:3).

Begin to refresh…have you missed godly fellowship and teaching? For they have refreshed my spirit and yours… (1 Corinthians 16:18) …on the seventh day He ceased from labor, and was refreshed. (Exodus 31:17).

Dwell in God's Word today, and see the difference it will make in you!

—Susan Miller

Prayer Starter: *Lord, let Your Word penetrate my heart and change my life.*

PRAYER

Be anxious for nothing, but in everything by prayer and supplication with thanksgiving let your requests be made known to God. (Philippians 4:6)

Over the years I have learned how different people pray. One friend of mine paces back and forth and is very dramatic as he talks with God. Another friend kneels at his bedside each day when he prays. Still another sits in the same chair at the same time each day as he communicates with God. Others pray as they go throughout their day at work, in the car, or even in conversation with others.

Which of these is the best? The answer is yes. They are all adequate in communicating with God. Learning to talk to God is like learning to talk when we were children. If our parents anticipated our every need, handing things to us before we asked, we would never have learned to talk. We wouldn't have needed to.

There are four main ideas that I think about with regard to my prayer life. In the next 2 months I will expound on these.

—Patrick Sullivan

Prayer Starter: *Heavenly Father, thank You for allowing me to come to You at anytime and anyplace. May I never cease to seek Your face.*

NOTHING "MEEK" ABOUT THE MEEK

Blessed are the meek, for they will inherit the earth. (Matthew 5:5)

Mark was a former college football player who also spent four years in the Army as an Airborne Ranger. "One of the hardest verses in the Scripture for me to think had any real application to my life was this verse in Matthew," he said. "I didn't want to be 'meek' even if it was something I was supposed to do or be!"

But then Mark went to seminary, and in a Greek class, found out that the original meaning of the word "meek" didn't mean wishy-washy or weak – it literally meant "to be teachable!" Someone being arrogant wasn't a learner but someone open to learning something new was teachable!

Being "meek" can help us gain ground both on earth and in Heaven! That's because dropping our pride and being willing to "learn" something new can go a long way towards building a strong marriage and friendships.

—John and Cindy Trent

Prayer Starter: *There are words like "meek," Lord that sound so foreign and so different from what we tend to value in our culture. But thank You for clarifying something that can help us know more about You – and about each other. Lord, we ask You to make us teachable. Decrease our pride or any feelings of "knowing it all." Keep us students of each other and of You.*

GODLY PRIVILEGE

God loves a cheerful giver… *(2 Corinthians 9:7)*

The Greek word for cheerful is *hilaros* which sounds like "hilarious." God loves everyone, but I believe giving is a godly privilege. What prevents hilarious giving? The text says "grudgingly" and "of necessity." Anyone who gives unwillingly or because he has to is not a cheerful giver. Giving as one can afford it prevents hilarious giving. This is giving that makes no demand on God's ability. People who give until it hurts just continue to hurt. But through prayer, God may put a number regarding your money or your time in your heart that is absurd, yes, hilarious. God will give us anything that we will use to glorify Him. And yes, He knows our needs as well (2 Corinthians 9:10). Will you go before God and ask Him to make you into a hilarious giver?

—William Anthony

Prayer Starter: *Lord, place on my heart what You want me to give for You.*

RENDER SAFE PROCEDURE

For we do not have a High Priest who is unable to sympathize with our weaknesses, but one who in every respect has been tempted as we are, yet without sin. (Hebrews 4:15)

At the height of the Cold War in the 1980s, I was an Army bomb disposal officer. We had filing cabinets full of procedures for safely handling a Soviet ordnance. Occasionally, however, we would come across a "first seen ordnance" - something we hadn't encountered before. We had clear procedures to follow and then we documented the "render safe procedure" so the next guy who encountered it would know what to do in order to avoid a harmful explosion.

When it comes to temptations, we don't have any "first seen ordnance." Jesus has already seen it all and He gives us clear procedures for safely handling these temptations and avoiding harm. We have his documented "render safe procedure" (the Bible). We can consult others (seek wise counsel). Most importantly, we can go to the acknowledged expert for guidance (prayer).

It's so easy to get overwhelmed, fearful, and discouraged when confronted with temptations. Even worse, the Father of Lies tries to make us believe we are alone in our unique trials...except they are not unique. Always remember that Jesus knows exactly what you are going through. Not only that, but He gives you the strength, skills, and route to escape (1 Corinthians 10:13). There is no such thing as a "first seen ordnance" with God!

—Jim York

Prayer Starter: *God, grant me the courage and strength to stand in Your will, when confronted with the temptations of this world.*

EXCEEDING ALL EXPECTATIONS

You have probably heard the old saying, "There are two great certainties: 1) death, and 2) taxes." But I believe that they forgot one of the most important certainties. For those of us who have accepted Christ's gift of salvation, we have a Heavenly home waiting for us. Jesus talks about it in John. In the last week of Jesus' earthly existence Jesus left us a promise. Jesus says,

"Let not your hearts be troubled. Believe in God; believe also in me. In my Father's house are many rooms. If it were not so, would I have told you that I go to prepare a place for you? And if I go and prepare a place for you, I will come again and will take you to Myself, that where I am you may be also." (John 14:1-3)

These are great verses, but the last phrase is actually the most comforting to me – "That where I am you may be also." I don't know a lot about Heaven, but if Jesus is there – I want to be there. "Death is not extinguishing the light from the Christian; it is putting out the lamp because the dawn has come." (Unknown author)

—Paul Wegner

Prayer Starter: *Thank You for Your promise Lord Jesus. To be with You will be everything.*

YOUR WORD IS A LIGHT

Your Word is a lamp unto my feet and a light to my path. (Psalm 119:105)

I want to encourage you as you begin to think about the lies you believe. God and His Word really can speak to you. Since He speaks to me through Scripture, He can do the same for you. Let me explain.

I usually start my day with quiet, solo walks with God. During the dark winter mornings I use a light. If it weren't for my flashlight I wouldn't see a thing. I wouldn't be able to see the rock I have to step over. I wouldn't even be able to see where the trail turns. Indeed my flashlight reminds me of the light of truth. God's Word is my guiding light that directs me over and around dangers and temptations. His Word illuminates the narrow path I need to follow for my own good and in order to be obedient to my Savior.

Just the other day, I worried about a good friend. After a few minutes of fretful thoughts, the Lord whispered 1 Peter 5:7 to me: "Cast all your anxieties on me because I care for you." His Word is light even to my deepest thoughts.

—Nonie Maupin

Prayer Starter: *Awesome…You are awesome Lord. I'm so amazed at the strength of Your Word and sovereignty of Your presence that I can barely speak.*

UNWAVERING CONFIDENCE

…But, the Lord helping me, I will drive them out just as He said. (Joshua 14:12c)

Caleb was one of the twelve spies who Moses commissioned to evaluate the land God had set aside and promised for Israel. After forty days, ten of the men emerged with a conclusion that, although the land appeared prosperous, it was an impossible military strategy to conquer its inhabitants. The giants in the land would easily destroy the followers of Jehovah. Caleb, however, was determined in his conviction that his all-powerful God was stronger than the giants and he was willing to risk his life for the cause.

All of us must also decide for ourselves what will be our convictions in every area of our lives. Will we, like Caleb, go against the majority when they are wrong? Will we believe in the true and living God and the power of His Word?

Caleb was an individual who was not afraid of the tough things of life. At the age of eighty-five, he requested permission to fight the Anakites, who were known as the giants of his day. These were the younger generation of giants who had frightened the original Israeli spies four decades before. Caleb even boasted that he was as strong in his eighties as he was in his forties! Are we like those who, when given the choice between courage or retreat, slip away in defeat and land up far short of God's desires for us?

In Joshua 14:12 Caleb spends no effort in determining his own personal resources. He simply proclaims that, "The Lord helping me, I will drive them out just as He said." Although he could no doubt handle a sword or other weapons of his day, Caleb refused to rely in his own abilities. Instead, he focused on the power of God for him.

Confidence is defined as a state of trust or intimacy. We are fools if we place trust in ourselves or any other temporal being. Like Caleb, we need a long-term intimacy with God who created the universe. God's best hope for us is that we will unreservedly focus our convictions, courage and confidence in Him.

—W. Sherrill Babb

Prayer Starter: *Lord, convict me in the power of You and Your Word so that I may have unalterable courage and unwavering confidence in You.*

HUNGER FOR CHRIST

He has told you, O man, what is good; and what does the Lord require of you
but to do justice, to love kindness, and to walk humbly with your God.
(Micah 6:8)

As we were created, we were given free choice to accept Christ or not. Since readers of this devotional are most likely to be believers, even further, He has given us the free choice to grow in our relationship with Him, or to live most of our lives apart from Him and His intimate influence.

His desire is that we'd choose to become all that He created us to be. He wants us to hunger for His influence in our daily lives. He wants us to crave the intimacy with Him that He offers each of us, for such is the walk of a humble man.

It is out of the "who we are," that the "what we do" comes. We cannot fool God, even though we often try. We frequently fool ourselves and miss His most abundant blessings.

Spend some time today talking to Him about it and choose to follow His heart for your identity. You'll find His heart on the subject is far more exciting than the identity we've followed from the world's eye view.

—Donald Farr

Prayer Starter: *Jesus, help me to crave You in my daily life. Help me to walk humbly with You each day.*

RENEW

But those who hope in the Lord will renew their strength. They will soar on wings like eagles; they will run and not grow weary, they will walk and not be faint. (Isaiah 40:31)

When a colleague of ours in Colombia was kidnapped and killed by guerilla forces, we were faced with many circumstances that called for strength, energy, and wisdom. As house parents at the school for missionary children, our focus was on the children we had been called to care for and we had a houseful at the time of the funeral. We set the children to gathering flowers to make a wreath for the grave.

After the service, the children in our home as well as those in the community asked if they could come to the children's home to be together. We had a time of sharing and praying and mourning–a time to revitalize, and a time to go forward in His strength. God met us in our sorrow and renewed our strength. God is faithful!

—Gary and Charlotte Shingledecker

Prayer Starter: *Praise the Lord for renewing our strength to soar and run without weariness.*

TAKING CAPTIVE EVERY THOUGHT

We demolish arguments and every pretension that sets itself up against the knowledge of God, and we take captive every thought to make it obedient to Christ. (2 Corinthians 10:5)

"You don't have what it takes." "You'll never measure up." "There's no way you can jump-start this relationship." "You aren't qualified to speak to that subject in your kid's life." "Face it, you're addicted, and there's nothing that can change that."

Have thoughts like these ever crossed your mind? Maybe I should ask if they have crossed your mind in the past 24 hours. It's amazing how debilitating thoughts like these can seize our heart and hold the high ground in our daily life. But there is one thing all of these thoughts have in common. They would never emanate from the heart of God.

We worship the "I can do all things through Christ who strengthens me" God (Philippians 4:13). We trust in the "cast all your cares upon me for I care for you" God (1 Peter 5:7). We pray to the "if God is for me who can stand against me" God (Romans 8:31).

As Jesus countered Satan's falsehoods with Scripture (Matthew 4:1-11), we need to counter Satan's negative prompts in our minds with the truth of God's Word. However, unless we know the Scriptures, it is going to be pretty hard to "take every thought captive and make it obedient to Christ."

—Tim Kimmel

Prayer Starter: *Dear Lord, please help me become a diligent student of Your Word so that I can align the thoughts of my heart with the truth of Your Word.*

FORGIVENESS IN THE PARKING LOT

Be at peace with all man, as much as is possible within you. (Romans 12:18)

Forgiveness is a complicated concept. Many of us have heard lessons that are confusing and often in conflict with each other on the subject of forgiveness. They sound like: "Forgive and forget. Time heals all wounds. Forgiveness is required if you follow Jesus. How can you accept your forgiveness from Christ, if you are unwilling to forgive others? The only way to forgive someone is for them to confess." I can hear you nodding!

Being at peace with someone as much as is possible within me is about my desire and offer to forgive. It is all about me and my heart.

At my birth there was a breach in my mother's family. The men in her family never forgave her or my father for the indiscretion of conception before marriage. This breach lasted until she died at age 76. Unforgiveness tore a hole in the fabric of our family.

When my mother died, her two brothers, who live in different states, did not attend her funeral. Their absence was painful to me personally. They just didn't come. No one said anything. During the year that followed, I took the advice of my mentor who told me that forgiveness was simple, just not easy, and that forgiveness changed your heart and allowed God to work in others. As I reflect on her words now, I know she was saying let go. God is the only one who can fix the problem.

I forgave my uncles and moved forward. Six years later, feeling prompted of the Lord, my husband and I made a trip to see one of the uncles. We had no agenda for the visit except to see him, perhaps for the last time, as he was nearly 90 years old.

We arrived at his home to find the conversation quickly went to my mother's past, and I was given a gift of unequal treasure. It was a photograph of me. For the first time in my 65 plus years, I saw a photo of myself as a toddler. My tears flowed, and I was certain this was God's plan for our visit.

However, God had a greater gift. The God of reconciliation meant for my mother's family and me to be united. My uncle could not wait to draw me aside. There we were, in the parking lot on a beautiful crisp day, while everyone else went inside. He said, "Forgive me, I should have come to your mothers funeral. I regret my decision." I wept. He wept.

Forgiveness is life changing. Because I had made peace with God and my uncle as much as was possible with me, I could receive my dear uncle fully, quickly and completely. It was freedom for both of us.

—Donna Otto

Prayer Starter: *Lord, help me to forgive…help me to do all I possibly can to forgive others.*

FORGIVENESS

"And forgive us our debts as we also have forgiven our debtors." (Matthew 6:12)

One of the greatest hindrances to an effective prayer life is having an unforgiving heart attitude. How can we know if we have truly forgiven another "from our heart?" The Puritan Thomas Watson in his <u>Body of Divinity</u> sets forth seven elements which are part and parcel of true forgiveness. He tells his readers to:

1. Resist thoughts of revenge (Romans 12:19).

2. Don't seek to do the other person mischief or harm (1 Thessalonians 5:15)

3. Pray for God's blessing upon them (Luke 6:28).

4. Grieve over their losses, heartaches and calamities (Proverbs 24:17).

5. Pray for each member of their household (Matthew 5:44).

6. If possible, seek reconciliation with them (Romans 12:18).

7. Always be willing to come to their relief (Exodus 23:4).

Praying about these seven things for ourselves and the one who needs our forgiveness, we will not only ensure that our forgiveness is genuine, but will become more and more conformed to the image of Christ who, while suffering the agony of the cross, was able to say: "Forgive them Father, for they know not what they do."

—John Politan

Prayer Starter: *Lord, give me a forgiving heart. By Your grace enable me to sincerely practice each one of these seven elements to Your glory.*

THROW THE PASS

…Salvation belongs to our God, who sits on the throne, and to the Lamb!
(Revelation 7:10)

Back in the late 1950's, professional football was just coming into how we know it today. Television was instrumental in that transformation. In those days my hero of all heroes was the quarterback for my favorite team - the Baltimore Colts, Johnny Unitas. He was a future Hall of Fame quarterback.

One day I was watching the Colts on TV and they were down by four points in the final seconds of the game. In their own end of the field, they were down to their last play. Johnny dropped back to throw a long pass. They would win if it was caught, or they'd lose if it was not. It's called a "Hail Mary" pass–for good reason. Johnny's favorite receiver, Raymond Berry, was streaking down the field, looking over his shoulder for the ball.

After the play, the split screen on TV showed repeatedly that while the pass was still in the air, Johnny removed his helmet, turned toward the locker room, and walked off the field. His back was to the completion of the play! Asked later by a reporter why he walked away before the play was over, Johnny said very simply, "My role was to throw the ball. It was Raymond's role to catch it. I had done my part and the game was over for me."

God has called us to share the Gospel, the good news of Jesus, with others. We often think that the result of that sharing, someone's salvation, is our responsibility. It is not. That is God's responsibility. Like Johnny Unitas, we throw the pass and God does the rest.

By the way, Raymond caught the pass and the Colts won! And God will, too!

—Bob Cain

Prayer Starter: *Lord, thank You for changing hearts. Help me to share You daily by word and deed.*

UNCHANGING LOVE

Who is a God like you... He does not retain His anger forever, because He delights in unchanging love. (Micah 7:18)

Change isn't easy. Just ask Mike.

Mike's father was a salesman who worked for an aggressive, expanding company. That meant that his family was always moving – twelve times in his first fourteen years.

Each move was a different city and a different school. In each place there was the need to make new friends for some sense of stability. And thankfully, Mike's father always made sure of one thing. No matter where they went, they picked a place to live near an outstanding church.

Amidst the myriad of adjustments, there was always a strong congregation that became an anchor for them. And while the scenery kept changing, God's love was unchanging and His people helpful and caring.

Even if you're in the midst of lots of "changes" and moves, it's very helpful to have a God who "delights in unchanging love."

—John and Cindy Trent

Prayer Starter: *Lord, You always go ahead of us and You know how much we need a "home." Thank You that a great church filled with Your people can give us that sense of "home" even if we're in the midst of change. Help us, Lord, to be a helpful part of Your church – not just to help our home but to be a help to others in need of a "home" as well.*

WORSHIP

God is Spirit, and those who worship Him must worship in spirit and truth.
(John 4:24)

Sometimes God makes a statement that is so simple that I'm embarrassed by how complicated we make it out to be.

Worship is one of those areas. Countless divisions exist over music preferences, preaching preferences, or a dozen other preferences. There is no shortage of opinions of what constitutes reverent, spirit-filled, edifying worship (or what falls short of these ever-evolving standards). We have managed to make worship a tragically complicated topic of the spiritual life.

God has said it simply: He wants us to worship. He wants us to connect with Him. To do that, He wants us to be fully engaged in our worship experience. He wants us to be fully connected in spirit. He wants us to incline our souls completely toward Him in our worship actions. He wants our songs to be sincere and not rote. He wants our prayers to be heartfelt and not distracted. He wants our praise to be authentic, not hindered by shame nor self-aggrandizing. God wants your spirit to be silent and submissive to receive the manna He will provide to nourish your soul, even while your song is loud, heartfelt, and without restraint.

God also wants you to worship Him in truth. He wants your thoughts about Him to be right as well as righteous. He wants you to know Him and understand Him correctly. He wants you to build your praise and adoration for Him upon a foundation of what He has revealed about Himself through His Word.

Interestingly, it is impossible to truly worship God if He is worshipped incompletely. Worship in spirit without truth is passionate idolatry. Worship in truth without spirit is condemnable legalism. However, worshipping God in spirit and in truth is a beautiful harmony that wholly engages the creation in devotion of the redeeming creator.

—Jamie Rasmussen

Prayer Starter: *God, help me worship You with my whole mind and spirit focused on You; my Savior, Redeemer and Friend.*

CONTENTMENT

*Command those who are rich in this present world not to be arrogant nor
to put their hope in wealth, which is so uncertain, but to put their hope in
God, who richly provides us with everything for our enjoyment.*
(1 Timothy 6:17)

I want to make a fall bouquet from my California garden. I select deep red roses—Chrysler Imperial with its sultry smell is a favorite. I add several Gold Medal blooms for autumn color--the largest golden rose you have ever seen. Here's a Chicago Peace that is mostly yellow with just a few tinges of pink. I finish by picking a Don Juan red rose for variety and, oh yes, an orange Gerber Daisy that I hastily planted in the flowerbed last year. Just one bloom, but it looks nice in the arrangement. Beautiful!

God gives us all things richly to enjoy. Aren't so many of our enjoyments simple pleasures: like gathering a bouquet, or watching a gorgeous sunset, or seeing puffy white clouds against a blue sky, or how the mountains look after a rain?

As I think about contentment, I realize that some of the things that please me most have nothing to do with money. They are available to each of us: a smile from a clean baby, the smell of the ocean, the desert at sunrise, a cup of tea early each morning, and the knowledge that I am deeply loved by God.

—Nell Sunukjian

Prayer Starter: *Dear Lord, may I be content and find joy in all You provide. Enable us not to put our hope in money, but to find enjoyment in simple delights. Help us to send our money on ahead by storing up treasures in Heaven.*

A GENTLE SPIRIT

Brothers, if anyone is caught in any transgression, you who are spiritual should restore him in a spirit of gentleness. (Galatians 6:1a)

Here's how I used to interpret this simple verse in my mind:

"Brothers (fellow Christians), if anyone in your church or community is caught in any transgression – no matter how serious, like adultery or stealing or even murder – you who are spiritual (the pastors and elders of the church) should restore him in a spirit of gentleness. Don't overreact, but calmly, lovingly, speak the truth and administer discipline – or let the governing authorities do so, as the case may be – in hopes that the offender will humbly recognize their error, and will gratefully receive the mercy and forgiveness so graciously offered to them, and eventually – not immediately of course – return to full fellowship – or even, possibly, to a position of leadership – in the church."

Our fifth child was born last summer, and this year I read something in a book called The Peace Maker, by Ken Sande that has intersected with my daily life circumstances and opened my mind to a another possible interpretation of this verse...something along these lines:

"Brothers and sisters and moms and dads, if anyone in your family is caught in any transgression – no matter how small, like refusing to finish their dinner, or forgetting to make their bed, or making the rest of the family late for an outing of some sort – you who are spiritual (any Christian with an ounce of spiritual maturity, but especially parents) should restore him in a spirit of gentleness. Don't overreact, but calmly, lovingly, speak the truth and administer discipline – or let the parents do so, as the case may be – in hopes that the offender will humbly recognize their error and will gratefully receive the mercy and forgiveness so graciously offered to them, and eventually – perhaps even immediately – return to full fellowship in the family."

—Joe Bubar

Prayer Starter: *Heavenly Father, thank You for reminding me that "love is not irritable." (1 Corinthians 13:5) help me love those closest to me with the affectionate love that You have shown me, and help me be a better steward of the influence – no matter how small – You've allowed me to have in their lives."*

LIVE IN THE MOMENT

Yet you do not know what your life will be like tomorrow. You are just a vapor that appears for a little while and then vanishes away. Instead, you ought to say, "If the Lord wills, we will live and also do this or that." But as it is, you boast in your arrogance; all such boasting is evil. (James 4:14-16)

How much of our lives do we waste in trying to control that which is not ours to control? "The mind of man plans his way, but the Lord directs his steps" (Proverbs 16:9). We are certainly called to consider the future and to lean on the wisdom God provides us in planning our way in this life, but when we go beyond that and try to control that way, we move into the arrogance about which James warned us. Even worse, since we have been "called according to his purpose" (Romans 8:28b), it is a sin when we try to rely on ourselves for the control of the future. Like all sin, our attempt to control the future is ultimately fruitless.

God does not want us to "live" in the future, which we cannot know, but rather simply in the moment, relying on His unfailing provision. Jesus said it best. "Do not worry about tomorrow; for tomorrow will care for itself (Matthew 6:33). We have enough trouble just handling today.

Embrace the freedom that comes from relying solely on God for the control of the future. Rely solely on God as you live each moment in the joy of an unfettered relationship with the Lord of the universe. Rely solely.

—Jim York

Prayer Starter: *Heavenly Father, grant me the strength and wisdom to rely solely on You.*

SYNCING UP

But as for me, my prayer is to You, O Lord. At an acceptable time, O God, in the abundance of Your steadfast love answer me in Your saving faithfulness.
(Psalm 69:13)

Synchronization or "syncing" is an important piece of technology that has come of age in this generation. We all know that data synchronization between our favorite devices is necessary to keep all of the facets of our daily lives organized and congruent.

However, I am thinking of a different kind of synchronization – the syncing up of my inner life – thought chatter going on inside my mind – with my outer life – the various events that affect my body and mark the passage of time.

As I think about it, the more proper way to describe what I am thinking may be the ability to be "in the moment" with both my body and my mind. One thing is certain – to be in the moment, I will need to slow down the rapid movement of the inner thought chatter.

I have heard the term "flight of ideas" to describe the meandering thought processes of a mind spun up on frenetic energy. Thoughts do literally fly through our minds in brilliant, imaginative and unrestrained ways. Slowing them down takes an intentional effort!

I picture two wheels of sensory input turning at different rates – an inner wheel and an outer wheel – which I then work to connect so that they sync together in tempo, speed and duration. Only then can I truly relax into the moment and not miss the significance of where I am on my spiritual timeline – time being the medium for the passage of predestined events throughout the course of my life.

Wow! Heady stuff! But it's necessary to understand the significance of the things that happen to me. Significance is so often obscure or indirect. My only hope is to be alert to the possibility of something having major significance even though it may be disguised and then hope and pray that I "get it" when it happens.

—Holly DelHousaye

Prayer Starter: *O Lord, slow me down to catch the significance of the events of my life. Help me get what You are trying to tell me. Help me commit to syncing up instead of being out of sync most of the time…You are my only hope!*

THANK YOU GOD

For I am convinced that neither death nor life, neither angels nor demons, neither the present nor the future, nor any powers, neither height nor depth, nor anything else in all creation, will be able to separate us from the love of God that is in Christ Jesus our Lord. (Romans 8:28,29)

You are the God of Abraham, Isaac and Jacob and You are my God. I marvel daily that You have chosen me to be one of Your own! My life is peppered with sin. My thoughts are not pure. My actions and deeds do not honor You. Yet Your love for me continues. Thank You for the Word You have given me in the Bible that says nothing can separate that love You have for me – nothing!

There are so many words to describe Your majesty and power, yet there are not enough words to begin to reveal all that You are to me today. As we talk, You are the Perfect Listener and the Perfect Responder. I humble myself before You and seek to bare my soul to You. Thank You for Your listening ear, although You already know my heart.

I confess I am a sinner of the worst kind and am not worthy to enter Your presence. However, because Your Son Jesus died on the cross to take the punishment of my sins, I can boldly and reverently speak to You with a humble heart. I love You with all my heart, soul and mind.

My prayer today is a simple one. I pray that all people would follow Your commandment to love one another. It would be a world that would live in harmony as You designed it. Specifically help me to be a loving person to everyone I meet, even those that are tough to love.

I love You today, Lord Jesus, but You love me more!

In the name of Jesus the Christ, the Messiah, the anointed one of God -Amen.

—Gary Phipps

Prayer Starter: *Most gracious and merciful God...*

SERMON ON THE MOUNT

When Jesus saw the crowds, He went up on the mountain; and after He sat down, His disciples came to Him. He opened His mouth and began to teach them, saying,... (Matthew 5-7)

Would you be willing to read Matthew chapters 5–7 every day for a month? These 111 verses take about 10 minutes to read. Get ready for positive change.

Jesus walked and talked humbly. The holy one never acted holier than thou. The One who knew it all never acted like a know-it-all. The One who owned it all never strutted it at all. Blessed are the poor in spirit, the meek, the merciful, the pure in heart. Pride is the ultimate sin and the complete antithesis of the kingdom walk. If pride is the ultimate sin, then humility must be the ultimate virtue.

The Sermon on the Mount says to keep your giving quiet, even a secret. The same is true when you pray—not by sounding a trumpet but quietly, humbly praying.

Now, I do not want to steal the joy of God speaking to you in these verses, but consider the possibilities: speaking the truth in love; thinking of others before yourself; keeping secrets; staying calm under stress; being willing to wait; doing what's right because it is right; loving God, not money; building your life on a rock. When Jesus says in the Lord's prayer, "Thy kingdom come, Thy will be done," He's asking that God's will be sought and obeyed, that our actions be pleasing to Him. Take the challenge. It may just change your life.

—Barry Asmus

Prayer Starter: *Dear God, help conform me to the image of Christ, "Who, for the joy set before Him endured the cross", so that I may be saved.*

MINISTRY

Let the Word of Christ dwell in you richly, teaching and admonishing one another in all wisdom, singing Psalms and hymns and spiritual songs, with thankfulness in your hearts to God. (Colossians 3:16)

The church is supposed to minister to God, to its members and to the world.

Ministry to God is done through worshiping Him. Paul tells us how to worship. Worship in the church is not merely a preparation for something else; it is in itself a fulfillment of a major purpose of the church, whose members were created to live for the praise of God's glory *(Ephesians 1:12).*

The church's ministry to its members is done through nurturing and building them up so that the church can "present everyone mature in Christ" (Colossians 1:28). As Paul said in Ephesians 4:12-13, the church's gifted leaders were given "to equip the saints for the work of ministry, for building up the body of Christ, until we all attain to the unity of the faith and the knowledge of the Son of God, to mature manhood, to the measure of the stature of the fullness of Christ."

The church's ministry to the world is done through preaching the Gospel to all people in word and in deed. What is your ministry?

—Wayne Grudem

Prayer Starter: *God, help me praise You in worship and reflect Christ to my family and friends and the world.*

SHARE YOUR HEART

Father, if You are willing, remove this cup from me. Nevertheless, not My will, but Yours be done. (Luke 22:42)

Just before Christ was arrested and eventually crucified, He went with His disciples to the Mount of Olives to pray. Christ had full knowledge of God's plan and the events to come, and yet He still prayed –"If you are willing, remove this cup from me." In this prayer Christ modeled to us the freedom we have to share the desires of our heart with our Father. Knowing we have this freedom we find peace in knowing that God remains sovereign, and yet He desires to hear our heart through our prayer requests to Him.

Perhaps today you are in dire circumstances financially, your marriage is in trouble, you have a child that is a behavioral challenge or does not know Christ, or some other situation that is heavy on your heart. Take these to the Lord – share your heart with your Father. Find rest and security in knowing that our Father is sovereign, and yet He desires to hear our heart through our prayer requests.

—Tom Sharda

Prayer Starter: *Father, we acknowledge that we have the privilege of living out the plans You have for us – for You are sovereign. We do however have desires of our heart – if You are willing, please grant us these requests.*

WISDOM FROM ABOVE

But the wisdom from above is first pure, then peaceable, gentle, reasonable, full of mercy and good fruits, unwavering, without hypocrisy. (James 3:17)

There is no shortage of so-called wisdom that the world, our culture, and media have to offer. But the wisdom that James refers to here comes down from above and manifests itself in fruit sprouting from the heart in which it has been planted. The fruit is not merely ornamental but is displayed in the faithful through character traits and behaviors.

This wisdom is pure, set apart, and free from sin and defilement. Like God Himself, this wisdom contains no double-mindedness, mixed motives, or wavering. The one who follows Christ faithfully, likewise, does not serve God and someone/something else, too. He or she belongs only to his or her Master and trusts and obeys because of His incomparable love and Holy Spirit empowering.

According to James, one possesses this wisdom when one's heart is set on Him, one's tongue or words are reflecting his or her heart, and one's thoughts, actions or behaviors are simply an outpouring of his or her heart set on Christ alone.

—David Walther

Prayer Starter: *Lord, grant me this wisdom, as I meditate on You alone. May I manifest this wisdom with peacefulness, gentleness, reasonableness, being full of mercy and good fruits, unwavering and without hypocrisy. In short Lord, may I be like Jesus today.*

SUBSTITUTIONAL SACRIFICE

For He [Jesus] has appeared once and for all at the end of the ages to put away sin by the sacrifice of Himself. (Hebrews 9:26)

Just think. Though Jesus was God, He made Himself nothing and took the form of a servant and became obedient to the point of death, even death on a cross. He was wounded for our transgressions, bruised for our inequities, and with His stripes we are healed. His suffering and death produced our salvation.

Have you ever stopped to think how often blessing comes after sacrifice? For example, pregnancy is often accompanied by sickness and birth always brings pain—one mother compared her delivery to giving birth to barbed wire. But then? No words can describe the joy of that precious, tiny, beautiful bundle of sheer love. The blessing now supersedes pain. But it is not a quid-pro-quo kind of blessing. It's now all-out, 100 percent attention and sacrifice for this new baby, where parents give up most of their independence and freedom for their children.

Tim Keller has said that "All life-changing love toward people with serious needs is a substitutional sacrifice. If you become personally involved with them, as you should, their weaknesses flow toward you as your strengths flow toward them." He's right. That is what Jesus has done for us!

—Barry Asmus

Prayer Starter: *Thank You God for Jesus' sacrifice. I lay my sacrifices at Your feet.*

HITTING BOTTOM

For My thoughts are not your thoughts, neither are your ways My ways…for as the Heavens are higher than the earth, so are My ways higher than your ways, and My thoughts than your thoughts. (Isaiah 55:8–9)

We try too often to figure it all out, and keep it all under control – in other words, to deliver ourselves from our affliction. We try to handle the fear, run from the pain. God says, "Humble yourselves under the mighty hand of God" (1Peter 5:7).

What's going on?

The issue is total dependence on God. Paul spoke of great affliction: "We were burdened excessively, beyond our strength, so that we despaired even of life; indeed we had the sentence of death within ourselves…" Why? "…in order that we should not trust in ourselves, but in God who raises the dead" (2 Corinthians 1:8–9). When Paul's own strength was gone, there was nothing else he could do. He had to trust God…or else curse Him, and die. (Job 2:9–10)

When we finally hit the bottom, we realize the bottom is the palm of God's hand.

It's been said that pain plants the flag of reality in the fortress of a rebel heart. Pain reduces us to a primary level, the level of dependence on our God.

That's why some of us have to hit bottom before we're willing to look up.

—Darryl DelHousaye

Prayer Starter: *God, help me to depend on You.*

HOPE

Turn back, my daughters, go – for I am too old to have a husband. If I should say I have hope… (Ruth 1:12)

The book of Ruth is the eighth book in the Bible. The word "hope" is first used in Scripture in the book of Ruth. The Hebrew word for "hope" carries the meaning of expectation – that for which I long. The root concept for "hope" comes from the idea of twisting or binding a rope and applies to strength.

As we read Naomi's words, in what is she hoping? Her tone appears quite mournful. As you ponder her comments to her two daughters-in-law in this passage, reading the remainder of verse 12 through verse 13, you might be thinking, "This is hope?" Naomi's speech sounds negative. Actually, Naomi is sarcastic. Naomi is downright bitter. Several verses later in chapter 1, Naomi is brutally transparent, talking to her friends. "Don't call me Naomi, call me Mara, for the Almighty has dealt very bitterly with me." Naomi is not exactly what you would call jubilant!

Circumstances in life might not appear hopeful to us. Sometimes our "hope" is merely, "I hope, I hope, I hope." In those times our hope is empty because the object of our hope is not Jesus. If our hope resides in anything apart from God, there is no strength. Our hope must have Jesus as its object. He is our Refuge, our Rock, our Strong Tower.

—Cathy Wilson

Prayer Starter: *I praise You Lord, for You alone are my hope and strength!*

FIRST-CALL LIST

Here am I. Send me! (Isaiah 6:8)

A last minute need for parents to supervise junior high students at an event found me uncomfortably deciding who to "cold-call" for help. Using a list of parents from a previous event, I first called the ones I knew best. Next, I tried people I knew less well, but had worked with before. Lastly, I called people I did not know at all, but who had been recommended by others I trusted. There were a few I skipped over, sensing they would not want to be called or that they would not be easy to work with. In the end, I was only able to enlist the help of Kathy and Lori. But with two capable, trustworthy people like these, it was enough!

As I thought about my own spiritual condition, I wondered whether I am on God's first-call list? Would He call me first when a need arises, confident that I would not let him down? Or would He pass over my name because I have proven untrustworthy or not very helpful?

It was hard work controlling all those junior high students that night, but it was a pleasure to work with Kathy and Lori. I want to be the kind of person that people are glad to work with, even on an unpleasant task.

—Lauren Locker

Prayer Starter: *If You can't call me for some reason, Lord, please change me. I want to be on Your first-call list.*

STANDING ON THE PROMISES

And this is the confidence that we have toward him, that if we ask anything according to His will He hears us. (1 John 5:14)

George Muller cared for ten thousand orphans over sixty years, relying only on faith and prayer. He never asked for money, though he regularly asked for more orphans. One morning, with no food on hand, he seated the orphans around the breakfast table and prayed. Just then, a knock came at the door. A baker told him, "I was awakened at 2 a.m. and felt I should bake some bread for you."

Within minutes came another knock. A milkman said, "My milk wagon just broke down in front of your place. I must get rid of these cans of milk." Muller meticulously recorded thousands of similar instances in his journals. To what did he attribute God's continual provisions? He always satisfied himself that he was doing God's will before he started a project. Then he stood on the promises of the Bible that God will provide.

—Joe Gordon

Prayer Starter: *Lord, shape my prayers with the Word of God so that I can stand confident with my requests.*

TOO MANY SAVIORS

For I am the Lord your God, the Holy One of Israel, your Savior. (Isaiah 43:3)

In our family, when a song sticks in your head and won't go away, we call it an "earworm." Lovely, I know. When I get a Chris Tomlin earworm, it's a caterpillar that becomes a beautiful butterfly in my mind, allowing me to meditate on the glory and wonder of God. When it's a Macarena earworm, the experience isn't nearly so glorious, and I begin combing through the radio stations looking for a new song to swoop in and devour the one currently chewing on my very last nerve.

Pastor Jamie recently shared a simple phrase that has become an earworm, boring itself deep into my brain. He wasn't even singing. I don't remember his exact words, but the earworm has reduced the message in my brain to, "You have too many saviors."

I have too many saviors. It wasn't an accusation. It was a warning.

I, like you, believe that Jesus alone is Lord. He is my Savior, my Lord, my King, and God. By no other name than Jesus is a person rescued from hell and restored into relationship with God forever.

This earworm, though, is a conviction to take inventory, and be honest with myself if there's anything that I'm propping up as a savior.

For the Christian, the "too many saviors" are the things that may look a lot like Jesus, or share some of the characteristics of Jesus, or may reflect Jesus, but aren't Jesus. Beliefs like: going to church will save me, or obeying the Ten Commandments justifies me, or volunteering my time earns me points toward salvation, or reading my Bible will earn my way to Heaven. If these things don't point to the person of the Savior Jesus, they are distracting from Him. The truth is, none of those dozens of distracting things that vie for your attention and devotion are a savior.

Only Jesus can save you.

If there's anything "not Jesus" that you're propping up as a savior, tear it down. Even if it's really "Jesus-y." May it be said of you that you have only one Savior, Jesus, and you share Him with others every chance you have.

—Bryan McAnally

Prayer Starter: *Lord Jesus, You are my only Savior. Help my focus to be entirely on You. Help me to share Your love and saving grace at every opportunity.*

RESTING IN JESUS

Yet those who wait for the Lord will gain new strength; they will mount up with wings like eagles, they will run and not get tired, they will walk and not become weary. (Isaiah 40:31)

Sometimes when we are overwhelmed and stressed out in life, we are often too busy and distracted from the one thing that will restore us. I remind you to "come near to God and He will come near to you" (James 4:8). Stay in God's Word. Run to the shelter of His arms and take everything to Him in prayer. Rest in Him and rely on His strength, not your own.

Your relationship with Christ is a vital part of taking care of yourself. At times you can feel physically exhausted. Emotionally you can feel drained. Spiritually you can feel dry. When you are running on empty, nothing can fill you like Jesus. "Come to me, all you who are weary and burdened, and I will give you rest" (Matthew 11:28).

—Susan Miller

Prayer Starter: *Oh God, I desperately need You! I am worn-out and weary from the heavy load I am carrying. Fill me with Your presence and Your peace. Give me rest and strength for each day. I run to You and yearn for Your arms of comfort.*

PRAYER

But seek first His kingdom and His righteousness, and all these things will be added to you. (Matthew 6:33)

The following are the first two ideas with regard to my prayer life.

1. Gaze and glance

I always want to remember that God is bigger than any of my situations. I want to spend most of my time gazing at Him and glancing at my situation and not the other way around. If I spend my time gazing at my situation and just glancing at God when I think I need Him, He becomes smaller than my situation. (Ephesians 6:18)

2. Seek the face of God before seeking the hand of God

Too often I have found myself only going to God when I needed something from Him. What I try and do now is remember who He is and what He has done in my life and thank Him for those things before bringing my requests to Him (as if He doesn't already know). One of the ways that I do this is by praying Scripture. Many of my thoughts have been captured by some of the biblical authors, especially in the book of Psalms. Many times I will open to one of the Psalms and read a verse or a phrase and then stop and talk to God about that verse or phrase. This helps me keep focused as I pray.

—Patrick Sullivan

Prayer Starter: *Heavenly Father, help me seek Your face first. I know You are bigger than any of my situations.*

GOD WITH US

After this I looked and there before me was a great multitude that no one could count, from every nation, tribe, people and language, standing before the throne and in front of the lamb. They were wearing white robes and were holding palm branches in their hands. (Revelation 7:9)

The sun cast long shadows across the valley floor, as the day was ending in this land of the Sabaot people of Eastern Africa. I was watching the children running back and forth. They were tending their goats and lean cattle from straying off the trail. The trail led to the crossing of a fast moving stream and then on to their village.

Then I saw her, being passed by the others, as she slowly moved along the trail. She was old and bent like the trees high on the mountain that struggle against the wind. A bundle of sticks were tied upon her back and a crooked one within her hand was used for a cane. I longed to sit with her and hear the stories of her life's joys, sadness's and fears, but I did not know the Sabaot language.

I imagined what they might be: joy as a child when she ran and laughed as the children on the trail today; sadness while burying some of her children at a very young age, as this is commonplace here; fear of tribal wars, or the elephants coming down the mountain eating their gardens and destroying the crops. They do not like to speak of these events as they fear talking of them may cause it to happen again.

The Larsons and the Leonards followed God's calling on their lives. Iver Larson and Henny Leonard spent years of their lives learning the Sabaot language. After learning the language they then proceeded to make an alphabet for the Sabaot. Using this they could then teach the people how to read and write their own language.

The people now say, "God is here with us and He speaks Sabaot! He has not forgotten us!"

—Roy Fritz

Prayer Starter: *I pray the old woman heard God's Word in her native tongue and the whole story of John 3:16. I would like to meet her at the wedding supper of the Lamb described in Revelation 19:9.*

TAKE GOD ALONG

...And behold I am with you always, to the end of the age.
(Matthew 28:20b)

The last words of Jesus, spoken at the end of the Great Commission, are often overlooked but they carry a great deal of importance to every Christian.

Isn't it awesome to know that God, revealed in Jesus and powered by the Holy Spirit, is with us all the time? He's there with us in the good times and the bad times.

This is not to put limits on God by putting boundaries on Him. Not only is He with each one of us, but He is omnipresent (always everywhere). However, we are privileged to have all of Him with all of us all the time!

Then a good question to ask ourselves would be: where are we taking God in our daily walk? Are we taking Him to places that please Him, or are we taking Him where He might not be so pleased to go?

Let's consider the day ahead. Do we want to take Him to an adulteress affair, a dishonest business deal, a day at the casino, a drunken night at a club or bar, a gossip session, or a situation where we use His name in vain? I don't see how these (plus many more) would be pleasing to Him.

Consider a few places, which are by no means exhaustive, that please Him: a Bible-based Christian church, a soup kitchen to serve hungry people, a quiet place where you can read and meditate on His Word, a hospital to visit a lonely person, or anywhere you can show His love to anyone.

I think we get the idea. God is with us everywhere we go! He is even with you as you are reading these few paragraphs. He loves you and wants the best for you. So today, consider what He has done for you and walk accordingly. Where are you taking Him today?

—Gary Phipps

Prayer Starter: *Loving God, thank You for being with me all the time.*

SO WALK…IN HIM

And now just as you trusted Christ to save you, trust Him, too, for each day's problems; live in vital union with Him. Let your roots grow down into Him and draw up nourishment from Him. See that you go on growing in the Lord, and become strong and vigorous in the truth you were taught. Let your lives overflow with joy and thanksgiving for all He has done.
(Colossians 2:6-7)

Can you remember the excitement of inviting Jesus into your heart – the desire to make Him Lord of your life, the unquenchable thirst to study His Word, the desire to know Him intimately? You said, "I'm a child of the King! I've been adopted into His family." And then you asked yourself, "What now? Where do I go from here? How do I learn to trust Him? What does it mean to 'walk in Christ?' "

Grasping the profound truth of walking by faith is a life-long journey, but the knowledge that we can have deep roots in our Savior gives us the resources and confidence we need to live each day for Him. The more we nourish our minds with the truth, the deeper our roots will grow, and the more we will experience the joy and peace that comes from God. Then, as we see and trust His hand in our lives, our hearts will overflow with gratitude.

—Archie Wright

Prayer Starter: *God, please help me to be rooted in Your love and truth and to learn more each day what it means to trust you and walk in You.*

LOSING GOD'S SPLENDOR

The women of my people you evict, each from her pleasant house. From her children you take my splendor forever. (Micah 2:9)

This is an amazing little phrase tucked into Micah that I know I have read over many times, but really never fully understood its meaning.

Basically the nation of Israel was going through very hard times. So apparently when the Israelite women (whose husbands were probably off at war or passed away) could not keep up on the payments for their houses, the rich landowners were kicking them out of their homes. What God says is that the message sent to the children when people act that way is that God could not take care of their family so they were kicked out into the streets. It says, "From her children you take My splendor forever;" meaning what child would want a God who cannot protect and provide for them?

Did you ever realize what message you send to a person in need when you share a cup of cold water in Jesus' name? You must have a generous God or why would you do it? The reverse is also true. Let's make sure people know that we have a gracious and generous God.

—Paul Wegner

Prayer Starter: *Dear God, let me reflect Your generous, kind and loving nature. Give me the opportunity to extend Your grace and love to someone in need today.*

GOD-BREATHED

Every Scripture is God-breathed – given by His inspiration… (2 Timothy 3:16)

The original Superman television show gave him quite an introduction. "Faster than a speeding bullet—more powerful than a locomotive—able to leap tall buildings in a single bound." What we have in our relationship with Christ is much more powerful and transformational. We who trust Christ as our Savior have the Holy Spirit and the Holy Scriptures. Realize, men and women, that the Bible is not mere words on a page. His truth is God-breathed. Say it with me: it is written…it is written…it is written! Superman was a fictional character, God is God.

When I'm tempted to believe that God expects me to be perfect, remind me that it is written: "Not that we are adequate in ourselves to consider anything as coming from ourselves, but our adequacy is from God…" (2 Corinthians 3:5)

When Jesus was tempted by the devil in the wilderness, He prayed Scripture against the tempter. (Matthew 4:1-11)

Therefore, when I am tempted to believe that I am the god of myself, remind me that it is written: "For from Him and through Him and to Him are all things. To Him be the glory forever. Amen." (Romans 11:36)

—Nonie Maupin

Prayer Starter: *Heavenly Father, I desperately need You moment by moment to clear away the cobwebs of deceit and cause Your truth to infuse my life.*

PRINCIPLES OF REFRESHMENT

Out of the most severe trial, their overflowing joy and their extreme poverty well up in rich generosity...they gave as much as they were able, and even beyond their ability...they gave themselves first to the Lord and then to us in keeping with God's will. (2 Corinthians 8:2,3,5)

At best, our life on earth is brief. After moving into my seventh decade this year, I looked back and reflected on some of the special, teachable moments that helped steer me straight in my life with our Lord Jesus Christ. There are lessons I have learned along the way that have become special "principles of refreshment." These principles have encouraged me to correct bad behavior, to make right decisions, or just simply recharge my battery when I needed a fresh jolt from our Lord Jesus Christ.

The Macedonian Principle

The Macedonian Christians were givers, not takers. As the Scripture above says, they gave above their ability to give. Great joy of the Lord comes to those who give themselves to Christ and then all they are and have for His ministry, even in the challenges of financial downturns. Why? Because God gets His work done through His people! God is searching for believers who are givers. In turn, He gives them more than they have (or think they have) in order to accomplish His work.

The Fort Knox Principle

It has been stated that the us government has 4,570 tons of gold bullion (147.3 Million ounces) buried in its bullion depository in Fort Knox! In addition, the US Federal Reserve Bank in New York City has a vault containing approximately 5,000 tons of gold, which is held in trust for banks and official international organizations. All of this wealth stored in vaults plus all the other riches on planet earth are meaningless in comparison with the valuable asset believers have in their Savior and Shepherd Jesus Christ. He alone provides peace and security with all the uncertainties we face. David experienced Him and recorded in Psalm 18:2a: "The Lord is my Rock and my Fortress and my Deliverer."

—W. Sherrill Babb

Prayer Starter: *Lord, in You I put my trust.*

MY IDENTITY

For we are His workmanship, created in Christ Jesus for good works, which God prepared beforehand so that we would walk in them. (Ephesians 2:10)

Consider where you most often find your identity. Is it in what you do, as it is for most men and many women in our society? Is that from God or is that from the world? Where do you believe Jesus wants you to identify yourself? Ponder these verses that may help you redefine your identity:

- You were known by God before the foundation of the world . (Ephesians 4:1,11)

- You were knit in your mother's womb by God. (Psalm 139:13)

- God knows the number of hairs on your head. (Matthew 10:30, Luke 12:7)

- God's thoughts of you are more numerous than the earth's grains of sand. (Psalm 139:17-18)

- You were created in God's image. (Genesis 1:27)

- Your citizenship is not here but in Heaven. (Ephesians 2:19, Philippians 3:20)

- You have been adopted by God. (Romans 8:15, Ephesians 1:5)

- You are loved by God and called by Him. (Colossians 3:12)

- You are a saint. (Ephesians 1:1, 1 Corinthians 1:3, Philippians 1:1)

- You are a child of God. (1 John 3:1-2)

- You are an heir to the kingdom of God in Heaven. (Romans 8:17, Galatians 4:7)

- You are redeemed, forgiven. (Ephesians 1:6-8)*

—Donald Farr

Prayer Starter: *Lord, I know in my head that my identity comes from You. Give me assurance in my heart that I might become all You created me for.*

UNIQUELY GIFTED

For we are God's workmanship, created in Christ Jesus to do good works,
which God prepared in advance for us to do. (Ephesians 2:10)

My mom started me on piano lessons at age seven with the notion of providing a future church pianist for our tiny congregation. Sure enough, by age eleven I was accompanying 4-part hymns (the musical staple back then). Although, I didn't mind. Not only was I gaining good experience, but I also found myself worshipping through the music even as I was benefiting my church family. I had invited Christ into my heart and was doing what God had designed me to do; but little did I or my mother know of the far-reaching ministry plans that eventually grew from "her idea."

Unlike career missionaries who reach the field in their 20s and 30s, the Lord touched our hearts for cross-cultural ministry in middle age while at Scottsdale Bible. We arrived on the field three years ago, subsequent to retirement. My husband walked away from a long career in electrical engineering and I left behind a lifetime of music ministry in various settings: the classroom, performance halls and the church.

God has blessed us so that we can bless others. What can you do better than anybody else because He has uniquely positioned and gifted you? What good works have your name on them for you to do?

—J. and S.W. (Missionaries in Middle East)

Prayer Starter: *Lord, I'm Yours. I give myself to You because You are worthy. You have distinctively made me as a tool for a specific set of good deeds, so I yield myself to You. One day at a time... Not running ahead or lagging behind, doing the things You've called me to do in the right time, in the right place, and the right way.*

THE CURE FOR A SPIRITUAL LIMP

But He said, to me, "My grace is sufficient for you, for My power is made perfect in weakness." (2 Corinthians 12:9)

I have issues. We all have issues. We have those things about us that consistently work to keep us off our game. Many times these "issues" are actually good qualities that gain center stage in our life at the expense of other good qualities. We articulate our thoughts well but don't listen carefully. We feel people's pain but struggle to speak hard truth about the source of their problems. We have a strong sense of justice but fall short when it comes to mercy.

These issues are most often the sum total of the way we were raised, the values we were handed, the choices we have made and the hardwiring of our God-given personality. And as such, they cause us to walk through life with a bit of an emotional and spiritual limp. This is where God's grace wants to shine forth in our lives.

God intentionally allows gaps in our personality, intellect, and physical abilities so that we have to depend on Him. But when we do, the real power of our faith rises to the surface. When we recognize how weak, flawed, and inadequate we are in our own power, it's much easier to invite our ego to take a back seat and hand the keys of our life over to God whose grace is always enough.

—Tim Kimmel

Prayer Starter: *Dear Lord, thank You…thank You… thank You for Your amazing grace.*

THANKSGIVING

All your works shall give thanks to You, O Lord, and all Your saints shall bless You! (Psalm 145:10)

A few years ago we had some guests from Australia at our Thanksgiving table. They were amazed our country takes an entire holiday just to express our thanks to God for all He has done for us. "How great to live in a Christian nation."

Pastor Darryl once said we aren't a Christian nation. We are a nation that has a Christian nation within it. For most Americans, thanksgiving is about food and football. But for Christians, Thanksgiving is a holiday that should express the everyday focus of our hearts.

God has done so much for us. He has created us, provided for our needs, and made sure we have enough air to breathe. He made the world colorful with many terrains and hills to climb and oceans to cross and rainbows to enjoy and flowers to smell. He provided taste-buds so we could enjoy different foods, and He gave us so much more than manna for our sustenance. Have you looked at an egg lately and pondered the creativity it took for Him to create those?

He has given us diverse people to meet and cultures to cross and friends to make. He gave us marriage and families and love. And most importantly, He gave sinful people a way of escape from judgment so we could enjoy our holy God for eternity. He gave us His Son. And He gave us His Holy Spirit at the time of our salvation. The list never stops.

I wondered how great a job we do at thanking God for His blessings in our lives? We work hard on menus and making sure the turkey isn't dry and that the mashed potatoes aren't lumpy. We decorate with fall colors and open our homes to those who have no family in town. We gorge ourselves on delicious food and try to eat as much as possible while saving room for dessert. But do we stop to express our true thanks to God?

This year, take time to privately and publically thank God for what He has done for you. Make it a priority during your prayer time to start with praise and thanks. Then you will be able to celebrate thanksgiving everyday of the year.

—Tracy Goble

Prayer Starter: *Lord, I thank You for all You have done for me…*

RELY ON GOD

And there were many lepers in Israel in the time of Elisha the prophet; and none of them was cleansed, but only Naaman the Syrian. (Luke 4:27)

In 2 Kings 5:1 and 5, Naaman is described as: 1) a military "captain" (professional success); 2) a "great man with his master" (political connections); 3) "highly respected for his military victories" (public acclaim); 4) a "valiant warrior" (physical prowess); and 5) possessing "10 talents of silver … and 10 changes of clothes" (personal wealth). The world highly esteems all these things: professional, political, and public acclaim, physical ability, and power. Yet none of those could rescue him from his situation. Only when he humbled himself in simple obedience to the Word of God (2 Kings 5:13-14) was his leprous flesh restored.

Have you been trying to approach God in your way, outside of the family of God and having never submitted to the cleansing power of forgiveness in the cross of Jesus Christ? Perhaps you are already in the family of God, but have drifted into relying upon things of the world instead of a faith striving for obedience to the Word of God in every area of life. Either way, you need to come (or return) to the cross.

—John Politan

Prayer Starter: *Dear God, I humble myself before Your mighty hand. Thank You, Jesus, for dying on the cross for me. Forgive me for my sin. Give me grace to obey Your Word today.*

FRAGRANCE OF THE SEASON

Through us, He brings knowledge of Christ. Everywhere we go, people breathe in the exquisite fragrance. Because of Christ, we give off a sweet scent rising to God, which is recognized by those on the way of salvation— an aroma redolent with life. (2 Corinthians 2:15)

Christmas is coming with its sounds, tastes, and fragrances. The fragrances of the season are the very first signal to my mind and spirit that Christmas is coming. Fragrance is the essence of something beautiful and I have precious memories of the scents of pine trees and gingerbread baking.

Sometimes I ponder in my heart, as Mary did, her experience that night so long ago when her Son was born. Can you imagine wrapped in a heavy robe sitting and holding onto a moving donkey, surrounded by the stars in the black night? The fragrances were so different from what we know or would even expect. The incense of the manger and later frankincense and myrrh, rich and valuable were the fragrances that welcomed Jesus our Savior into our world. They were fragrances that Mary treasured her entire life as she reflected on what we know now as the very first Christmas.

So as Christmas draws near, let us open our hearts and focus on the essences of our sweet Jesus and dwell on it. Be aware of Christmas and search every day for the fragrance of the season.

—Jessica Neill

Prayer Starter: *Lord Jesus please be the sweet fragrance in our lives this Christmas that points others to You.*

DOING NEW THINGS

Your mercies are new every morning; great is your faithfulness.
(Lamentations 3:23)

Long ago, Madison Avenue advertisers learned that people respond to certain key words when shopping – and one of those words is "new." We like to have the "latest and greatest." People don't want the "old" model. They're looking for what's "new" and just assume that it's better. Sometimes "new" things really are better. In John 13:43, Jesus tells the disciples, "A new commandment I give to you, that you love one another; as I have loved you, that you also love one another."

People in Christ's time were used to the rules and regulations of the Scribes and Pharisees. The Pharisees literally had hundreds of laws the people were to observe each day. Then Jesus showed up with a "new" rule that we "love one another." This is the kind of love He demonstrated – that self-sacrificing "agape" love that was His hallmark and needs to become ours too.

God's love and His "mercies" are new every morning. That's great news for us imperfect people. But thankfully, His faithfulness shows up every day – as we seek to live out that "new" kind of love.

—John and Cindy Trent

Prayer Starter: *Lord, we want to have a "new" kind of love for You and each other. Help us show the kind of love to each other that Jesus demonstrated. Help us make the sacrifice of time and effort and attitude and action that demonstrate that love.*

HIS DWELLING PLACE

In Him you also are being built together into a dwelling place for God by the Spirit. (Ephesians 2:22)

When I became your pastor in 2007, we moved from Cleveland, Ohio, and found a home for our family. Once we found a house that met our needs, we began that process almost everyone experiences at various times over their years: "moving in." We brought in our furniture, our pictures and our "stuff." We brought in everything that brought comfort, familiarity, and identity into this house to make it our home. This house is where we rest and prepare for work. It is where we laugh and love and live. This house is our dwelling place.

When God rescues you, you become His dwelling place. While your salvation is immediate, His "moving in" takes time because He graciously also has to deal with you as the "previous tenant." Make no mistake though; God is committed to making you His home. He is committed to filling you with His grace, His love, His peace, His compassion and His nature. He fills you with His "stuff," and in the process, you become the dwelling place of God.

This is also true for the church. As God brings people together into a community of faith, His Spirit builds them together as a corporate body that is His dwelling place. It is within and amongst and through the people of the church where God extends grace, demonstrates mercy, performs miracles and advances His kingdom.

—Jamie Rasmussen

Prayer Starter: *Use me as Your dwelling place with grace, mercy, shelter and strength to further Your kingdom.*

PREPARE THE WAY

The voice of one crying in the wilderness: prepare the way of the Lord. Make straight in the desert a highway for our God. (Isaiah 40:3)

From the time that sin entered the world, God has been announcing that a Redeemer would arrive. Throughout the pages of Scripture, God unfolds His plan of salvation through Jesus. The profile of the Redeemer is revealed to us within the Old Testament. The Redeemer is Jesus; He is God. He is the One who would be coming. This one who announces Jesus' entrance is John, the baptizer – John, the son of Zacharias. John is the one spoken of by Isaiah the prophet.

John would be the herald for the Messiah. In the history and culture of the day, it was the custom of some eastern monarchs to send heralds before them to announce that they were on their way. An envoy would be commissioned to ensure that the roads were safe. Obstacles had to be cleared away and crooked roads needed to be straightened. John was calling the people to prepare their hearts because the king was coming.

John boldly proclaimed that the Messiah would come as the ultimate sacrifice for sin. Do you know when the announcement of John's birth was given to his father, Zacharias? At the time of sacrifice in the Temple in Jerusalem!

—Cathy Wilson

Prayer Starter: *Lord, prepare our hearts this Christmas to truly celebrate Your first coming and to marvel again at Your glorious sacrifice, so that we may have eternal life with You!*

ATTITUDE CHANGE

Finally, all of you, have unity of mind, sympathy, brotherly love, a tender heart, and a humble mind. Do not repay evil for evil or reviling for reviling, but on the contrary, bless, for to this you were called, that you may obtain a blessing.
(I Peter 3: 8,9)

One of the great benefits of being married to Georgann is that she loves to shop. I do not. So, it has worked very well for her to do all the birthday and Christmas shopping for our family. But it does not relieve me of the need to shop for her presents. One of the reasons I never liked shopping – especially around Christmas (and Georgann's birthday is a couple of weeks after Christmas!*)* – is because the other shoppers were so rude. They always elbowed me out of the way and, more times than not, I would push back – gently, of course.

It was not until I was in my mid-forties that I asked Jesus into my life. So with the "new me" guided by the presence of the Holy Spirit, I approached Christmas shopping with a new attitude. I still was not looking forward to it, but I was going to be polite, courteous, and respectful. Remember "WWJD?" The most amazing thing happened that year. The stores were still crowded, but all of the shoppers seemed to be so polite, courteous, and respectful. At first I thought it was just an unusual day. But the more I applied the new attitude, the more noticeable the change I observed in others.

Might there be an attitude that you could adopt that would cause a pleasant, and perhaps unexpected, response from those with whom you associate?

—Bob Cain

Prayer Starter: *God, I confess that I have demonstrated a bad attitude about certain things.*

ALL IS CALM...ALL IS SILENT

God said, "Go out and stand on the mountain before the Lord,

> *For the Lord is about to pass by." Now there was a great wind, so strong that it was splitting mountains and breaking rocks in pieces before the Lord, but the Lord was not in the wind; and after the wind an earthquake, but the Lord was not in the earthquake; and after the earthquake a fire, but the Lord was not in the fire; and after the fire a sound of sheer silence. When Elijah heard it… (1 Kings 19:11-13)*

"Silent night, holy night, all is calm."

Calm and silent? It is Christmas. More like hectic and loud!

This familiar and well-loved Christmas carol begs us to remember what these days preceding our Christmas celebration can be like.

The celebration of Christ's birth, as seen in most of our land, does not lend itself to calm. In fact, most of what we see, do, and are asked to do, does not lend itself to calm, but rather brings weariness and emptiness.

When I am too busy, I cannot concentrate on my Lord. I cannot hear His voice. I cannot do His work.

Jesus calmed the seas. Jesus tells us to, "Take care and be calm. Have no fear." He has done His part in bringing calm into my life. The rest is up to me. He ordained that I participate.

Will you join me this Christmas month in making "Silent night, holy night, all is calm," your desire and goal?

—Donna Otto

Prayer Starter: *Lord, amidst all the noise and business, help me to center on You and remain in Your peace.*

'GOD BLESS US, EVERYONE!'

For He makes His sun to rise on the evil and the good, and sends rain on the just and the unjust. (Matthew 5:45b)

When A Christmas Carol was first published in 1843, it met with instant success and critical acclaim. Charles Dickens touched a nerve with his character of Ebenezer Scrooge who undergoes a complete transformation after supernatural visitations from his former business partner, Jacob Marley, and the ghosts of Christmases past, present and future.

Apparently many people related to Scrooge. When his pinched, cold heart is restored to the innocent goodwill he had known in his childhood, readers jumped to their feet in their hearts clapping with abandon. And, before long, they were evaluating their own hearts and lives in light of the startling challenges found in the story.

Today, we need the same strong ideological, ethical and emotional transformation we see in Scrooge.

How can I return to the joyful enthusiasm of my own childhood in the celebration of Christmas? Joy returns when I fill the tradition with the truth, compare my attitude to the plumb line of Scripture, and then let it transform me.

In Matthew 5:45 we read that our Heavenly Father "makes His sun rise on the evil and on the good, and sends rain on the just and on the unjust." God generously sprinkles common grace and care upon all of His creatures. And, therefore, because we call ourselves disciples of Jesus, we are to imitate God and love both our neighbors and our enemies.

It may interest you to know that A Christmas Carol has never been out of print. God's blessing rests upon the timeless truth of "good will toward men" that is found as a theme in the story because it is bathed in the truth of God's common grace falling on the just and the unjust.

So, Tiny Tim's prayerful benediction is indeed appropriate! God bless us, everyone!

—Holly DelHousaye

Prayer Starter: *Lord, help me spread Your joy to everyone I meet.*

FULFILLED PROPHECY

Then she arose with her daughters-in-law that she might return from the country of Moab, for she had heard…that the Lord had visited His people. (Ruth 1:6)

A most joyful Christmas season to you as we look into the book of Ruth. The book of Ruth? Yes! The entire Bible anticipates and celebrates Jesus' birth, observes His death, and rejoices in His resurrection and soon return. And so, we're in Ruth where we read that following a famine in the land, the Lord visits His people – in Bethlehem. And so, Naomi returns to her home in Bethlehem because God had provided for His people by giving them bread. Jesus, when He came to earth, said, "I am the Bread of Life." The book of Ruth is prophetic – looking ahead to the incarnation–Jesus' first coming—His coming as Immanuel, God in the flesh.

On our calendar, it's Advent, a time of preparing as we wait expectantly. "Advent" means "a coming into being." At this time of year we look forward to celebrating what God had promised mankind. At Christmas, we are celebrating fulfilled prophecy. God visited His people. He invaded our world. How is He invading our lives?

As we interact and fellowship with people this Christmas season, what will they say is most important in our celebration of Jesus' birth?

—Cathy Wilson

Prayer Starter: *We praise You, Lord, for Your promise – Jesus! May those around us see in our lives, the impact of Your invading of our hearts!*

USE OF RESOURCES

So then, as we have opportunity, let us do good to everyone, and especially to those who are of the household of faith. (Galatians 6:10)

The concept of responsible stewardship before God requires that believers use all their property and possessions in ways that are pleasing to God and faithful to His teachings in Scripture.

1. Some resources should be used to support oneself and one's family. God tells us to work quietly, earn our own living, enjoy the resources of the earth with thankfulness to Him. He warns us against loving money or being wasteful with it or being deceived by it.

2. Another morally good use of some resources is to save for future needs. In James it states that this is wise because "you do not know what tomorrow will bring." However do not let accumulated savings tempt you to sin. Jesus tells us to lay up our treasures in Heaven not on earth.

3. A third use of resources, one repeatedly emphasized in Scripture, is giving money to those in need or to the Lord's work in the church and in missions. The New Testament places emphasis on generous, abundant, cheerful giving.

—Wayne Grudem

Prayer Starter: *Help me lay up treasures in Heaven and be a faithful steward here on earth.*

ADVENT

And the Word became flesh… (John 1:14a)

I must confess: I love Christmas. I enjoy the parties, the gift giving (and receiving!), The functions, and even the pace of life this time of year. Most of all, I love it because I have come to see a unique meaning behind the child in the manger.

In knowing God, J.I. Packer writes: "…the supreme mystery with which the Gospel confronts us [is] not in the Good Friday message of atonement, nor in the Easter message of resurrection, but in the Christmas message of incarnation." Packer argues that the King of all Kings stooping to become lowliest of all, is the most improbable miracle. And for Packer, the Incarnation, the "supreme mystery" of Scripture, demonstrates God's ability and willingness to do absolutely anything to accomplish His redemptive plan.

Each Christmas we celebrate that God's living Word became flesh. For me, this most improbable miracle is also a compelling reminder of God's power and of His commitment to accomplish His purpose and plan.

Do you find it difficult to trust God at times? Think on the Incarnation and let it remind you that God can accomplish anything.

— Lucas Cooper

Prayer Starter: *Father, as I think about the incarnation this Christmas season—that You, mighty God, became a baby boy—allow it to remind me of Your great power and ability to accomplish Your plan.*

INCREASE MY FAITH

But he must ask in faith without any doubting, for the one who doubts is like the surf of the sea, driven and tossed by the wind. For that man ought not to expect that he will receive anything from the Lord, being a double-minded man, unstable in all his ways. (James 1:6-8)

Lord, help me yield myself to You, every desire, thought and behavior, every cell and molecule. It is too easy to be swayed by the diverse temptations of the world: I am too vulnerable, too weak. I know I was built and designed to function properly only in utter dependence on You: perfect love.

Every waking moment, every breath is a gift from You. My heart beats because of You, perfect Designer. I want to be pleasing to You. Turn my eyes to You only and my allegiance be undivided. There is none like You, my precious King, Redeemer. You pulled me out of the dark places and cause me to remain in light. Stabilize me. Help me.

—David Walther

Prayer Starter: *Lord, I ask in faith; increase my faith! Make me trust in You without wavering, whatever it takes, whatever may befall me, make me run to You.*

TRUST *(AND GROW)*

We live by faith, not by sight. (2 Corinthians 5:7)

Have you ever been disappointed in God? Has the Bible ever helped you see your situation differently? For example, take the story of Joseph in Genesis 37–50. He was a beloved son, supreme in his father's eyes; a suffering servant, betrayed by his brothers; and finally, a savior of Egypt. Every good deed done by Joseph turned to terrible disappointment. Envious brothers sold him into slavery. Resisting a sexual advance by King Potiphar's wife got him thrown into prison. Interpreting a dream for a cell mate was quickly forgotten. Might Joseph have had moments of: "God doesn't care about me; I'm disappointed, alone, and forgotten; or life is not fair?" Have you ever said that?

As God "pulls back" and allows things to unravel in your life, could He be pushing you to a new level of maturity? Are you learning patience? Have you ever wished for more courage? What happens in your life when you trust Him fully? Speaking to his brothers in the last chapter of Genesis, Joseph said, "As for you, you meant evil against me, but God meant it for good" (Genesis 50:20). God always redeems hardship, even yours.

—Barry Asmus

Prayer Starter: *Lord, let me trust in You with all my heart and not lean on my own understanding. In all my ways, help me to acknowledge You. Please direct my paths. (Proverbs 3:5-6)*

THE SCENT GOES GODWARD

We are a fragrance of Christ to God. (2 Corinthians 2:15)

Paul speaks of how "The sweet aroma of the knowledge of Him" is manifested through our lives (2 Corinthians 2:14); we are vessels or instruments through which the fragrance is released. "We are the fragrance of Christ to God among those who are being saved and among those who are perishing. (2 Corinthians 2:15)" the scent goes Godward, and is pleasing to Him, regardless of the response. Just having His Son shared is joy to the Father, though the response of people will vary. God is pleased whenever His Son is declared.

Paul then lays down the ultimate exclusives: "…to the one an aroma from death to death, to the other an aroma from life to life." When all the dust settles and the philosophical chattering ceases, it comes down to this: either you are moving in life to life, or in death to death—literally "out of life into life," or "out of death into death." Whether those living in death will respond to the message of Christ is not your responsibility, but His. It is He who draws, and the Holy Spirit who convicts of sin (John 16:8–9).

Paul says, "For we are not like many, peddling the Word of God, but as from sincerity, but as from God, we speak in Christ in the sight of God" (2 Corinthians 2:17). Ours is not to market this thing, to "peddle" the Word of God. Personal gain, fame, or even acceptance is not our aim.

We share in sincerity. The fragrance is to please Him by sharing and declaring His Son!

—Darryl DelHousaye

Prayer Starter: *God, help me to please You by sharing Your Son.*

JUST THE RIGHT TIME

In the fullness of time, God sent forth His Son, born of a woman, born under the law. (Galatians 4:4)

What a Christmas verse! At just the right time, with everything lined up the way God had orchestrated, Jesus entered the world.

I'm suggesting that Mary and Joseph, from their perspective, probably didn't travel to Bethlehem from Nazareth to fulfill Bible prophecy. They traveled to Bethlehem because God had orchestrated the events! God used pagan Caesar Augustus to issue a decree that would tax the Jews, thereby further oppressing them. But God was at work. And so – we marvel!

Are we seeing "but God" moments in our lives? Do we detest some of the circumstances surrounding us? Can we say "but God?" Can we marvel at what He is doing? Joseph in Genesis 50:20 told his brothers, "You meant evil against me; but God meant it for good…" we need to focus on "but God!"

Caesar Augustus was moved by the Spirit of God at exactly the right time. He unknowingly fulfilled Micah 5:2 which tells of the One who would be born in Bethlehem. Caesar Augustus hailed himself as the savior of the world. As he sought to tighten his grip, the decree he issued played into the fulfillment of the birth of the One who would eventually reign over the world!

—Cathy Wilson

Prayer Starter: *As I begin this day, may my heart and mind be focused on You. As the enemy continues to seek to accuse me, may my entire being embrace the truth that You are God and that You reign supreme!*

JESUS OUR HOPE

Now may the God of hope fill you with all joy and peace in believing...
(Romans 15:13)

Christmas scenes from children's storybooks belie a much grittier reality: an oppressive Roman occupation, rising taxes, a pregnant teen threatened with stoning, a long journey ending in an inconveniently timed labor, and a narrow escape to foreign exile. That first Christmas was full of danger, fear, pain, death, and hardship.

Plus, Jesus arrived! Angels rejoiced, wise men brought gifts, and a few recognized that hope had arrived – a future hope. The Romans did not disappear. The slaughtered infants were not reborn. Mary's stigma of being an unwed pregnant teen remained.

Colossians 2:16-17 says that celebrations are just a shadow of what is to come, but the substance belongs to Christ. Christmas is a shadow of what is coming. And just as for the people in the original story, life goes on around us with its hardship and sadness and danger and death.

But like Mary and Joseph, we can focus on God's mercy, provision, protection, and sovereignty. Yes, God is in control. He will help me in my distress. He will fulfill every one of His promises through Christ. That gives me hope, making it possible to say with sincerity, "Merry Christmas!"

—Lauren Locker

Prayer Starter: *Lord, may I find my joy not in pleasures, but in the hope You have wondrously provided.*

BEST GIFT OF ALL

And going into the house they saw the child with Mary His mother, and they fell down and worshiped Him. Then, opening their treasures, they offered Him gifts, gold and frankincense and myrrh. (Matthew 2:11)

We're told in the Bible that the Magi gave three gifts to the baby in the manger. Do you remember what they were? They were myrrh, frankincense and gold.

Upon first glance, two of these gifts seem a little less than spectacular.

Myrrh is a resin from a tiny shrub used for embalming. It would be like presenting your bundle of joy with a junior mortuary kit.

The frankincense is hardly better. Frankincense is a perfume. We all know that if you're doing last minute shopping, buying perfume or cologne is one of the easiest gifts, requiring the least amount of thoughtfulness.

But the third gift, the gold, saved the day. At least that's what economists say about gift giving.

Economists say that when it comes to giving gifts the best gift is cash. Why? It's because people know their own preference best.

Of course psychologists disagree from economists here. A dollar will always have a psychological value of a dollar. But a specific gift can deliver so much more.

In all seriousness, when you're given something, you want to analyze it and try to figure out why this person gave it to you. In other words, every gift given says something about your need and it also says something about the character of the person who gave it to you.

God has given us Jesus Christ. Take a moment and think about what this gift says about our need. What does this gift say about God?

—Joe Gordon

Prayer Starter: *Thank You, Father, for the gift of Jesus Christ. You knew our needs better than we do. We receive this gift again with appreciation and praise.*

NEVER BEYOND REPAIR

I praise You, for I am fearfully and wonderfully made. Wonderful are Your works; my soul knows it very well. (Psalm 139:14)

I'm not very handy. I appreciate those stories of home restoration and improvement because they are so foreign to my own experience. As I see the finished results of others, I marvel at what is possible in the hands of a skilled craftsman.

My own stories have beginnings like, "Once I tried to fix my faucet and ended up power washing the kitchen ceiling." And virtually every tale ends with, "And that's when I gave up and called the plumber/repairman/fire department/9-1-1."

The Bible's King David is known as "the man after God's own heart." He's also the man who committed some pretty huge mess-ups along the way. He was at times deceptive. He was adulterous, compounded by cover-up conspiracies. His offenses included massive collateral damage that devastated loyal families, and even generations of his own family. In even a casual reading, it'd be fair to call him a "fixer-upper," and hard to label him "wonderfully made" using even the most generous of criteria.

But I absolutely believe David got it right when he was writing out his praise to God. I do believe he was wonderfully made, and I believe you are, too. Perhaps what is so ingenious about how God designed us is that we are never, ever beyond repair.

There are probably plenty of times in your life when you can identify with David when he was in his worst moments of disrepair. Times when you blew it, broke it, or outright destroyed whatever measure of life you were using as a barometer of success. You might think you should be condemned and razed, flattened and forgotten.

But like David, you're not beyond repair. God can fix you. He can restore you. You are wonderfully made because God can restore you, whenever you fall apart.

Understanding and embracing this, David wrote in that same entry, "How precious to me are Your thoughts, O God! (Psalm 139:17)" when you aren't feeling well-constructed and like you're about to collapse, remember that you are wonderfully made, and only a heart's cry away from God doing a masterful work of restoration in you.

—Bryan McAnally

Prayer Starter: *Jesus, thank You that You love and save me in spite of my sin. Thank You, thank You.*

BELIEF NOT DOUBT

And Zacharias was troubled...and fear gripped him... and blessed is she who believed...what has been spoken to her by the Lord. (Luke 1:12,45)

Have you been silenced by fear and doubt? When Zacharias, a righteous and blameless priest, went before God, he knew he was standing in the presence of God. Yet, when an angel appeared before him, he was gripped by fear and he doubted the message given to him. His doubt did not limit God's fulfillment of his purpose or the answer to Zacharias' prayer (Elizabeth still became pregnant). However, when Zacharias questioned God's response to his prayer, his doubt took away the joy of receiving God's response. His joy was limited and his voice (influence) was silenced because he recognized that he failed to believe when God answered his prayer (Luke 1:5-25).

Contrast Zacharias' response with that of Mary, who unlike Zacharias believed what was spoken to her (Luke 1:45). Mary's soul was overflowed with joy (Luke 1:46-47). When belief replaces fear and doubt, the Holy Spirit is enabled to release His power to speak through us (Luke 1:64-79).

When you pray, are you praying expectantly that God will answer your prayer? And when He does answer your prayer, are you inclined to respond more like Zacharias or Mary?

—Mark Upton

Prayer Starter: *Lord, right now I am gripped by fear and doubt about ...*

PRAYER

*Finally, brethren, pray for us that the Word of the Lord will spread rapidly
and be glorified, just as it did also with you; and that we will be rescued
from perverse and evil men; for not all have faith. But the Lord is faithful,
and He will strengthen and protect you from the evil one.
(2 Thessalonians 3:1-3)*

These are the last two ideas with regard to my prayer life. (See November 11)

1. Better to pray with someone than to just pray for them

In the past as someone would give me something to pray for, I would say "Yes I will" and then promptly forget to pray. What I decided to do to remedy this problem was to stop right there and pray for that need. I did not forget to pray, and the person whom I was praying for felt valued.

2. Perception of my affliction

As I look at Paul's affliction in 2 Corinthians 12, I am reminded that God does not take away all of our afflictions just because we ask Him to. However, as in the case of Paul, He can change my perception of the affliction. For Paul learned that it gave him assurance knowing God would provide sufficient grace and divine strength to sustain him regardless of his trials. Having learned the lesson that Jesus taught him through the thorn, Paul experienced an attitude change and got a different perspective on his situation.

—Patrick Sullivan

Prayer Starter: *Heavenly Father, help me to see my afflictions through Your eyes. Help my attitude be one of thankfulness to You at all times.*

GOD'S CREATION & GOD'S GIFT

Like the appearance of a rainbow in the clouds on a rainy day, so was the radiance around Him. (Ezekiel 1:28)

My wife and I lived in Kenya for two years as missionaries and had the privilege of attending Nairobi Baptist Church. The congregation had people from many different countries. Visitors were asked to give their names and the country of their origin. What a joy to hear and meet so many different people. The singing and preaching were a great blessing to us.

I remember how Pastor Gichinga's teaching from Ecclesiastes 1:3 of a man's toils under the sun blended with his life's experiences which touched my heart and soul. The pastor's mother gave birth to him, her first-born son, under a tree. God had his hand on this child. God chose to make an outstanding preacher of him.

The choir was outstanding because they loved being together and to sing! One Sunday while listening to them singing, I realized there probably was no other choir on earth that could equal them. I saw the Bantu people of Kenya with their women in bright, colorful dresses, next to the tall brown Cushitic people of Kenya and mingled with them were the brown Indian descendents of workers brought in to build the railroad in years gone by, with their clothes of colorful fabrics and textures. The white people of British and European descent added a colorful mix with shades of hair from golden blonde to red and tones of brown along with the silver-gray of the mature. The British men with their suits and ties and the Australian and Americans with their less formal dress, shorts, blue jeans and open collars added their own colors. I could not imagine the number of ethnic groups and the different languages spoken as some spoke as many as five languages! Only God could bring such a diversified group in one place to raise their voices in praise and celebration to God because they had the joy of loving Him and loving each other!

God used the creation of the sun to make a rainbow that Ezekiel uses to describe the radiance and the glory around God! God gave His Son to redeem man and show His love to the world, which enabled this choir to be so inspiring and so colorful! We will probably see all these people standing before God in Heaven which I believe will be another one of his rainbows!

—Roy Fritz

Prayer Starter: *Father, Your glory is radiant and fills me with praise! Thank You for the gifts of Your rainbow in the sky and Your rainbow of people in Your family.*

PROPHECY FULFILLED

*Blessed is the Lord God of Israel, for He has visited and redeemed His people,
and has raised up a horn of salvation for us in the house of His servant David.
(Luke 1:68-69)*

This is a Christmas verse? Yes! This verse so aptly connects the dots between the Messianic prophecies in the Old Testament and their fulfillment in the New Testament. God had promised Israel a Deliverer. That Deliverer, the Messiah, was about to be born. God is faithful. He delivers on His promises.

What did the people in that day know about "Christmas?" How did they celebrate? Zacharias declared this prophecy recorded in Luke at the circumcision of his newborn son John (whom we know as John the Baptizer). Immediately before this, we read that the people of Judea marveled. I love that word, "marveled." The people in Judea who had witnessed all the happenings surrounding the birth of John were filled with awe. Why? They were anticipating God to move.

Are we marveling today as we celebrate Jesus' birth? The people in Zacharias' day were marveling – and the Savior of the world hadn't made His entrance. What compelled them to "marvel?" They were living in the excitement of the coming of their deliverer – the Messiah – because God had promised.

Jesus has come and we can celebrate with joyful hearts as we "marvel" at God's indescribable gift. Are we living in the excitement of Jesus' second coming? Are we anticipating God to move? He has promised!

—Cathy Wilson

Prayer Starter: *Lord, may we marvel anew as we look forward to the celebration of Christ's birth – His first coming. May You fill us with excitement because He is coming again. We know because You promised!*

GETTING PREPARED

Prepare your hearts for the Lord and serve Him only. (I Samuel 7:3b)

When I think of being prepared, I think of getting organized, making my list, planning ahead, and getting focused. Every year I always say I am going to start earlier getting ready for Christmas. Somehow that just doesn't happen like I want it to. Sometimes I can be fully organized, but not prepared at all.

Think about Mary, a young maiden God chose to be the mother of Jesus, our Lord and Savior. Do you think she had time to prepare to be Christ's mother? Probably not in the way we think of being prepared, but I do believe she was prepared for Christ's coming or God would not have chosen her to be the mother of His Son. Her heart was prepared, she was tender toward God and she had a willing spirit. She was called the handmaiden of the Lord.

Preparing is not all about planning ahead and organizing our lives for Christ's coming. Preparing is opening our hearts to be willing to listen when He calls. It may mean surrendering ourselves and our own agenda. It may mean being open to the Spirit's leading in ways we would never have imagined. Corrie Ten Boom put it this way, "Lord, prepare me for what You are preparing for me." Are you willing to lay aside your plans for God's plans and purpose for your life? Are you prepared for Christ's coming?

—Margi Galloway

Prayer Starter: *Lord, help me to open my heart to You and be willing to allow You to use my life.*

YOUR GOD WILL BE MY GOD

…where you go, I will go, and where you lodge, I will lodge. Your people shall be my people, and your God, my God. (Ruth 1:16)

In the ancient Near East most people believed in local deities, so Ruth's response to Naomi makes sense: "…where you go, I will go, and where you lodge, I will lodge. Your people shall be my people, and your God, my God." But why would Ruth ever want Naomi's God? He certainly does not take very good care of His children – letting Elimelech die, and then Mahlon and Chilion. What kind of a God is this that treats His people so poorly?

Thus I wonder what it was that caused Ruth to make such a commitment to Naomi? Was it what she saw in these Yahweh followers? I don't know what caused Ruth to cling to Naomi, but I certainly have a great respect and appreciation for Ruth and her commitment to Naomi. I don't believe Ruth was making this commitment because of what she would get out of it. She was a very kind woman, showing *hesed* (the Hebrew word for "loving-kindness") to Naomi.

I hope that I am the same kind of person as Ruth and that I show "lovingkindness" to others so that they can see my God and want to love Him.

—Paul Wegner

Prayer Starter: *God, help me to love others as a reflection of You and the way You love me.*

IT IS WRITTEN

For the Word of God is living and active and sharper than any two-edged sword… (Hebrews 4:12)

When I am tempted to believe that life is too hard, remind me that it is written: "…let us run with endurance the race that is set before us, fixing our eyes on Jesus, the Author and Perfector of faith…" (Hebrews 12:1-2)

When I am tempted to believe that people hurt me and can't be trusted, remind me that it is written: "…and let us consider how to stimulate one another to love and good deeds." (Hebrews 10:24)

When I am tempted to believe that God is inadequate to handle my life and I must worry, remind me that it is written: "in the world you have tribulation, but take courage; I have overcome the world." (John 17:33b)

When I am tempted to believe that my fearful feeling is truer than God's Word, remind me that it is written: "be strong and courageous. Do not tremble or be dismayed for the Lord your God is with you wherever you go." (Joshua 1:9)

Or when I'm tempted to believe that God couldn't love me, remind me that it is written: "For God so loved the world that He gave His only Son, that everyone who believes in Him will not perish but have eternal life." (John 3:16)

—Nonie Maupin

Prayer Starter: *We can take God at His Word.*

PRINCIPLES OF REFRESHMENT

I know that my Redeemer lives, and that in the end He will stand upon the earth. And after my skin has been destroyed, yet in my flesh I will see God; I myself will see Him with my own eyes – I, and not another. How my heart yearns within me! (Job 19:25-27)

The Lighthouse Principle

This has become special to me along my way with Jesus Christ. Along the eastern coast of the United States, there are hundreds of sunken ships, which have failed to heed the warnings being beamed by the brilliance of a lighthouse. One still stands near me on the New Jersey coastline by the name of Barnegat Lighthouse, having faithfully protected mariners for over 100 years. I have been out in the Atlantic Ocean on a rather small fishing boat as the sun was going down and I was very thankful for "Old Barney," as fishermen affectionately call it. Job, in the Old Testament, reminds me of a man who focuses his faith in times of difficulties and disappointment on God. When his health and wealth hit bottom, Job's spiritual eyes targeted the shining light of his Redeemer.

The Motel 6 Principle

There is always guaranteed comfort and refreshment to be found in our Lord even when the seas are rough. He stands as a lighthouse on the horizon calling us to faith in Him and His promises. Psalm 34:4,8 reads: "I sought the Lord, and He answered me, He delivered me from all my fears…taste and see that the Lord is good, blessed is the man who takes refuge in Him." Let us take refuge in the lighthouse of our God!

—W. Sherrill Babb

Prayer Starter: *Lord, You are my beacon. Help me to always look to You for my direction and comfort.*

CHANGE MY HEART

Blessed are those who hunger and thirst for righteousness, for they shall be satisfied. (Matthew 5:6)

Do you hunger for Christ throughout your day? Is your life a visible testimony before others that you are "different'"– a maturing full life follower and disciple of Christ? When bumped by the things of life, like being cut off by another driver, or having your spouse or friend hit your 'hot' buttons, is your response one that points them to Christ in attractive ways? Or, is your reaction one that leaves the observer saying, "He calls himself a Christian? I sure don't want any part in that!"

When we find ourselves thinking or reacting in ways that do not bring honor to the King of Kings, (and we all have), there is something we can do about it – right then and there. I believe the first thing is to consider whether we care if we hurt others by our reaction to them or the issue at hand.

Then, if we care (and even if we do not), ask God to forgive us and to show us the response He would have us make instead. Then ask forgiveness, if possible, of the one who observed your first behavior.

Fundamental in that process is what we discover about ourselves, if we admit to God that we didn't care if we hurt someone else. As we come before Him with that in mind, He alone can change our heart to that broken place where we do care about the pain we cause others. This pain we caused them is the same pain in our lives when others hurt us.

As we grapple with that, we also begin to get a small sense of the pain our sin causes God. We sense the suffering that Christ endured because of our individual sins, as He bore them on the cross.

—Donald Farr

Prayer Starter: *Father, make those changes in me that You desire. Give me a continuing burden in my heart until I soften and respond.*

SHEPHERDS AND GOD'S GRACE

And behold, an angel of the Lord stood before them, and the glory of the Lord shone around them, and they were greatly afraid. (Luke 2:9)

Why would an angel of the Lord appear to shepherds? Why was the announcement of the Messiah's birth first proclaimed to shepherds in a remote field, on the outskirts of Bethlehem? Is there any significance in this part of the Christmas account? Have we pondered this?

Shepherds were the lowest of the low. Shepherds were under a rabbinical ban – a prohibition issued by the Rabbis. Because shepherds spent long hours with their flocks in the fields, it was impossible for these protectors of the sheep to follow all the religious regulations concerning washings and perhaps dietary rulings. Shepherds were shunned by the Jewish community.

I love this scene in Luke's Gospel. Here are these shepherds, the lowest of society, visited by an angel of Almighty God! I don't know about you, but I'm praising God! In this account we see—in neon—God's grace extending to the likes of us!

And, once again, I'm marveling!

—Cathy Wilson

Prayer Starter: *Lord, You are indeed a marvelous God whose love extends to even me. May I be glued to that truth today, and may I marvel anew!*

THE WITNESSING TOOLBOX

Or do you show contempt for the riches of His kindness, tolerance and patience, not realizing that God's kindness leads you toward repentance? (Romans 2:4)

If you put a bunch of evangelistically minded people in a room and asked them the singular most important tool for reaching people for Christ, it would be interesting to see what they'd suggest. The usual suspects would be:

• A clear and articulate Gospel presentation.

• A succinct personal testimony.

• An arsenal of strong apologetic arguments to counter the standard pushbacks of unbelievers.

Although these are helpful tools, they aren't the ones Paul thinks are most important. In the book of Romans, Paul uses his testimony, apologetics and a clear presentation of the Gospel to set forth his case. But the singular tool that he says had the greatest influence in turning the Roman believers to faith in Christ was the kindness, tolerance and patience of God shown to them by other believers.

Today, we all have an opportunity to play the role of ambassadors of the kingdom of Heaven. It's nice to know that, if asked, we could outline the Gospel, tell them our own story and deal with their intellectual concerns. But the greatest thing we can do to share our faith today is to love people. It's God's grace with sweat all over it.

—Tim Kimmel

Prayer Starter: *Dear Lord, give me a chance today to be not only Your voice to lost people, but Your hands, Your feet, Your eyes and Your heart.*

SACRIFICE FOR SIN

*Now there were in the same country shepherds living out in the fields, keeping watch over their flock by night. (**Luke 2:8**)*

Didn't these shepherds know it was winter and it was too cold to watch sheep in a lonely field out in the middle of nowhere? While we sing, "O little town of Bethlehem" at Christmas, it might be good to know that a specific area of the city of David is mentioned – "Ephrathah" (Micah 3:2). Sheep that were destined for temple sacrifice were kept in fields within a certain radius from the Temple in Jerusalem. Ephrathah was within that radius.

The account of the shepherds in the Gospel of Luke pointedly highlights the reason for Jesus' first coming; to die for sin and to offer Himself as a sacrifice for sin. The announcement to the shepherds speaks of the Messiah who came as our Passover Lamb. The Messiah came first as the suffering Servant who died for our sins.

He's coming again, isn't He? Time has gone by and we're waiting. Are we waiting expectantly? And, are we marveling? Luke 2:17-18 tells us that the shepherds made it widely known what they had seen and heard. "And all those who heard it, marveled at those things which were told them by the shepherds."

—Cathy Wilson

Prayer Starter: *Lord, may we boldly proclaim what You have revealed to us in Jesus. May many who hear our words marvel at Your amazing gift of grace!*

PERSISTENCE

Ask, and it shall be given to you; seek, and you shall find; knock, and it shall be opened to you. (Matthew 7:7)

The words "ask…seek…knock" are probably better translated "keep on asking…keep on seeking…keep on knocking" and imply a persistence in prayer. Except for the failure to pray at all, the failure to persevere in prayer is our most common problem. Remember that prayer is not only our calling out to God, but it is God speaking back to us through His Word as well. God wants us to persevere – to keep on knocking, as it were, on the gates of Heaven.

Why does God desire such perseverance? The reason is simple. God is a God of relationship. The more we communicate with someone, the deeper, the richer, and more meaningful that relationship becomes. God does not want us to follow some set formula – He wants us to live in genuine relationship with Him. Persevering prayer deepens that relationship.

The German evangelist George Muller was a man of persevering prayer. His diary reflects he prayed for two friends to come to Christ for over 50 years. One of them reportedly gave his life to Christ shortly before Muller died, and the other at Muller's own funeral. May we all be encouraged to pray in such a manner without ceasing.

—John Politan

Prayer Starter: *Lord, by Your grace enable me to persevere in communing with You.*

GLORY OF GOD

The Word was made flesh and dwelt among us and we beheld His glory.
(John 1:14)

Jesus is the glory of God revealed at His birth – the celebration we call Christmas. Christmas is Jesus' first coming. At His second coming, Jesus will return in His blazing glory, which Matthew 24:30 describes as "great glory."

The literal meaning of the "glory" of God is "weight, abundance, riches." The glory of God manifests all of His attributes – all who He is.

Are we beholding God in all His glory? Do we think of Christmas as a time of beholding Him? In Psalm 34, King David describes those who trust in the Lord. I love verse 5 of Psalm 34 which states that "They looked to Him and were radiant…" the radiance in our lives that is ignited by Christ far exceeds the brightness of Christmas lights! Do we long for this radiance?

As we continue to read Psalm 34:5, the Holy Spirit through King David, tells us that those who behold God and are radiant are not ashamed. We are told that "Their faces" are not ashamed! As we truly behold God, our outward expression will display our confidence in Him. What a description of a lovely countenance! Do we long for such confidence in Him – confidence that is clearly seen by others?

—Cathy Wilson

Prayer Starter: *Lord, cause me to behold you this Christmas and always. Lord, I don't want to miss beholding Your glory!*

CARRYING HIS NAME

So they shall put my name on the children of Israel, and I will bless them.
(Numbers 6:27)

Individuals and businesses proclaim who they are in various ways. Companies emboss their names on pens. Construction sites announce, "future home of…" sports teams want their fans to wear a hat or a T-shirt with their logo.

God finds it important to "put His name" on His children as well. And when we understand what that means, it's a tremendous blessing.

One man named Eric read this verse and knew just how important someone putting their "name" on you meant. Orphaned at seven years old, he spent the next five years bouncing between foster homes and orphanages. Several times he was paraded before prospective "parents" but was never "chosen." That is until he was twelve years old and finally ended up in a foster home that became his permanent home.

The foster parents couldn't have children of their own but felt God was leading them to be parents. They asked the orphanage for a child who had been "passed over" and were given Eric. Three years and many court dates and lawyer fees later, Eric gladly "took their name." Having their name meant so much to him. It still gives him a feeling of security and love he can't explain, but gratefully accepts.

—John and Cindy Trent

Prayer Starter : *Lord Jesus, thank You that You put Your "Name" on us. You chose us and purposefully made us a member of Your family. Help us to add security and love to our home – and to always "choose" to be there for our loved ones.*

CHRISTMAS

And she gave birth to her firstborn Son and wrapped Him in swaddling cloths and laid Him in a manger, because there was no place for them in the inn. (Luke 2:7)

It's always amazed me how the Son of God was more than willing to enter into our chaos. For years people have tried to sanitize the Christmas story with greeting cards that show a serene baby with a glowing head or public manger scenes that display some "Little House on the Prairie" look or even hymns that state "all is calm and all is bright." But none of these truly capture the picture of the incarnation that the Bible presents.

The Gospel writers present the birth narrative of Jesus as one filled with chaos. There was societal chaos with abusive politicians and oppressive taxes—fragile peace on the brink of rebellion. There was personal chaos as Joseph and Mary are found separated from family—having to give birth to their first child in a dark cave surrounded by smelly animals. Like so much of our lives today there was chaos surrounding the primary players in this well-known Bible story. And God, in the form of Jesus, chooses to enter into chaos.

And into this chaos Jesus brought hope and peace. That's the message of Christmas. God is not afraid to enter into a fallen world filled with lots of sin. He is not afraid to enter into our mess—for when He does He brings forgiveness, hope, peace and joy. And we are changed.

—Jamie Rasmussen

Prayer Starter: *God, may Jesus' joy and peace be ours this Christmas in the midst of the storm.*

VICTORY IN JESUS

Unto the hills will I lift up my eyes, from whence does my help come. My help cometh from the Lord, maker of Heaven and earth! (Psalm 121:1)

Psalm 121:1 shouts to the reader – remember, rejoice, worship, anticipate – thus, be renewed in your faith.

Psalm 12:1 is one of the "Songs of Ascent" (Psalm 120-134) which the Jewish pilgrims chanted on their way up to Jerusalem to celebrate the feasts of the Lord. (Psalm 122:3-4a proclaims, "Jerusalem is built as a city that is compact together where the tribes go up…").

Throughout the Old Testament, God continually called upon the children of Israel to remember what He – the Creator, the Deliverer, the Provider – had done on their behalf. God told them to rejoice in His provision and in His power to deliver. They were to worship Him as they rejoiced and lived in hope. Hope necessitated anticipating His continued provision and help. Hope also came in anticipating the ultimate deliverance of the Messiah, Jesus, to whom the entire Old Testament points.

Are we, as believers in Jesus, who have the gift of the indwelling of the Holy Spirit, remembering His finished work on the cross on our behalf? Are we living in that victory? Are we rejoicing and worshipping Him? Are we anticipating His return, "our gathering together to Him" (2 Thessalonians 2:1)?

—Cathy Wilson

Prayer Starter: *Lord, cause us to move forward in our walk with You from the place of victory which You have already won!*

CELEBRATE LIFE

Be devoted to one another in brotherly love. Honor one another above yourselves.
(Romans 12:10)

One of the things I remember enjoying about my time as a student at Wheaton College, was the feeling that I could be interacting at any time with the "next Billy Graham" (Wheaton's most famous alum), the "next Jim Elliott' (martyred missionary), the "next John Nelson" (conductor), the "next John Piper" (pastor/author), "Dan Coats (U.S. Senator), "Don Nelson" (basketball coach), or "Wes Craven," – yes, the writer and director of the "Nightmare on Elm Street" film franchise is also a Wheaton grad!

Some years after graduation, I had a dream that I returned to campus for a homecoming visit, and all my friends had gone on to become quite famous. I had no idea what they were famous for, but I just knew that they had gone on to make a significant impact in their chosen field, and had somehow become household names here in the United States. And in my dream, with every encounter, I felt this pervasive sense of "celebrity," this awareness and awe of the importance of the people around me. In seeing many of my former classmates, friends, professors, administrators, and mentors, I wanted to celebrate their lives – to discover everything I could about them: "What have you been doing? Where have you been living? How are your children like you? Where are you going to church and what's it like?" The questions in and of themselves might not have been any different from ones I would have asked in real life, but—as with any intense dream—the feeling of awe and wonder was palpable.

I've heard much protesting about the ills of our "culture of celebrity" in America today, and I'm a guilty accomplice. But the inherent meaning of "celebrity" is "a celebrated life" – and celebrating life is a great quality for any culture, but especially for the Christian community. The Lord's apostle to the Gentiles points out here that true Christian love should be characterized by a devotion to others that might at times rival that of a Hollywood tourist for a movie star, or a fan who camps out over night to get front row tickets. I know I don't treat my family this way often enough, let alone my neighbors, and certainly not my enemies, but this must be the "manner of love the Father has lavished on us!" (I John 3:1).

—Joe Bubar

Prayer Starter: *Heavenly Father, give me a love like this – a love like Yours – that thinks more highly of others than I think of myself.*

PUTTING CHRIST FIRST

In everything you do, put God first, and He will direct you and crown your efforts with success. (Proverbs 3:6)

It's never too late to get organized, clean out clutter, and make plans for the months ahead. This can apply to your spiritual life, too.

When reorganizing your life, put Christ first in the order of your priorities. Clean out old habits and patterns of doing things that do not reflect Christ in your life. Have a plan for how you will be intentional about growing in Christ. You might want to get into a Bible study to grow deeper through God's Word and through fellowship. You might want to cultivate a more faithful prayer time each day, or read Scripture as a personal devotion. Think not just about what you will do; think about who you will become during the process.

—Susan Miller

Prayer Starter: *Lord, my heart has a hunger and a thirst to know You. Guide me as I begin to clean out the clutter that keeps me from You. Give me a clear plan for how I can get to know You more intimately. I love You, Lord, and I commit to putting You first in my life.*

LONELINESS

And the Lord will guide you continually and satisfy your desire in scorched places and make your bones strong; and you shall be like a watered garden, like a spring of water, whose waters do not fail. (Isaiah 58:11)

Sometimes loneliness overwhelms and a good metaphor to describe how it feels is a playground with only one child on it – me! It is painful to work hard to surround yourself with people you have given to, encouraged, supported, rooted for – only to find yourself in a predicament where you are more lonely than ever before.

Where is the encouragement for the heart during times like this?

My heart has been touched by a passage of Scripture that jumped out to me during a sermon I heard recently. It is found in John 7:38 which says, "Whoever believes in me, as the Scripture has said, 'out of his heart will flow rivers of living water.' "

These verses explain that anyone who believes (present tense participle) – meaning a continuing act of believing here and now – will only find satisfaction in coming to Jesus, drinking of Him, believing in Him. Rivers will flow out of his or her innermost being and these rivers bring enlightenment, joy and power.

All this adds up to the fact that when I am lonely I must turn my focus inward to the source of life and energy and vitality. I must remember I am weak and that I depend on God for the very sustenance of my life.

It seems so difficult to get back to this profoundly simple thought. I know I must become empty and depleted to once again be filled up with the fullness of God. Out of the fullness of my heart flow all the thoughts and words and choices of my life.

—Holly DelHousaye

Prayer Starter: *God, You are my strength…my focus….My all.*

THE MAGI

Now after Jesus was born in Bethlehem of Judea in the days of Herod the King, behold, wise men from the east came to Jerusalem saying, "Where is He who has been born King of the Jews?" (Matthew 2:1-2)

The Magi, the wise men, appear on the scene following a gap of time from the birth of Jesus. The shepherds found Jesus at His birth, lying as a babe in a manger (Luke 2:12,16). The wise men saw the star when Jesus was born and then traveled a great distance. When the wise men found Jesus, they found Him as a "child in a house" (Matthew 2:11).

The shepherds, who were watching over flocks destined for temple sacrifice, found the perfect passover lamb in Bethlehem Ephrathah. The Magi had their GPS programmed for Jerusalem where they intended to find the King of the Jews.

Who were these Magi? They were approvers of kings. During the time the Jewish people were in exile in Babylon, Daniel was assigned as the chief administrator over the Magi *(Daniel 2:48).* Daniel boldly proclaimed the Messiah who would one day reign from King David's throne in Jerusalem.

The shepherds' account speaks to Jesus' first coming when He fulfilled His role as the perfect Passover Lamb who died for sin. The Magi's account speaks to Jesus' second coming when he will come as the conquering King.

And so we wait expectantly as we marvel at the details laid out for us in Scripture by our awesome God!

—Cathy Wilson

Prayer Starter: *Lord, Your detailed plan laid out in Your Word thrills our hearts as we cry, "Even so, come, Lord Jesus!"*

NEXT

On the next day, when they had come down from the mountain, a great crowd met Him. (Luke 9:37)

It's been a great year, hasn't it? We looked back to praise God in remembering the amazing feats that he has accomplished through Scottsdale Bible church over the past fifty years. We looked around and rejoiced at all that God is doing right now in our church, too. And we have looked forward, renewing our commitment to serve Jesus, obeying all that He has commanded and loving others with God's matchless grace.

Truly, it has been a mountaintop year. It was a time where God revealed Himself to us many times. We have been blessed to be in His abiding presence. We have shared many experiences of community; of honoring the unique favor that God has shown us. It would be easy to agree to just "camp out here" to bask in the goodness that this last year has offered.

Yet, we desire to renew… renew our commitment to serve Jesus in all we do. We strive to march forward by faith. To do this, we have to come down from the mountain. When Jesus, Peter, James, and John came down from the mountain, there was a great crowd waiting for them. It is likewise so for us.

All around us, people need Jesus. Around Scottsdale, families need the grace that Jesus offers. Around Phoenix, men and women need the hope and healing that Jesus alone provides. Around Arizona, souls are crying out for Christ's saving mercy. Around the nation and around the world, humanity's only hope is Jesus.

The crowd awaits. So we renew. I am excited to meet the crowd along with you so together, we experience the great things that God has prepared to do through and with us!

—Jamie Rasmussen

Prayer Starter: *Lord I want to renew my commitment to You…*

CPSIA information can be obtained at www.ICGtesting.com
Printed in the USA
BVOW031638100112

280149BV00002B/9/P